BNCOD-8

Proceedings of th...
British Nat
on I

Ec...
Alan Brown a... ...er **Hitchcock**
Computer Science Dept, University of York

Pitman

PITMAN PUBLISHING
128 Long Acre, London WC2E 9AN

A Division of Longman Group Limited

© Longman Group UK Limited 1990

First published in Great Britain 1990

Printed and bound in Great Britain by
Biddles Ltd, Guildford and King's Lynn

ISBN 0 273 08837 8

Contents

APPLICATIONS

INTERFACES AND OFFICE INFORMATION SYSTEMS

Preface

For a number of years, the British National Conference on Databases (BNCOD) has provided the main forum in the UK. for the promotion and discussion of database and information system issues. It is a forum at which both database researchers and industrialists can share their experiences, and obtain reports on the latest developments in their areas. The eighth conference in the series (BNCOD-8) took place from the 9th to 11th July 1990 at the University of York.

While primarily aimed at the UK. database community, it is interesting to see that half of the papers were submitted by representatives of institutions outside the UK. While most of them were from mainland Europe, submissions also arrived from the USA. and Australia. The presentation of international work at this UK. conference is certainly a pleasing trend of the recent BNCOD conferences.

Throughout its existence, BNCOD has encouraged the submission of papers from as wide a research area as possible, and thus BNCOD-8 received a large number of papers on a diverse range of issues such as database systems theory, information system standardisation, and numerous database application areas. From these submissions the Programme Committee selected 12 papers for presentation at BNCOD-8. Together with 2 invited papers, these papers are reproduced in full in this book in the order that they were presented at the conference.

The papers can roughly be divided into four categories:

1.   Database Architectures.
2.   Theoretical Issues.
3.   Applications.
4.   Interfaces and Office Information Systems.

Database Architectures

The first paper in this section is an invited paper by William Kent, one of the foremost researchers in the area of databases and data modelling. In this paper Kent discusses the future of database systems as a component of more general object systems, arguing that in such a context databases as we now know them may not survive as an identifiable entity.

The second paper by Jean Louis Cheval continues the object-oriented theme by describing a version model which can be used within an object-oriented database. In particular, Cheval proposes a dynamic approach to version modelling based on evolution rules which are placed within each object type definition.

In the third paper, Gray and Poole report on a project which is investigating the use of transputer-based parallel hardware to improve the performance of database software. In particular, they report on a prototype 4th Generation Language (4GL) which produces Occam code for subsequent execution on a transputer-based system.

In the fourth paper of this category, King *et al.* discuss the design and implementation of a binary relational storage architecture, and the database languages that can built upon such a platform. One of the main issues which they address is the efficient implementation of a binary relational storage architecture.

Theoretical Issues

The first paper of this category, by Thomas Ludwig, discusses the compilation of complex DATALOG programs. The compiler which Ludwig describes has two phases. The first phase translates DATALOG into a set of Extended Feature Term Algebra (EFTA) templates, while the second phase makes use of the templates in executing the program.

In the second paper, Wang *et al.* investigate the use of semantic information to optimise database transactions. In particular, they make use of integrity constraints either to replace expensive operations with equivalent cheaper operations, or to ignore operations which have no effect on the database state.

In the third paper, Peter Wood examines the expression of recursive database queries using a graph-based approach. Graph views on relational databases are discussed, and two languages for querying these views are developed; one is itself graph-based, while the other is an extension to SQL.

Applications

The first paper of this section, by Deborah Thomas, discusses the STandard for Exchange of Product model data (STEP), an emerging standard for engineering data exchange. In particular, Thomas examines the logical data model which forms the basis of STEP, and the use of a relational database for capturing, controlling, and integrating information at that level.

In the second paper, Greg Nicholls and Steven Demurjian describe the Ozone software development environment, concentrating on the object-oriented database design of the environment data that is required by Ozone for supporting its tools.

In the third paper, by Fredrich Lohmann and Karl Neumann, a high-level database language for geoscientific applications is developed. Elements of the language are discussed, and the language is illustrated with a substantial example.

Interfaces and Office Information Systems

The first paper of this section is an invited paper by David Gradwell. In his capacity as Chairman of the ISO Technical Committee on the framework of the Information Resource Dictionary System (IRDS), Gradwell discusses the IRDS standardisation effort, and its likely impact on the future of commercial database systems development.

In the second paper, by Celentano *et al.*, the authors discuss the importance of direct access to document semantics in an office information system. A set of guidelines for the development of a suitable semantic model for office documents is then defined.

In the third paper by Sillitoe *et al.* the benefits from using existing database technology in the implementation of hypertext systems is discussed. The authors present a system which implements the storage and retrieval of trails through hypertext.

The fourth paper, by Brown *et al.* examines the relationship between the database system interface and the user interface using a paradigm known as "surface interaction". Initial results from experiments using this principle are analysed, and future directions of the work are indicated.

Acknowledgements

Organising a conference is inevitably a team effort, and it is my privilege to acknowledge the important contributions that have been made by others.

- The members of the Programme Committee for their efforts in reviewing a large number of papers, and in selecting a varied and interesting programme for BNCOD-8.

- The members of the Steering Committee for their help and advice on how to deal with the many problems which arise in organising a conference. Alex Gray and Mike Shave have been particularly helpful in this regard.

- Peter Hitchcock and Rebecca Wise, my colleagues at York whose contribution to the smooth running of the conference has been as much (if not more) than my own.

Alan W. Brown
University of York.

BNCOD-8 Committee Members

Steering Committee

M.J.R. Shave, University of Liverpool (Chairperson)
A.W. Brown, University of York
W.A. Gray, University of Wales
A.F. Grundy, University of Keele
P. Hammersley, Middlesex Polytechnic
P. Hitchcock, University of York
J. Longstaff, Leeds Polytechnic
E.A. Oxborrow, University of Kent
H. Williams, Heriot-Watt University

Programme Committee

P. Hitchcock, University of York (Chairperson)
T. Bourne, Independent Consultant
A.W. Brown, University of York
I.W. Draffan, Sheffield City Polytechnic
D. Gradwell, Analyst Workbench Ltd.
P.M.D. Gray, University of Aberdeen
W.A. Gray, University of Wales
A.F. Grundy, University of Keele
P. Hammersley, Middlesex Polytechnic
K.G. Jeffery, Science and Engineering Research Council
R.G. Johnson, Birkbeck College, University of London
J. Longstaff, Leeds Polytechnic
J.K.M. Moody, University of Cambridge
E.A. Oxborrow, University of Kent
G.C.H. Sharman, IBM UK. Laboratories Ltd.
M.J.R. Shave, University of Liverpool
C. Small, Birkbeck College, University of London
R.M. Tagg, Consultant in Information Management
H. Williams, Heriot-Watt University

Organising Committee

A.W. Brown, University of York
P. Hitchcock, University of York
R.S. Wise, University of York

The Evolving Role of
Database in Object Systems

William Kent

Hewlett-Packard Laboratories
1501 Page Mill Road
Palo Alto, California 94304 USA

Abstract

In the context of object systems, database as we know it today may not
survive as an identifiable entity. The distinction between behavioral
and structural object orientation will diffuse the database interface,
while the management of transient and persistent objects will blur the
distinction between application run-time environments and database
environments.

1. Introduction

The nature of database in object systems will be profoundly influenced by
two factors: the distinction between behavioral and structural object orientation,
and the relationship between transient and persistent objects. These factors have
opposing effects. Behavioral and structural object orientation will divide a single
interface into two, while the management of transient and persistent objects will
unify two interfaces into one.

Other factors will also be influential, and predictions are risky. But a plausible extrapolation suggests that database as we know it today may not survive as an
identifiable entity distinct from other system components.

2. Behavioral and Structural Object Orientation

2.1. Two Levels of Interface

Today's applications use database operations to manipulate data structures.
There is a single interface between user programs and the system code managing
the database (Figure 1). The semantics of the operations at this interface are
defined in terms of the system-supplied data structures.

Object-oriented database introduces a new middle ground [2] (Figure 2).
Object-oriented applications no longer directly manipulate data structures. In

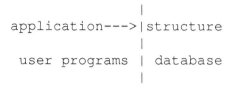

```
                    |
application--->|structure
                    |
user programs  | database
                    |
```

Figure 1.

keeping with the object-oriented principle of abstraction, applications apply operations (send messages) to objects without knowing the implementation of such objects.

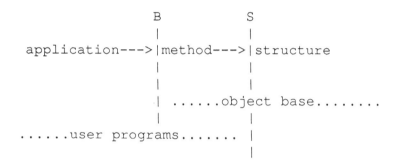

```
               B              S
               |              |
application--->|method--->|structure
               |              |
               |              |
               | ......object base........
               |              |
......user programs....... |
                              |
```

Figure 2.

Applications use operations defined to be meaningful in the application domain. Working on documents, applications might use operations that return the next line after a given line, or insert a paragraph or a diagram between two other paragraphs. Other operations might identify or retrieve the authors of the document, or define the contract between the publisher and authors, or manage the records of royalty payments. The applications would not manipulate arrays or lists or pointers or tables. The structure of a document, as well as its other related information, could be implemented in various ways using such data constructs, which should be of no concern to the applications.

The operations are implemented by methods, which are programs in the object base that access the underlying data structures. An operation may have various implementations in terms of different method programs and different data structures, so long as they all provide the same behavior to the application.

The boundary between application and object base no longer coincides with the boundary between user programs and data structure. User programs exist both as applications and as methods in the object base. The object base includes both method programs and data structures. Applications do not manipulate data structures, but invoke operations implemented by methods which manipulate data structures.

In a certain sense, the whole notion of data structure is an illusion supported by a hierarchy of levels of abstraction. The application is using operations implemented by methods designed to provide the semantics of documents. Those methods in turn look like applications using operations implemented in, say, a relational data manager to provide the semantics of relations. The relational data manager in turn looks like an application using operations implemented in a file system and an operating system, to provide the semantics of files and buffers. This layering of abstraction illusions cascades down until we get to physical behaviors that support the semantics of binary digits implemented in magnetic and atomic phenomena.

Where is database in this picture? It depends on what you mean by database. Database is suffering an identity crisis at dual interfaces.

In its traditional role as a manager of structured data, the database exists to the right of the interface we have labeled "S" for "structure". A database is "structurally object oriented" [1] if this interface supports complex data structures that physically mirror the structural composition of objects. In a structurally object-oriented database, a document might be represented as a data structure including all of its text and diagrams as well as lists of authors, contracts, royalty records, etc. Operations to manipulate such data structures are provided by the database management system.

However, in its other traditional role of providing the interface by which applications manipulate data, the database exists to the right of interface labeled "B" for "behavior". A database is "behaviorally object oriented" [1] if this interface supports operations defined to be meaningful in the application domain.

The behavior of complex objects can be described without reference to the implementing data structures, in terms of propagation of operations. For example, a diagram behaves as though it were contained in a document if the diagram is displayed, copied, or destroyed when the document is displayed, copied, or destroyed.

At this level, from the viewpoint of the application, database is evolving from its traditional role of supporting structure to a new role of supporting behavior. Structure is hidden from the application by the methods implementing the behavior.

Structural and behavioral object orientation are orthogonal. Either can be provided without the other. Structural object orientation without behavioral retains the configuration of Figure 1, the difference lying in the complexity of data structures available to applications. More complex data structures allow applications to model more complex structures of objects. Applications still manipulate data structures, and are still sensitive to differences or changes in the structures used to implement the applications. In this configuration, the database management system itself constitutes the methods implementing the operations used by the applications.

Behavioral object orientation without structural allows applications to be expressed in terms of operators which are semantically meaningful to the application domain, without benefit of complex data structures that might improve the efficiency of the applications. Applications can be designed in object-oriented fashion, yet implemented with methods that map to conventional data storage such as files or relational databases. Such applications are relatively data independent and robust, enjoying most of the benefits of object orientation: ease of development, extensibility, maintainability, adaptability, interoperability, etc. They can be migrated to more efficient implementations, including various forms of structural object orientation as they become available, in object-oriented fashion by altering the methods that implement the operators.

2.2. Corollaries for Data Analysis and Design

This realignment of interfaces implies corollary realignments in the roles of data analysis and design.

Data analysis produces a conceptual schema formally capturing the semantics of the data requirements, generally expressed in terms of entities and relationships in current methodologies. The design phase then transforms the conceptual schema into a data model specifying the data structures in the database which will be used by applications. There is currently a "semantic gap" between the concepts and structures in which the conceptual schema expresses requirements and the concepts and structures in which applications manage information (Figure 3). Data analysts and application developers speak different languages.

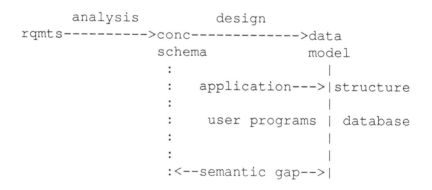

Figure 3.

The methodology will obviously adapt to object orientation by expanding concepts. The notions of entities and relationships will be enriched to encompass such object-oriented features as subtypes, behavior, polymorphism, etc. Data design will encompass more complex data structures.

Perhaps less obvious is a shift in boundary alignments, the closing of the

4

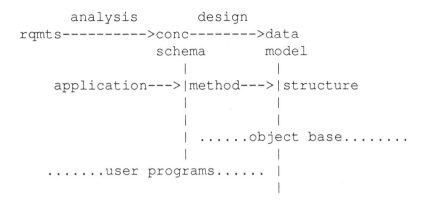

```
        analysis          design
   rqmts---------->conc-------->data
                   schema          model
                     |               |
       application--->|method--->|structure
                     |               |
                     |               |
                     | ......object base........
                     |               |
       .......user programs...... |
                                     |
```

Figure 4.

semantic gap (Figure 4). In effect, although the major phases of data analysis and design remain much the same, their "clients" will shift. The conceptual schema, now expressed in terms of objects, is directly usable as the interface to which applications are developed. The specifications produced by the design phase are for the benefit of method writers, not application developers.

3. Transient and Persistent Objects

Object-oriented programming emerged as a way to enrich the data structures available to programs while making the programs less dependent on the implementation details. Object orientation was realized in terms of enhancements to run-time libraries, binding of variables, storage (heap) management, type checking, and similar programming facilities.

Typical objects were extensions of familiar programming constructs, such as lists, arrays, queues, and stacks. These objects were used in the course of some computation, vanishing when the program terminated. Then, for some applications, a need was realized for such objects to persist, to remain available for later executions of the same or different programs.

File systems provide the first approach to persistent objects. Objects are made persistent by writing them to files. When referenced, they are read back from the files into the run-time environment (Figure 5).

Many influences are currently at work, and it's not entirely clear how to present them in a historical or logical sequence. It may not matter, since the various paths are likely to converge (evolution progresses along many paths), and debates over how we'll get there aren't that important.

Longevity isn't enough; persistent objects need other database-like services such as recovery, concurrent usage, and security. Database techniques for optimizing data access can sometimes eliminate the need to move entire objects into program space. Those objectives, as well as requirements to understand the scope of

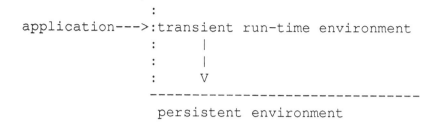

```
                    :
application--->:transient run-time environment
                    :       |
                    :       |
                    :       V
        -----------------------------------------
              persistent environment
```

Figure 5.

copy and delete operations, mean that the database must understand more of the semantics of objects, such as object properties, inter-object references, and sub-object containment.

Database management systems provide a persistent execution space as well as secondary storage. Executing methods in the persistent space of the database management system rather than in the application's transient run-time environment allows optimized data retrieval, and avoids the double movement of data from disk to database buffers to application space.

As more and more of the semantics of objects move into the persistent space, object services appear redundantly and often inconsistently in both spaces. This includes such services as the definition, installation, and maintenance of types and classes; resolution of polymorphism; type checking; and storage management and garbage collection. Other facilities are also provided unevenly, such as complex queries and set-oriented processing.

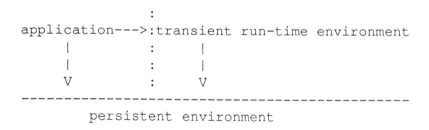

```
                    :
application--->:transient run-time environment
     |              :       |
     |              :       |
     V              :       V
        -----------------------------------------
              persistent environment
```

Figure 6.

These factors sometimes lead to a configuration which requires applications to be aware of such differences and interact separately with programming facilities and database facilities (Figure 6).

The existence of all these interfaces may not be recognized. There is often a feeling that the application and its run-time environment are intimately bound together, while the file system or the database are alien, on the other side of some fence. The boundary to the persistent environment (file system or database) is recognized as an interface, while the boundary between the application and its run-time environment might not be.

Trying to extrapolate logically into the future (always a risky business), it seems we ought to evolve to a unified object management architecture (Figure 7).

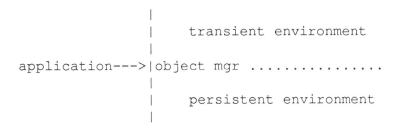

Figure 7.

Here applications deal with a unified object management interface, behind which are managed transient and persistent objects in a consistent and integrated fashion. The boundary between applications and object management becomes more defined, while the distinction between transient space and persistent space may become less so.

We can get there by several paths: extending persistent programming objects to provide database capability, or extending databases with object-oriented capability. The two forks will merge in a unified facility, and the debates over how we'll get there won't matter.

Database seems to have merged here with the run-time program environment, likely to be reflected in a unified database programming language (DBPL). Thus, while the distinction between transient and persistent objects remains, other object services are provided in a coordinated and consistent fashion. As mentioned earlier, object services include such things as the definition, installation, and maintenance of types and classes; resolution of polymorphism; type checking; and storage management and garbage collection. A unified DBPL would also provide other services uniformly, such as complex queries and set-oriented processing.

Arriving at such a unified DBPL will require some innovation in program and operating system technology to coordinate such things as process and storage management, and to be able to bind program variables directly to persistent space (e.g., database buffers) at run time.

7

4. Conclusion

Combining the two lines of development, we arrive at the configuration of Figure 8.

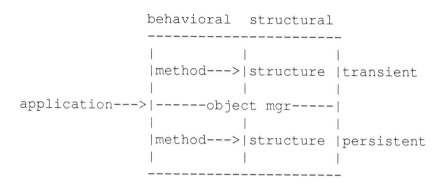

```
                    behavioral   structural
                    -----------------------

                    |          |          |
                    |method--->|structure |transient
                    |          |          |
   application--->|-------object mgr-----|
                    |          |          |
                    |method--->|structure |persistent
                    |          |          |
                    -----------------------
```

Figure 8. Where's the Database?

Once again, where's the database in this picture? We've already seen its identity split between behavioral and structural, depending on whether you think of database as the application's interface to data or as the manager of stored data structures. Now it's in danger of losing its identity as something distinct from the management of transient run-time program data. There is so much in common in the management of transient and persistent objects that the concept of database may give way to the unified notion of object base, integrating the management of transient and persistent objects.

We've only considered some factors here. Other requirements seem to work against such a monolithic approach. Rather than a simple dichotomy of transient and persistent spaces, we may need a spectrum of varied capabilities. Truly process-local data may need minimal services, but query and set-processing capability might be desirable. File systems provide persistence with a minimal degree of other database services, though security might be wanted here. Persistence may come in a range of durations, reflecting the varied lifetimes of short and long or nested transactions. Private databases (e.g., locally checked out data) may not need concurrency or security control. Distributed systems and client/server architectures also suggest dispersal of capabilities. The management of application operators strongly overlaps the technology of network message management.

Thus the configuration of Figure 8 may be too simplistic, but it is a reasonable intermediate stage of extrapolation. Other investigations [3] are exploring how the various facilities of object and database technology can be mixed and matched in different contexts.

8

Acknowledgements

This work evolved in discussions with Kevin Wentzel of Hewlett-Packard and Mary Loomis of Object Sciences in the course of working on a reference model for the Object Management Group.

References

1. K.R. Dittrich, "Object-Oriented Database Systems: The Notion and the Issues", Proceedings 1986 IEEE International Workshop on Object-Oriented Database Systems, Asilomar, Pacific Grove, California, Sept. 23-26, 1986 (K.R. Dittrich and U. Dayal, eds).

2. William Kent, "Object-Oriented Database: New Roles and Boundaries", InfoDB 4(3) Fall 1989.

3. Craig Thompson et al, "Open Architecture for Object-Oriented Database Systems", Texas Instruments Information Technology Laboratory Technical Report 89-12-01, December 6, 1989.

A Version Model
for Object-Oriented Databases

Jean Louis Cheval

Laboratoire LGI
B.P. 53X
38041 Grenoble Cedex
France
E-mail : cheval@imag.imag.fr

Abstract

This paper presents an extension to an object-oriented model in order to model object evolution. In the first part, the abstraction mechanism is used to structure the different object evolution levels and emphasize the basic concepts of the version model : evolution constraint, value inheritance mechanism via the evolution-of relationship and properties linked to the evolution hierarchy. In the proposed model, different evolution strategies are expressed in the object type definition with the help of evolution rules. The approach is dynamic : each rule describes the event which triggers off object evolution and the action which must be perform to generate a new version. Several examples are given to illustrate the use of the evolution model.

1. Introduction

Today, in database domain, many researchers aim at defining models and tools suited to new applications : CAD, software engineering, office information.... . A fundamental point appears from the study of these new applications : the **very evolutive nature** of the information which is handled. On the one hand, application objects are of big complexity and very numerous, so they cannot be designed and produced "once for all". On the other hand, in these applications, we don't only have to compute and store informations but also to explicitly manage the evolution of these informations throughout their lives. **Time** and **version** are now fundamental concepts of the new applications [Adiba 87].

Up to now, object evolution problems have been mainly resolved in two ways :

1) by use of version management tools such as SCCS [Rocking 75], RCS [Tichy 85] in the Unix environment,

2) by the development of specific application tools. Many projects have been proposed and achieved : [Batory 85, Chou 86, Ecklung 87, Fauvet 88, Katz 86a, Klahold 86] in CAD, [Estublier 88, Perry 87, Repps 88, Winkler 87, Zdonik 86] in software engineering.

If we want to take stock of the different solutions proposed in the version domain, we may stress the following remarks :
    • the version concept is not part of the data model and the semantic expression of object evolution is generally very poor and limited to derivation links,
    • the solutions are too general or too specialised. The tool approach handles objects of too big granularity (file). Specialised version models are too fixed once for all and cannot be altered when the domain evolves.
    • version management is mainly manual. A user generates a version by creating a copy of the object and by modifying it afterwards. This operation mode is still necessary. But in the new applications where evolution conditions are better and better known, a new approach is possible : the automatisation of the version generation process. Control mechanisms are however necessary to limit the number of versions.

The proposed version model is based on the object-oriented model concepts. Indeed, on the one hand, these models offer abstraction mechanisms, which come from semantic models such as generalization, specialisation and classification, which are very powerful to model the different object types. On the other hand, they take the operations into account. These models are thus well suited to express the object evolution behaviour. Several solutions to the version problem are already proposed with an object-oriented approach [Beech 88, Kim 88, Naraya 88, Penney 87, Skarra 86, Zdonik 86]. Compared with these solutions, our model is limited to the object value evolution and must be rather seen as a design model (i.e. which is used at the design level), because it permits the application designers to define the evolution characteristics of the objects they design.

The original aspects of this version model are :

    1) the expression of **evolution rules** which are adapted to each application object [Cheval 89]. These rules are expressed in the object type definition, in accordance with the object design philosophy of the object-oriented approach.

    2) the expression of a **precise evolution semantic**. The evolution rules permit the designers to describe both the exact value transformation and the generation conditions of each version.

    3) the **consistency proof** of evolution specification expressed on the application objects and an **automatic** version generation mechanism.

This paper is mainly limited to the presentation of two aspects : the definition of the basic object evolution concepts which are introduced in the second chapter and the version model which is described in the third chapter. The fourth chapter presents several application examples of this version model use.

2. Basic Evolution Concepts

2.1. Object-Oriented Model

Our version model is an extension of an object-oriented model. Since 1986, several object-oriented models have been proposed in the database domain [Banerjee 87, Bloom 87, Fishman 87, Lecluse 87, Maier 86]. We shall sum up below the basic concepts which are common to these model's and which are necessary for our study :

Type : a set of common object attributes and operations,

Object : an instance of a type defined by an unique object identifier,

Attribute : an object property identified by a name which can be simple, constructed or computed,

Sub-type : a specialization of a type by attribute or operation adjunction. An **is-a** link between an sub-type and its types ensures inheritance mechanism.

Method : an object manipulation operation, defined into the type,

Class : an object set built for a given type ; any object which is instancied for a given type by default belongs to a general class called "maternal" class.

Sub-class : object set of a mother class build from a criterium,

Our proposition also assumes persistence concept is supported by the O.O. model.

We shall now be using an abstraction mechanism to emphasize the basic concepts of our version model. We shall start by describing the different abstraction levels.

2.2. Abstraction Levels

Versions of an Oi object are values of this object which have been stored at different instants. In general, these versions have the same properties as the Oi object : they belongs to the same type. Hence, an object which evolves in different versions represents an **abstraction** for these versions, as a type is an abstraction for objects of this type.

Figure 2.1 represents three abstraction levels corresponding to the three entities - type, object and version - and the relationships between these levels.We have assigned significant values to entity attributes, which we are now explaining :

1) at **type level**, the type entity describes a general structure which defines attributes (A, B, C) and their domains,

2) at **object level**, the object entities have the same structure as the type entity. Each object has some attributes with values assigned (here A) which are generally called "key attributes". They define the identity of each object. These key attributes are classically fixed by a constraint called **identity constraint**. An identity constraint requires only one value assignment for key attributes and checks identity value unicity.

3) the **version level** contains version entities with the same structure as that of the object entity. All versions of the same object have the same object identity value (for example A=a1). Their difference comes from the values of one or several attributes, except for key attributes (here B).

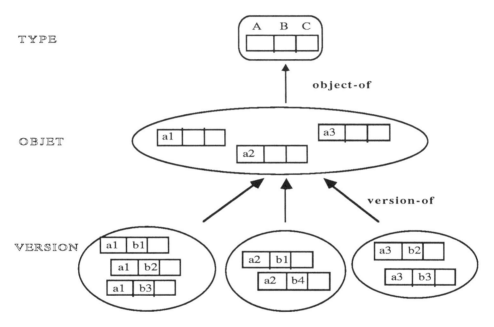

Figure 2.1 : Abstraction level example

This decomposition process by abstraction level may be repeated by now considering a Vi version as an abstraction for the VVi versions derived from the Vi version. In this way, we introduce the concept of **version of version**.

4) version of version entities have the same structure as that of the version entities. Common properties of the version of version entities of the same version are the attribute values of the previous level entity from which they are issued (here A and B). In turn, their difference comes from the values of one or several other attributes (here C, in figure 2.2).

The version of version concept comes from the fact that the value evolution of the C attribute at the version of version level depends on the B attribute value at the version level, the evolution of the latter depending itself on the A attribute value at the object level.We may now present the basic evolution concepts.

2.3. Evolution Constraint and Evolution Scope
At each abstraction level, a constraint called **evolution constraint (EC)** defines the set of attributes which are significant of the evolution corresponding to this level. We call **evolution scope** this set of constrained attributes. So, there is an evolution constraint for each evolution level.

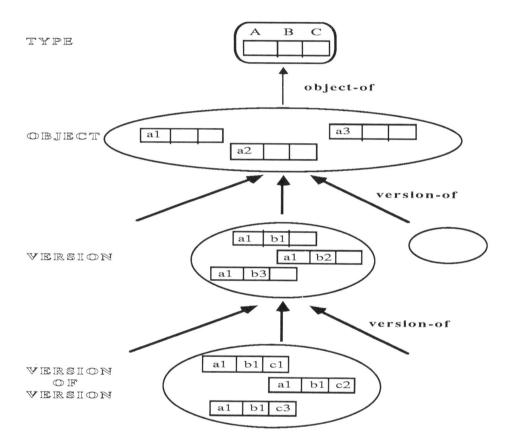

Figure 2.2 : Version of version example

Remarks :
1) for practical reasons of the presentation of figures 2.1 and 2.2, we have limited the type definition to three attributes and the evolution constraint definition to a single attribute. In general, the type attributes are not all systematically constrained and each evolution constraint may have several

14

attributes. If there is no evolution constraint on an attribute, it means there is no entity representing its value evolution.

2) the object identity constraint is also an evolution constraint which imposes to check the identity value unicity of objects. Therefore, it is a stronger constraint than the evolution constraint.

2.4. Value Inheritance

This modelling approach shows the uselessness of an inheritance mechanism based on the type specialisation between the evolution levels. On the other hand, this approach needs a value inheritance mechanism between an entity of an i level and the evolution entities which are derived from it at the i+1 level. [Katz 86b] had already mentioned the need for several kinds of inheritance, in particular the value inheritance. [Berkel 88, Naraya 88, Wilkes 88] have the same conclusion : if the IS-A relationship is necessary to refine the design of object types by allowing an inheritance mechanism between type and sub-types, this relationship is insufficient to model the object evolution. They stress the interest of a value inheritance mechanism ("instance inheritance") between an object and its versions, particularly useful in the domain of design applications like CAD, software engineering, ...

These concepts are summarized in figure 2.3 which represents a V entity of the i level, its VV evolution entities at the i+1 level and the **evolution-of** relationship which induces value inheritancé mechanism between the two levels for an EC **evolution constraint** :

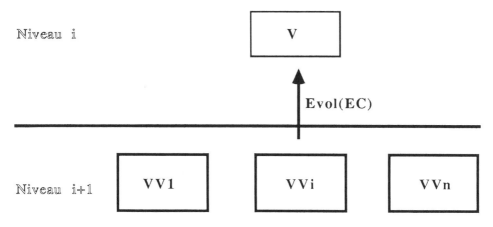

Figure 2.3 : Evolution concepts

2.5. Evolution Constraint Inheritance

The value inheritance concept may be explained by the way of evolution constraint :

  • an evolution constraint defined at an i abstraction level is inherited by the following levels (i+1, ...),

15

• an evolution constraint at an i level is the conjonction of an evolution constraint defined at the i level and the evolution constraints inherited from the previous levels (i-1,...).

Inheritance of evolution constraint corresponds to a **value specialization** of the entities. From the example of figure 2.2, we show this progressive value specialization for each evolution level :

  • at the **type level**, the evolution constraint on the T type entities is initially :

  evolution-constraint (T) : domain(A) **and** domain(B) **and** domain(C)

  • at the **object level**, the evolution constraint scope is the A attribute. The constraint on an object, for example O1, is :

  evolution-constraint (T, O1) : (A=a1) **and** domain(B) **and** domain(C)

  • at the **version level**, the evolution constraint scope is the B attribute. The constraint on a version, for example V1 of O1, is :

  evolution-constraint (T, O1, V1) : (A=a1) **and** (B=b1) **and** domain(C)

  • at the **version of version level**, the evolution constraint scope is the C attribute. The constraint on a version of version, for example VV1 of V1 of O1, is :

  evolution-constraint (T, O1, V1, VV1) : (A=a1) **and** (B=b1)
  and (C=c 1)

2.6. Approach Generalisation

Until now, we have supposed that only one possibility of evolution, i.e. only one evolution constraint definition, exists between entities of two consecutive levels. For example, in figure 2.1, all object versions are characterized by the value evolution of the B attribute.

We think that the model possibilities are too restrictive. Actually, in design applications, an object frequently evolves in several ways. Also we generalize the approach by permitting that several **evolution-of** relationships exist between an entity and its evolution entities. Each relationship is labelled by its own evolution constraint.

The three **evolution-of** relationships with their own evolution constraints (EC1, EC2 and EC3) in figure 2.4 characterise three evolution possibilities. This evolution form is called **multiconstraint evolution**. At the i+1 level, all the entities wich are constrained in the same way compose an **evolution family**.

16

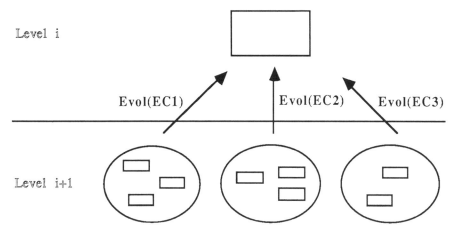

Figure 2.4 : Multiconstraint evolution

The approach allows now to describe a more general evolution structure of entities of a given type. Figure 2.5 represents a multiconstraint evolution hierarchy.

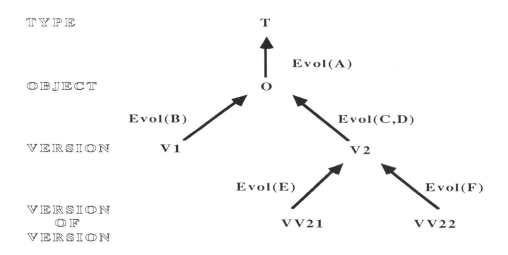

Figure 2.5 : Multiconstraint evolution hierarchy example

2.6.1. Evolution Tree

From this hierarchy, we can deduce the evolution tree (figure 2.6) which represents dependencies between the evolution constraint scopes. An interpretation of the tree of figure 2.6 is the following :

- for each A value, an object potentially exists,
- for an A value, for each B or (C, D) value, an object version

potentially exists,
   • for an A and (C, D) value, for each E or F value, a version of version of an object potentially exists.

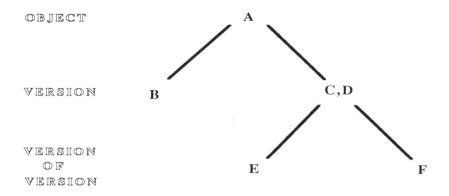

Figure 2.6 : Evolution tree example

The different evolution possibilities are then obtained by the different paths of this evolution tree. We call these paths **evolution paths**.

2.6.2. Evolution Constraint Properties
The evolution tree structure emphasizes properties which must be satisfied in order to assume a non ambiguous value for each evolution entity. We defined three interesting properties :

   1) evolution constraints are hierarchised,

   2) at an evolution level, evolution constraints must have distinct scopes,

   3) on an evolution path, an attribute has only to appear once.

Each evolution level is thus mapped by distinct type attributes. These properties are used in the evolution model (cf chapter three) in order to verify the consistency of object evolution specification expressed by application designers.

2.6.3. Extension : Evolution Lattice
We have limited our approach to a hierarchised evolution structure. This approach ought to be sufficient for most applications. We can however admit a more general evolution structure: an evolution lattice. This structure would mean that entities belonging to entity families of the same level evolve in turn according to the same evolution constraint. This form of evolution specification is not familiar but not incorrect. Nevertheless this evolution lattice structure is delicate to understand and manage.

2.7. Short conclusion

This study emphasizes two fundamental concepts for an evolution model : the **evolution constraint** on entity attributes defined at an abstraction level and the **evolution-of** relationship which induces a **value inheritance** mechanism between an entity and its evolution entities. A multiconstraint evolution hierarchy can be defined.

3. The Version Model

The proposed version model is an extension of an object-oriented model which includes the above evolution concepts. This model enables application designers to express evolution rules in the type definitions of the objects they build. We think this approach matches well with the object-oriented approach which tends to include all the object characteristics in the type definition : their structure, their operations, ...

3.1. A Dynamic Approach

Two approaches of object evolution specification are possible :

    1) a **static** approach which is limited to the expression of the different object evolution constraints. This approach already enables to identify each evolution level and to manage the different links between evolution entities, i.e. object versions.

    2) a **dynamic** approach which adds a detailed specification of how evolution entities are generated.

We have choosen the dynamic approach because on one hand it includes the static approach (we can always restrict it), on the other hand it seems us more promising for the new applications. According to this dynamic approach, an **evolution** can now be define as the process which generates a new entity from a source entity.

The entity which is generated can be a new object, or a new version or a new version of version,... depending on the value transformation, i.e. on the evolution constraint which is applied to the source entity. Actually, the notion of object evolution or version evolution or version of version evolution or... is significant when we compare two entities itselves.

For example, figure 3.1 shows the generation of a new version because the evolution constraint (here EC(P)) is supposed defined at the version level. This would be a version of version evolution if the evolution constraint was defined at the version of version level.

Vocabulary

We used afterwards the term of *entity* each time it represents the evolution of a general entity and the term of *object* or *version* each time it represents the evolution of the corresponding entity.

19

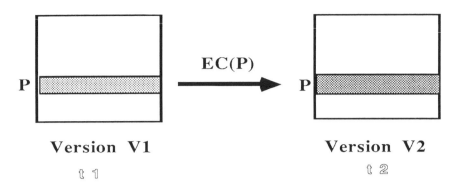

Version V1   Version V2

t 1   t 2

Figure 3.1 : Version evolution

3.2.   Hypothesis
The hypothesis for our version model are as follows :

1) we have deliberately limited our model to the specification of version evolutions. Thus, the model doesn't permit to express dynamic instantiation of objects. But the inheritance mechanism of evolution constraints requires that the identity constraint be known by the levels : version, version of version, ... Thus the definition of this identity constraint will be part of the evolution model.

2) any entity of a given type can be source of evolution,

3) only one evolution is possible at a given instant,

4) an evolution generates only one version from a given entity.

The above hypothesis mean that the version model allows to express the generation of only one version from a given type entity at a given instant.

3.3. Evolution Parameters
A version evolution may be expressed by the following expression :

$$V2, t2 \longleftarrow \textbf{evolution} \ (V1, t1, EC(P))$$

This expression means that V2 is a version generated at the t2 instant from the V1 version according to the evolution constraint EC whose scope is P. It is not enough to express the dynamic characteristics. Some parameters are missing. They are :

1) the **event** which triggers off the evolution,

2) the **condition** which limits the generation to the only useful versions,

3) the **action** which precises the version generation characteristics.

20

Event, condition and action are concepts used in active databases [Adiba 88, Dayal 88, Hanson 89, Kotz 88, Rolland 83] to implement functions such as : integrity constraint, access constraint, support for inference,... Because they are well suited to our problem, we have decided to use these concepts for the object evolution expression, by the way of evolution rules.

3.4. Evolution Rules

We call **Evolution Rule** the evolution specification of an object expressed in the following form :

> **when** *<event>*
> **if** *<condition>*   **then** *<evolution-action>*

The different evolution rules, as well as the identification rule, are expressed in object type definitions. The designer can express zero, one or several evolution types.

We are now going to describe more precisely an evolution rule.

3.4.1. Evolution Rule Event

An event triggers off an evolution rule. There are two kinds of events :

1) events tied to value modification operations,

2) temporal events (not described here).

For each update operation of a type attribute, event may be attached which is triggered off when the attribute is modified. **update**(ATT) is a predefined event of the model which is triggered off before the ATT attribute is updated. In the following examples, we use the **update**(WIDTH) event which is attached to the WIDTH attribute of a MECHANIC-PIECE type (not described in this paper).

Example :
> **when update**(WIDTH)
> **if** *<condition>* **then** *<evolution-action>*

3.4.2. Evolution Rule Condition

An evolution rule condition allows or doesn't allow to generate a version. It limits this generation even if the rule event is triggered off. It is a logical expression builded from type attributes and logical operators.

Example :
> **when update**(WIDTH)
> **if** new.WIDTH < LENGHT / 2 **then** *<evolution-action>*

Before a **new** value is assigned to the WIDTH attribute and if this new value is smaller than the half of the LENGTH attribute value, then perform the rule evolution-action.

3.4.3. Evolution Rule Action
An evolution rule action defines the **mode** and the **scope** of the evolution :

1) the evolution mode expresses how versions are linked each others at the same evolution level. Two modes are proposed :
- the **altern** mode (contraction of alternative version) requires no time constraint. It permits thus to generate a version from any already existing version. It permits the parallel development of object versions.
- the **succ** mode (for successive) requires that the new version always be generated from the most recent version. This additional constraint permits to build the historic evolution of all or a part of the object value.

2) in chapter three, we have introduced the evolution scope and the evolution constraint concepts : an evolution scope defines the list of attributes which are significant of an evolution level. This list is a parameter of the rule mode. It contains the attributes updated and possibly other attributes which depend on these attributes.

Example :

> **when update**(WIDTH)
> **·if new.**WIDTH < LENGHT / 2 **then succ** (WIDTH, SURFACE)

For a mechanical piece, when the WIDTH attribute is updated, if its new value is smaller than the half of the LENGHT attribute value, then generate a new successive version with the new values of the WIDTH and SURFACE attributes.

Note : if the rule scope is empty, then the corresponding rule generates version copies.

3.4.4. Rule Declaration
Evolution rules and identity rule are expressed in an **evolution** and an **identity** paragraph of the object type. A type may contain zero, one or several evolution rules.

Parallel with the abstraction model
If we refer to the abstraction model of the chapter 3, we can assert:
- the lack of evolution rules in a type definition means the existence of only one abstraction level : the object level,
- the presence of only one evolution rule means the existence of an **evolution-of** relationship between an object and its versions and thus the existence of only one version level,
- the presence of several rules means the existence of several **evolution-of** relationships between an object and its version or perhaps between a version and its versions and thus perhaps several version levels.

4. Examples

We may now illustrate this version model by giving several examples with different evolution strategies defined for different object types.

4.1. Successive Version

Type PERSON ;
NAME : **string[12]** ;
AGE : 0..120 ;
ADDRESS : **string**[50] ;
PHONE : **string**[10] ;
DEGREE : **string**[10] ;
GRADE, SAL-GRAD : **integer** ;

identity
    NAME
evolution
    when update(ADDRESS)
    if true then succ (ADDRESS, PHONE) ;
type-end ;

a) Interpretation

The designer has defined a PERSON type where each person entity is identified by its NAME. The three parts of the evolution rule indicates that he wants to build the historic evolution of the adress and phone number of a person each time its adress changes. There is no restrictive condition.

b) Analysis

The evolution part contains only one rule. Thus, there is only one version level. The **succ** mode imposes some constraints :
    • a new version is generated if the source version is the most recent one,
    • the attribute values of the new version may be modified as long as a new successive version is not generated. These attribute values are afterwards frozen. This strategy is imperative to maintain temporal consistency of successive version values. Let note that the ADRESS attribute evolution implies the PHONE attribute evolution.

4.2. Version of Version

We reuse the same PERSON type and add new evolution rules.

Type PERSON ;
NAME : **string[12]** ;
AGE : 0..120 ;
ADDRESS : **string**[50] ;
PHONE : **string**[10] ;
DEGREE : **string**[10] ;
GRADE, SAL-GRAD : **integer** ;

identity
    NAME

evolution
    when update(ADDRESS)   / rule 1 /
    if true then succ (ADDRESS, PHONE) ;

    when update(DEGREE)
    / rule 2 /
    if new.DEGREE > **old.**DEGREE
    then succ (DEGREE, GRADE, SAL-GRAD) ;

    when update(GRADE)
    / rule 3 /
    if new.GRADE > **old.**GRADE
    then succ (GRADE, SAL-GRAD) ;

type-end ;

a) Interpretation

The evolution part contains now three rules, with the same **succ** mode.
The second rule builds the historic evolution of the degree, grade and grade-salary of a given person if the grade value increases.
The third rule builds a more precise historic evolution since it keeps track of each grade and salary-grade value when the degree of a person increases.

b) Analysis

The analysis of these evolution rules shows that the two first rules have distinct scopes while the third rule has a scope embedded in the second one. So we have the following evolution tree :

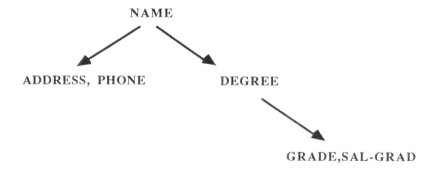

Figure 4.1 : Evolution tree

This evolution tree allows to verify the correctness of the evolution specification, i.e. that the evolution properties (cf §2.6) are satisfied, and to deduce two evolution levels :

1) a first (successive) version level with the corresponding evolution constraints :

EC11 (ADDRESS, PHONE) ; EC12 (DEGREE)

2) a second (successive) version level with the corresponding evolution constraint :

EC2 (GRADE, SAL-GRAD)

This example is interesting because it brings up the following question : how are generated the successive versions when they belong to different levels ? There is only one answer, for the same above mentionned reason of temporal consistency of the successive version values : a new successive version must always be generated from the most recently version and the values of previous successive versions are frozen.

Figure 4.2 shows several successive versions generated by the triggering off of evolution rules of the PERSON type. For each evolution, we have mentionned the corresponding ECii evolution constraints. The attributes concerned by a value evolution are on a white background. Let note the particular generation of t5 version.

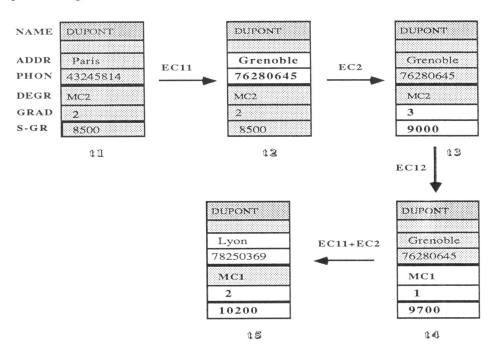

Figure 4.2 : Successive versions of versions

4.3. Alternative and Successive Version

This last example is issued from the module representation in software engineering. A module is composed of an interface and a body. A body *realizes* one interface and *uses* several interfaces. The below type describes a module body.

25

Type MODULE-BODY ;
REALIZE : INTERFACE ;
AUTHOR : **string**[20] ;
SOURCE : **text** ;
LANGUAGE : TLANGUAGE ;
USE : **list of** INTERFACE ;

identity
    REALIZE

evolution
    when update(SOURCE)
    if new.SOURCE **<> old**.SOURCE
    then succ (SOURCE, USE) ;

    when update(LANGUAGE)
    if unique (**new**.LANGUAGE)
    then altern (AUTHOR, SOURCE, LANGUAGE, USE) ;

type-end ;

a) Interpretation

The identity rule defines that each module body is identified by the REALIZE attribute value.

The first evolution rule builds the historic evolution of both source texts and used interfaces of each module body, each times the source text is edited and modified.

The second rule generates an alternative version if a new and unique (**unique** function) language value is proposed.

b) Analysis

The analysis of each rule shows that their scope are embedded, defining the two following version levels :

    1) a first (alternative) version level with the evolution constraint :
        EC1 (LANGUAGE, AUTHOR)

    2) a second (successive) version level with the evolution constraint :
        EC2 (SOURCE, USE)

For each alternative version, there is a **family** of successive versions. Because of this evolution hierachy and because the evolution mode of the first version level is alternative, the temporal constraint of the successive mode is specific to each successive version family.

Several activations, simultaneously or not, of these two rules lead to the development of the following version structure :

26

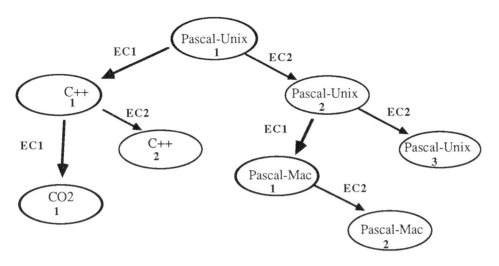

Figure 4.3 : Alternative and successive version evolution

5. Conclusion

In the first part of this paper, we have first used an abstraction mechanism to emphasize the basic evolution concepts : evolution constraint, evolution scope, value inheritance mechanism. The latter had already been presented in [Katz 86b, Naraya 88, Wilkes 88]. We have then generalised the approach thus allowing us to describe multiconstraint evolution hierarchy. Eventually we have defined properties which must be satisfied in order to model correctly object evolutions.

The second part has been devoted to the description of the version model. The original feature of this version model seems to be the application designers to describe the evolution of their objects with a greater semantic expression. They can specify several evolution rules in an object type. Each rule defines at the same time the evolution causes (event and condition), the evolution granularity (constraint scope) and the evolution mode (alternative or successive). Multiconstraint and multilevel version evolutions can be easily expressed. The analysis of evolution rules permits to verify the correctness of an evolution specification and to deduce from it the different evolution levels with their corresponding constraints. It can therefore be seen as a help for the designer.

This version model is a part of the research of the Aristote project which is a joint research project between Laboratoire de Génie Informatique and BULL Research Center at Grenoble.

6. References

[Adiba 87] M.ADIBA, N. BUI QUANG, C.COLLET :
Aspects temporels, historiques et Dynamiques des Bases de Données
TSI, vol. 6, N° 5, 1987.

[Adiba 88] M.ADIBA, C.COLLET
Management of Complex Objects as Dynamic Forms
Conference VLDB 1988, Los Angeles.

[Banerjee 87] J.BANERJEE, H.T.CHOU, J.GARZA, W.KIM et al.
Data model issues for Object Oriented Applications
ACM TOIS, Vol 5 Num 1, january 1987.

[Batory 85] D.S.BATORY, W.KIM
Modelling Concepts for VLSI CAD Objects
ACM Transactions on Databases Systems, Vol. 10, N° 3, Sept.1985.

[Beech 88] D.BEECH, B.MAHBOD
Generalized Version Control in an Object-Oriented Database
4th Int. Conf. on Data Engineering, Los Angeles, Feb. 1988.

[Berkel 88] T.BERKEL,P.KLAHOLD,G.SCHLAGETER,W.WILKES
Modelling CAD-Objects by Abstraction
Proc. 3rd Int. Conf. on Data and Knowledge Bases, Jerusalem, June 1988.

[Bloom 87] T.BLOOM, S.B.ZDONIK
Issues in the Design of Object-Oriented Database Programming Languages
OOPSLA 87, October 1987.

[Cheval 89] J.L.CHEVAL
Une Extension aux Modèles Orienté-Objets : Règles d'Evolution
Congrès Inforsid, Nancy, Mai 1989.

[Chou 86] H.CHOU, W.KIM
A Unifying Framework for Version Control in a CAD Environment
Proc. of 12th Conference on VLDB, Kyoto, 1986.

[Dayal 88] U.DAYAL, A.P.BUCHMANN, D.R.McCARTHY
Rules are Objects too : a Knowledge Model for an Active Object-Oriented Database System
Lecture Notes in Computer Science, Advances in Object-Oriented Database Systems, Sept. 88.

[Ecklung 87]   D.J.ECKLUNG,E.F.ECKLUNG,R.O.EIFRIG,F.TONGE
DVSS : a Distributed Version Storage Server for CAD Applications
Proceedings of the 13th VLDB Conference, Brighton, 1987.

[Estublier 88]   J.ESTUBLIER
A Configuration Manager : the Adele Database of Programs
Proc. of the Workshop on Software Version and Configuration Control, Stuttgart, January 1988.

[Fauvet 88]   M.C.FAUVET
ETIC : un SGBD pour la CAO dans un Environnement Partagé
Thèse de Nouveau Doctorat de l'Université de Grenoble 1, Sept. 88.

[Fishman 87]   D.FISHMAN, D.BEECH, H.CATE, E.CHOW et al.
IRIS : an Object-Oriented Database Management System
ACM TOIS, Vol 5, Num 1, January 1987.

[Hanson 89]   E.D.HANSON
An Initial Report on the Design of Ariel : a DBMS with an Integrated Production Rule System
Sigmod Record, Vol. 18, No.3, September 1989.

[Katz 86a]   R.H.KATZ, E.CHANG
Managing Change in a Computer Aided Design Database
Proc. ACM Sigmod Conference, Washington, May 1986.

[Katz 86b]   R.H.KATZ
Inheritance Semantics for Computer-Aided Design Databases
Proc. of the Int. Workshop on Object Oriented Database Systems, Pacific Grove, California, 23-26Sept. 1986.

[Kim 88]   W.KIM, HONG-TAI CHOU
Versions of Schema for Object-Oriented Databases
Conference VLDB, Los Angeles, Aug. 1988.

[Klahold 86]   P.KLAHOLD, G. SCHLAGETER, W.WILKES
A General Model for Version Management in Databases
Proc. of 12th Conference on VLDB, Kyoto (Japan), 1986.

[Kotz 88]   A.KOTZ, K.DITTRICH, J.MULLE
Supporting Semantic Rules by a generalized Event/Trigger Mechanism
Proc. Intern. Conf. on Extending Database Technology, March 1988.

[Lécluse 87]   C.LECLUSE, P.RICHARD, F.VELEZ
O2, an Object Oriented Data Model
Rapport Technique Altaïr 10-87, septembre 1987,
Proc. of the ACM-SIGMOD Conference, Chicago, 1988.

[Maier 86]   D.MAIER, J.STEIN, A.OTTIS, A.PURDY
Development of an Object-Oriented DBMS
OOPSLA 86, Sept. 86.

[Naraya 88]   K.NARAYANASWAMY, K.V. BAPA RAO
An Incremental Mechanism for Schema Evolution in Engineering Domains
4th Int. Conf. on Data Engineering, Los Angeles,Feb. 1988.

[Penney 87]   D.J.PENNEY, J.STEIN
Class Modification in the Gemstone Object-Oriented DBMS
OOPSLA 87, Oct. 1987.

[Perry 87]   D.E.PERRY
Version Control in the Inscape Environment
9th Int. Conf. on Software Engineering, Monterey, California, 30 March 87.

[Reps 88]   T.REPS, S.HORWITZ, J.PRINS
Support for integrating Program Variants in an Environment for Programming in the Large
Proc. of the Int. Workshop on Software Version and Configuration Control, Stuttgart, January 1988.

[Rocking 75] M.J. ROCKING
The Source Code Control System
IEEE Trans. on Software Engineering SE-1(4), Dec. 1975.

[Rolland 83] C.ROLLAND
Database Dynamics
Revue ACM Data Bases (Spring), 1983

[Skarra 86]   A.H.SKARRA, S.B.ZDONIK
The Management of Changing Types in an Object-Oriented Database
OOPSLA 86, Sept. 86.

[Tichy 85]   W.F. TICHY
RCS : a System for Version Control
Software-Practice and Experience 15(7), July 1985.

[Wilkes 88]   W.WILKES
Instance Inheritance Mechanisms for Object Oriented Databases
Lecture Notes in Computer Science, Advances in O.O. Database System, Sept. 1988.

[Winkler 87]   J.F.H. WINKLER
Version Control in Families of Large Programs
9th Int. Conf. on Software Engineering, Monterey,
California, 30 March 87.

[Zdonik 86]   S.B. ZDONIK
Version Management in an Object-Oriented Database
Int. Workshop on Advanced Programming Environments,
Trondheim, Norway, June 1986.

A Transputer Based Implementation of a Parallel Database System

J P Gray and F Poole

Department of Computer Studies
Sheffield City Polytechnic
Pond Street, Sheffield S1 1WB, UK
Email: JANET R806@uk.ac.scp.vmt

Abstract

A sophisticated database application generation system, Data Base 4th Generation Language (DB4GL), incorporating an object-oriented self-describing data model, has been developed at Sheffield Polytechnic. A recent extension to the DB4GL research has been an investigation into a possible parallel implementation of DB4GL on transputer hardware. A prototype Parallel-DB4GL (P-DB4GL) system has been designed and implemented. In P-DB4GL, the application code modules generated by DB4GL have been redesigned as concurrent Occam [Inmos88b] processes. Results have been obtained which show significant performance improvements when applications are run on small (one to four processors) transputer networks. The principal benefit comes from the ability to perform multiple concurrent disc input/ouput, thus increasing disc throughput, and hence improving overall application performance. Development and testing of the prototype P-DB4GL has confirmed the feasibility of using transputer based parallel hardware for DB4GL applications, and indicated where further performance gains can be obtained in the full working version of P-DB4GL, currently under development.

1. The DB4GL Project

DB4GL (Data Base 4th Generation Language) [Ewin84] [Ewin85a] [Ewin85b] [Hird89] [Poole87] is a database applications prototyping tool that has been developed at Sheffield Polytechnic. It is a result of research conducted in the

Department of Computer Studies over the past six years in the area of database applications prototyping and Fourth Generation Languages (4GL's). DB4GL generates single user database applications to run on an IBM PC AT microcomputer. DB4GL is a collection of tools - report generators, screen painters, code generators - based around a data dictionary; and can be used for either "throw-away" requirements analysis prototyping, or for "evolutionary" prototyping in which the final prototype is the eventual product [Dearnley83] [McCraken82] [Horowitz85]. The DB4GL data dictionary is active, in that, applications are generated from the specifications stored in the data dictionary at generation time, the data dictionary does not just passively describe applications. The DB4GL data dictionary is itself maintained by DB4GL generated applications. DB4GL uses its own hybrid self-describing [Mark85] [Mark86] [Roussopoulos85] data model [Hird89] [Poole87], originally based on the Entity-Relationship approach [Chen76] [Howe83] but also influenced by other data models, for instance, DIAM [Senko73] [Senko76] and CODASYL [Olle78].

Central to the generation of DB4GL applications is the concept of "the architecture of a database application program", essentially this is a generic structure, or template, from which particular instances of database applications are derived (see Figure 1). Conceptually, a DB4GL database application is composed of a set of Presentation Objects (PO's). Each PO comprises:
- an Information Unit Group (IUG), that is, a group of data entities processed by the PO;
- a Process Schema, with a number of Process Tasks for processing the IUG;
- a Presentation Format, describing the user interface of the PO;
- a set of Integrity Rules, controlling updates to the IUG.

This database application structure is implemented by a collection of separate code modules performing generic processing, user interface, and data access functions (see Figure 2). These modules can be broadly classified into User modules (Screen, Window, and Process modules, that process user requests and send commands to the data access schemas) and Data Access modules (Schema handler and Entity handler modules, that retrieve and store persistent application data in the filestore).

In order to generate a particular database application (that is, create an instantiation of the generic application structure), it is necessary to first enter a specification of the required application into the DB4GL data dictionary. This is done using a DB4GL generated database maintenance application, and the specification includes three types of information (see Figure 3):
- **data model description**, in terms of entities, attributes, domains, and schema links (access paths);
- **processing requirements**, in terms of standard maintenance operations and query and report producing functions defined over the entities and attributes of the application;
- **user interface**, in terms of screens and windows of input and ouput data requested and produced by the processes specified above.

33

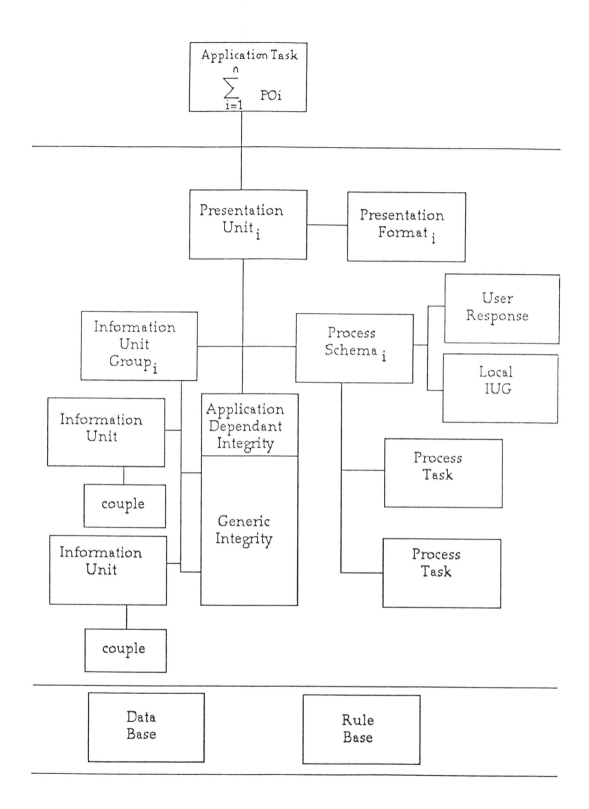

Figure 1 - Architecture of a DB4GL application

34

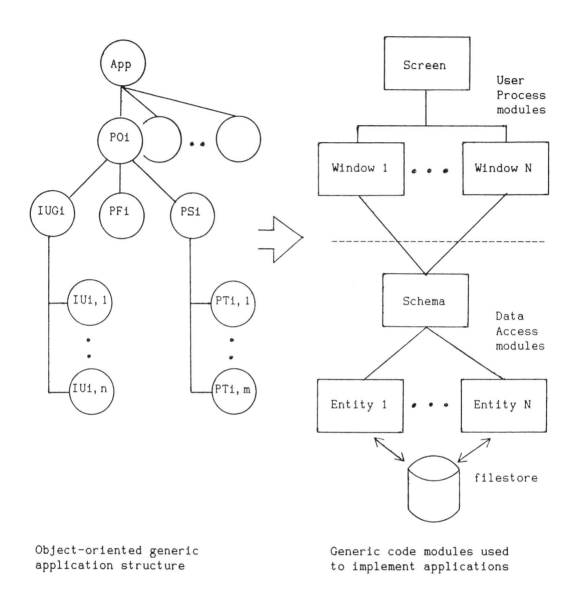

Object-oriented generic
application structure

Generic code modules used
to implement applications

Figure 2 - Implementation of DB4GL applications

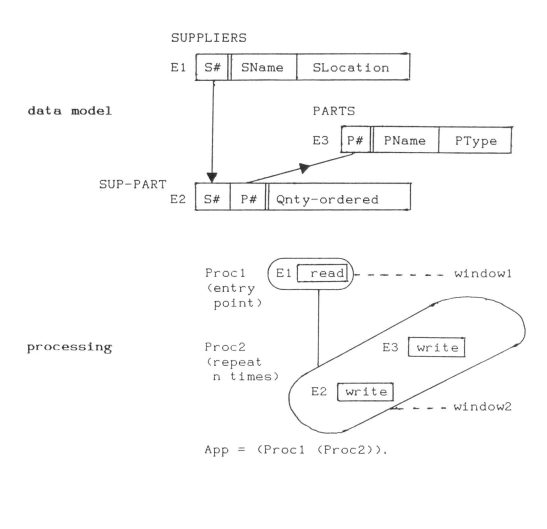

data model

processing

```
SUPPLIERS
E1   S# ‖ SName │   SLocation

                        PARTS
                        E3  P# ‖ PName │  PType

SUP-PART
         E2  S# │ P# ‖ Qnty-ordered
```

```
Proc1    ⎛ E1 │ read │⎞ - - - - - - window1
(entry
 point)

Proc2                        E3 │ write │
(repeat
 n times)
              E2 │ write │
                                  - - - window2

App = (Proc1 (Proc2)).
```

user interface

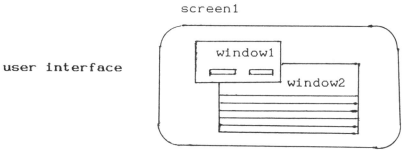

screen1

window1

window2

Specification of a simple DB4GL application to process a
small (3 entities) Suppliers-Parts database

Figure 3 - Information for application specification

The DB4GL application generation tools use this specification to produce an application consisting of a number of separately compiled COBOL program modules. The separately compiled modules are reusable, with several applications sharing many of the same modules (see Figure 4). This application generation procedure is summarised in Figure 5. Generated applications have an overall hierarchical control structure, individual code modules execute sequentially passing parameters (see Figure 6).

DB4GL places emphasis on the attribute as the primary data object, and this is reflected in the attribute-based Basic Communication Unit (BCU) communication protocol used in the implementation. However, for the efficient implementation of data storage, data is aggregated into records. All DB4GL data is stored as normalised relations (known as entities), and individual records (or entity occurrences) are accessed by a primary key. Entities are considered to be sorted on primary key which may be composite. Each entity is maintained by an entity handler module, which provides the entity's interface to the filestore. Currently, each entity is supported by a single indexed-sequential file. Thus, individual records identified by primary key, and single record-level operations constitute DB4GL's data access/storage interface. This type of interface (record level operations) is present in all current and planned implementations.

An Information Unit (IU) is a group of related attributes. A prime view IU (supported by a prime entity) is accessed via the key attribute(s) of the entity. A non-prime view IU is accessed via non-key attributes, using a closely coupled entity formed from the concatenation of the non-key attribute with the key attribute(s) (see Figure 7). The non-prime (or coupling) entity is closely coupled, in that, updates to the coupling entity can only be performed by the prime entity to which it is coupled. Thus, a coupling entity (supporting a non-prime view IU) can be seen as a form of "secondary key" or index to a prime entity (supporting a prime view IU).

For a given application, the set of all IUG's in the PO's of the application are collectively known as the application's schema (see Figure 8). A schema handler module controls access to the entities of a schema. Schema links define access paths from one entity to another. The schema handler module uses schema links to prefetch (or realise) entity occurrences (records) of a subordinate entity (target entity of the link) when the corresponding superordinate entity (source entity of the link) has itself been realised (ie a record is read or written to file).

2. Transputers, Occam, and Databases

Transputers are a family of programmable VLSI devices produced by Inmos Ltd [Inmos89b]. Transputers are principally designed for the construction of parallel processing architectures based on local memory and point-to-point serial communication [Inmos89a]. The family of devices includes: microprocessors;

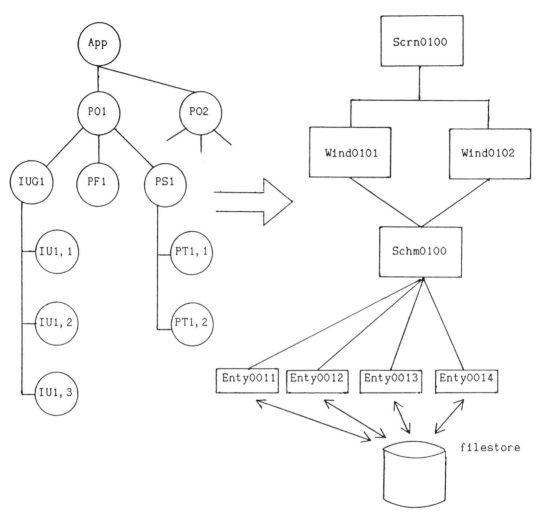

A simple database application as an instance of the generic application structure

Instantiated code modules generated by the DB4GL application generators

Figure 4 - Database applications as instantiations

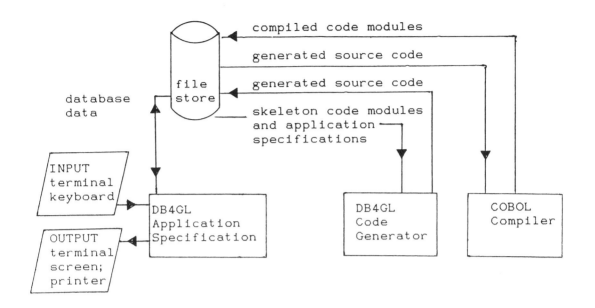

Figure 5 - DB4GL application generation

e⟶   - denotes parameters

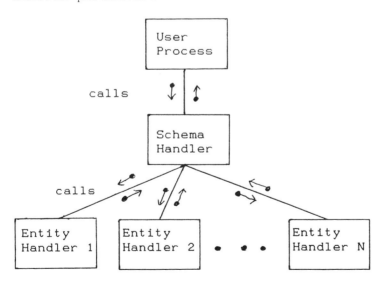

Hierarchical control structure of separately compiled code
modules, calling and passing parameters that communicate
control and data information

Figure 6 - Modular structure of a typical DB4GL application

39

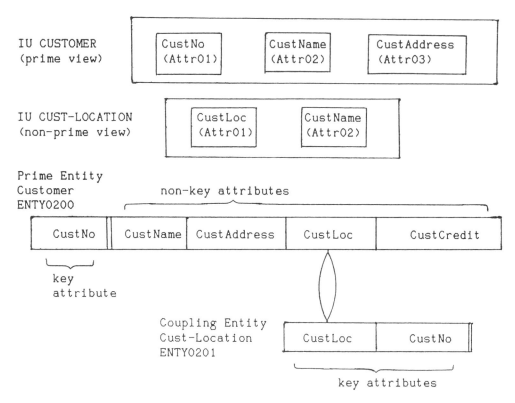

The prime view IU CUSTOMER is supported by the prime entity Customer (ENTY0200), the non-prime view IU CUST-LOCATION is supported by the coupling entity Cust-Location (ENTY0201) defined over attribute Cust-Loc

Figure 7 - Prime and non-prime views

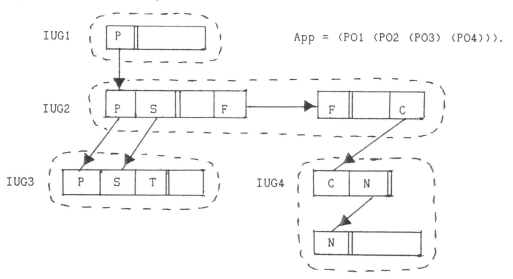

The schema of an application, with four Presentation Objects (PO's) and associated Information Unit Groups (IUG's)

Figure 8 - Schemas, IUG's and access paths

40

dedicated peripheral controllers; digital signal processors; and communications devices. A typical transputer 32 bit microprocessor (eg T414-20) contains in a single integrated circuit: a CPU; internal memory (2K on-chip RAM); an external memory interface; four high-speed (20 Mbit/s) bidirectional serial links, and is capable of 20 MIPS (peak) instruction rate (see Figure 9). Transputer microprocessors have a low level microcoded scheduler which enables any number of processes to execute together on a single processor, with each process sharing processor time.

Occam [Inmos88b] is a high level programming language designed for concurrent programming and derived from Hoare's CSP language [Hoare78]. Occam is based on a process model of computing, and uses unbuffered unidirectional point-to-point channels for inter-process communication, with the communication between connected processes synchronizing otherwise independent processes (see Figure 10). The transputer and Occam were designed together, every transputer implements the Occam concepts of concurrency and communication, and the transputer instruction set contains instructions for the optimal implementation of Occam [Inmos88d].

Using transputers, parallel systems are built as networks of microprocessors and peripheral controllers connected by the devices' point-to-point serial links. Various network topologies can be constructed, for example, rings, trees, regular arrays, and hypercubes. Because there is no shared memory or communication bus connecting the processors, the communication bandwidth of a transputer based system grows in proportion to the number of processors present. Thus, transputer based parallel architectures tend to be very scaleable, it is usually just as simple to construct a ten processor network as a thousand processor network. However, not all parallel algorithms can benefit from such large numbers of processors, and though the parallel hardware may be readily scaleable, many parallel algorithms are not.

When a transputer network is programmed in Occam, configuration information has to be supplied to an Occam program. This configuration information places particular processes at numbered processors in the network, additionally, the Occam channels connecting processes have to be mapped onto the point-to-point serial links connecting the transputers. Configuration information is static, and fixed when a compiled program is linked. All the code intended to run on a processor must be explicitly placed on it during configuration. Occam programs do not allow one process to remotely invoke another process placed on a separate processor. Operating systems, providing facilities such as dynamic load balancing of networks, message routing, program scheduling, and filestore management, are now becoming available for transputers [Perihelion89] [Grimsdale89] [Oakley89]. However, it is more usual for transputer applications to run without operating system support; applications are typically developed on a host computer (such as a PC), then the compiled, linked and configured programs are loaded onto the target transputer network.

i) Typical Transputer Microprocessor Architecture with memory, processor, and communication links on a single integrated circuit

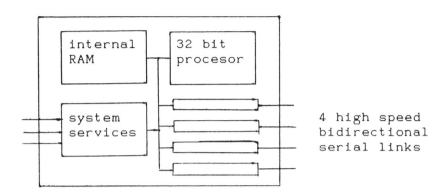

ii) Networks of Transputers connected together by their serial links

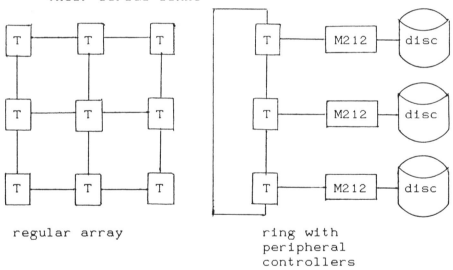

regular array

ring with peripheral controllers

Figure 9

i) Concurrent programs using the PAR construct

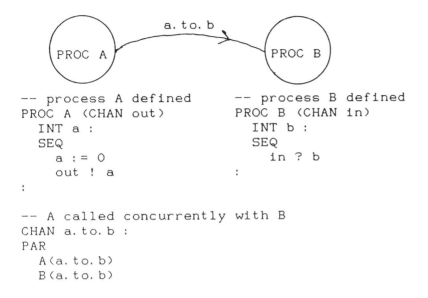

```
-- process A defined          -- process B defined
PROC A (CHAN out)             PROC B (CHAN in)
   INT a :                       INT b :
   SEQ                           SEQ
      a := 0                        in ? b
      out ! a                    :
:


-- A called concurrently with B
CHAN a.to.b :
PAR
   A(a.to.b)
   B(a.to.b)
```

ii) Placing code on hardware for parallel execution

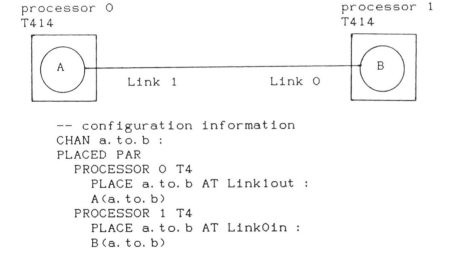

```
      -- configuration information
      CHAN a.to.b :
      PLACED PAR
         PROCESSOR 0 T4
            PLACE a.to.b AT Link1out :
            A(a.to.b)
         PROCESSOR 1 T4
            PLACE a.to.b AT Link0in :
            B(a.to.b)
```

Figure 10 - The Occam language

Transputer based parallel architectures are being used for database applications in a number of ways. One approach, for example [Stringer89], is to download an entire database into a transputer network, all the database data can then be searched in parallel, with each processor searching the database partition held in its own local memory space. Obviously, such an approach is only possible if the database is small enough to be temporarily held in main memory. A 32 bit transputer has a maximum address space of 4 GigaBytes, and the total available memory in a network can grow proportionately with the number of processors; but, the considerable time needed to transfer a large database from disc to memory before searching could commence, would tend to restrict such an approach to applications with (relatively) small databases which are never, or infrequently, updated and subject to a limited range of queries. For applications with very large amounts of updateable data, different approaches are being tried. One is DRAT [Kerridge87], a design for a relational database machine using dynamically reconfigurable networks of transputers. Another approach is LSDM [Rishe89] for a database system based on a Semantic Binary Model, this proposes a hypercube architecture of many transputers each with its own small local disc.

The main advantages of transputer based architectures for database systems can be summarised as:

- scaleability of communications and memory bandwidths in proportion to increasing numbers of processors;
- tight coupling between processors and discs, made possible by the processors' on-chip serial links and peripheral controllers using these high speed links;
- high disc I/O bandwidth, made possible by a large number of discs, these can be small cheap Winchester discs.

All the above features have been utilised in the design of Parallel-DB4GL (P-DB4GL), but the P-DB4GL system has not been designed for a specific network topology.

The Department of Computer Studies has a number of transputer resources available to the DB4GL project. This includes: several boards containing transputers; a development environment, the Transputer Development Environment (TDS) [Inmos88c]; compilers (C and FORTRAN); and a transputer controlled hard disk board. These resources have been extensively used in the development of the prototype P-DB4GL system.

3. Developing a Parallel DB4GL

3.1 P-DB4GL Overview

The Parallel-DB4GL (P-DB4GL) project is an extension of the Department's database research, in which parallel architectures are being considered for executing database applications and 4GL's. DB4GL is based on an application program architecture with a high degree of inherent parallelism. The component Presentation Objects (PO's) in a DB4GL application are, in principle, concurrently executable. Data dependencies between PO's enforce some sequential processing, for example, a PO defined over a subordinate ORDER-LINE entity cannot begin processing ORDER-LINE occurrences until the superordinate ORDER entity PO has realised an ORDER occurrence. Currently, DB4GL runs on an IBM AT microcomputer, but research [Hird89] suggests that performance gains could be achieved from the conversion of DB4GL to run on parallel-processing hardware, such as transputer networks [Inmos88a]. The aim of the P-DB4GL project is not to produce a design for a general purpose parallel relational database machine, for example [Kerridge87], but to develop suitable parallel processing hardware and software architectures for a specific product, that is, the DB4GL database application generation system. The parallel hardware - PC expansion boards containing transputers [Inmos88a] and disc drives - is transparent to the end users of the generated applications. The P-DB4GL applications should look and behave exactly like the sequential DB4GL, the only difference being improved execution times.

3.2 Design and Implementation

It was decided that the best approach to evaluating the parallelism in DB4GL was to construct a prototype P-DB4GL system. This prototype system would implement a few of the most important code modules generated by DB4GL - prime entity handlers, coupling entity handlers, schema handlers, and screen/window modules. These code modules are sufficient to construct simple database applications which would be functionally equivalent to the applications generated by an early version [Ewin85a] of DB4GL. Results from the prototype would test the feasibility of a transputer-based P-DB4GL implementation, and identify the key areas of development in a fully functional P-DB4GL.
All of the DB4GL system had been implemented in COBOL, but at the start of the P-DB4GL project a COBOL compiler was not available for transputers. It was therefore decided to develop the protytype P-DB4GL system in Occam, the native high level language of the transputer. The version of Occam chosen was the latest release, Occam 2 [Inmos88b]. It may be possible to re-compile, and incorporate into P-DB4GL, some of the old DB4GL code when a COBOL compiler becomes available for the transputer.

P-DB4GL retains both the data model and the "application program architecture" of DB4GL. The overall classification of software modules, into User and Data Access modules, is also retained, but in P-DB4GL the generated applications are

45

Occam [Inmos88b] programs cosisting of a number of separately compiled code modules capable of parallel execution and communicating via message passing down Occam channels. The applications are run by loading the program onto a network of transputers contained on the PC expansion boards, application data is stored on multiple transputer controlled disc drives and the host computer is simply used as a terminal interface to the application user (see Figure 11).

The sequential control structure of the DB4GL generated database applications, with a hierarchy of code modules, calling and passing parameters, is an implementation technique that has been used to allow the DB4GL application designs to execute on a single-tasking microcomputer. DB4GL applications conceptually are modelled as collections of concurrently executable objects that communicate with each other by passing control and data messages [Hird89]. The DB4GL application implementation is an inversion of the original design. The inversion implementation technique used in data-driven software design methodologies such as JSD and JSP, is documented in [Jackson83], [Cameron86], and [Storer88]. In P-DB4GL, an inversion transformation from a concurrent message-passing objects design to an implementation with a hierarchical contol structure of sequential code modules, is not necessary; because, the target programming language and hardware (Occam and transputers) directly support concurrency. The independently executable message-passing objects of DB4GL, can be implemented in the Occam language as separately compiled concurrent processes that communicate by sending messages along Occam channels. When run on transputer networks, P-DB4GL can execute in parallel.

A uniform communication protocol for inter-P-DB4GL module message passing has been used that accommodates both control and data messages. This protocol, known as the Basic Communication Unit (BCU), is modelled on the BCU described in [Ewin85a] and [Hird89] for inter-DB4GL message passing. In DB4GL, message passing is effected by parameter passing between calling and called code modules. In P-DB4GL, this is replaced by a two-way Request-Reply protocol (see Figure 12): if module1 wishes to send a message (control or data) to module2, a BCU-Request is sent to module2 suspending module1's execution; after reception and processing of the BCU-Request, module2 sends a BCU-Reply to module1; upon receipt of BCU-Reply, module1 continues its execution.

As with many database applications it is the disc access that is the limiting factor to overall system performance, in DB4GL the processing time of the user modules is negligible compared to the time it takes the data access modules to retrieve and store records. In P-DB4GL the data access modules (Schema handlers and Entity handlers) have been redesigned to execute in parallel, but still provide the same functionality and operate with the same data model as the original non-parallel DB4GL. The entity handlers of a P-DB4GL application are capable of concurrent access to their files of records stored in a transputer contolled parallel filing system. This has three main benefits (see Figure 13):

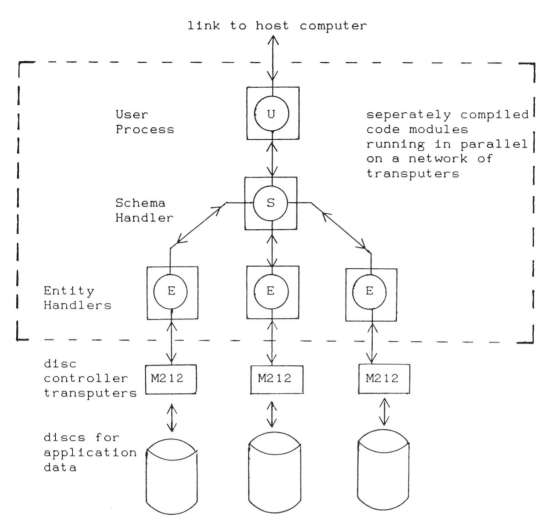

Figure 11 - A typical parallel-DB4GL application

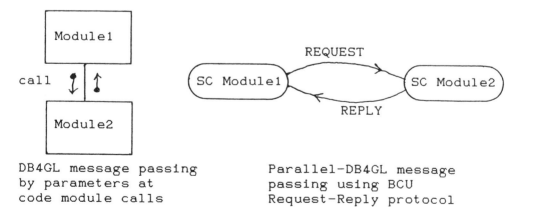

Figure 12 - DB4GL and parallel-DB4GL message passing

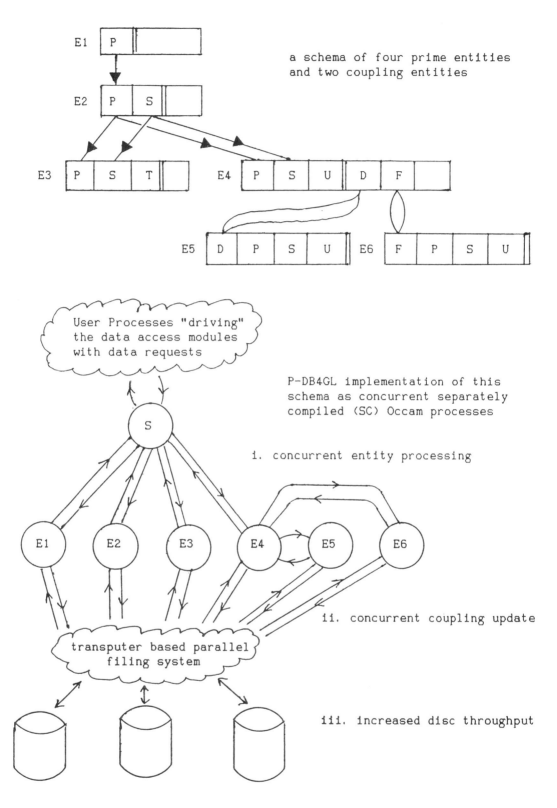

a schema of four prime entities
and two coupling entities

User Processes "driving"
the data access modules
with data requests

P-DB4GL implementation of this
schema as concurrent separately
compiled (SC) Occam processes

i. concurrent entity processing

ii. concurrent coupling update

transputer based parallel
filing system

iii. increased disc throughput

Figure 13 - Concurrent execution of data access modules

48

i.   an entity handler in a schema can access records independently of, and concurrently with, other entities in the schema;
ii. a prime entity can concurrently update all of its coupling entities;
iii. total disc/application data throughput is increased by the ability to access multiple discs in parallel.

P-DB4GL has a coarse grained level of concurrency, the unit of distribution suitable for allocation to a processor is the DB4GL module (i.e. Entity handler, Schema handler, Process schema, Process task). A processor may be allocated more than one module, but usually a module cannot be decomposed into further levels of concurrent execution. When a P-DB4GL application is run on a tranputer network, code modules have to be allocated to processors, and logical communication channels between modules have to be mapped onto physical point-to-point serial links. This configuration information is supplied to the Occam program at compile time. The P-DB4GL software has been designed without any pariticular link topology in mind. The simple test applications used so far, have required only simple mappings of code modules and communication channels to processors and links and this mapping has been done on an ad hoc basis. However, this is an area that requires further development, the fully functional P-DB4GL system will incorporate a message routing kernal allowing applications to be completely topology independent.

Results have been obtained from a number of test runs on small transputer networks (one to five processors), with a range of different configurations, for several simple applications (typically five to ten entities). A typical test configuration is shown in Figure 14. The purpose of these tests is to determine the benefit of two things:

1)   the advantage of concurrent data access algorithms over sequential data access algorithms for an application running on one transputer;
2)   the improvement gained from running concurrent data access algorithms on more than one transputer.

The Occam language does not support files, filing is achieved via processes connected either to a host filing system or to a dedicated device such as the M212 disc controller. In a fully functional P-DB4GL, filing processes using the M212 will be implemented, but the prototype system has been developed using a simulation of a parallel filing system. This simulation is implemented by the Filer and Disc processes, it is possible to alter both, the number of simulated discs, and, the mapping of entities to discs (see Figure 15). For concurrent algorithms, the best performance is obtained with a maximum number of discs (that is, a mapping of one entity per disc), however, for some test runs an optimum performance can be gained with mappings of many entities to a disc.

A number of functionally equivalent versions of the data access modules have been implemented. These versions differ in the degree of concurrency of their algorithms:

49

i) Test application schema SCHM0003

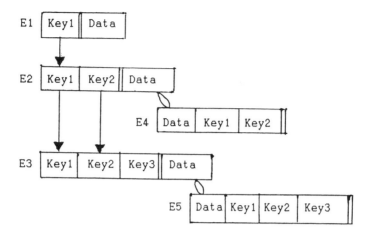

ii) SCHM0003 - DBMS Code (Filer Harness not shown)

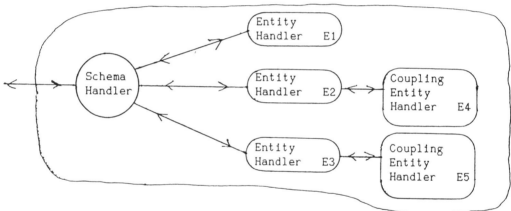

ii) Configuration - placing code on hardware

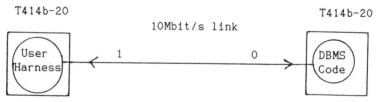

Both processors are T414 parts running at 20 MHz and connected with 10 Mbit
per second links.   The first processor runs the User Process Harness, as an
EXE under TDS, and communicates with the second processor through link 1.
The second processor runs the Data Access modules and Filer Harnesses, as a
PROGRAM loaded by the TDS, and communicates with the first processor by
Link 0.   The BCU protocol is supported by two unidirectional unbuffered
occam channels (BCU. Request and BCU. Reply) mapped onto the bidirectional
serial link between the two processors.

Figure 14 - A test configuration

i) Mapping one entity to one disc

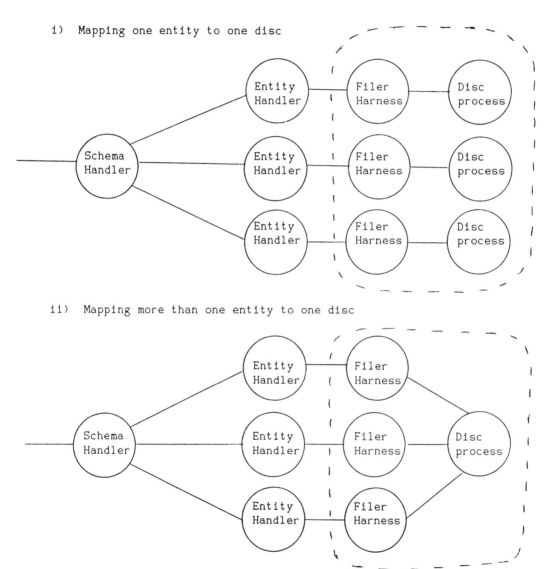

ii) Mapping more than one entity to one disc

Figure 15 - Mapping entities to discs

1) "original" sequential handler versions (v1) - in which, the data access modules receive a request message from the User process, process that request, and return a reply message;

2) "modified" sequential handler versions (v2) - in which, the (sequential) data access modules execute concurrently with the User process, processing data during the inter-message delays;

3) concurrent handler versions (v3) - as (v2), but the sequential data processing performed by the data access modules is replaced by equivalent concurrent algorithms;

4) concurrent handler versions (v4) - as (v3), but with improved concurrent data processing algorithms, the prime entity update of coupling entities is performed concurrently.

Under normal circumstances, the data access modules of a P-DB4GL application would be "driven" by the user process modules that interface with the database user and generate data storage and retrieval requests. However, genuine P-DB4GL user process modules have not yet been developed, so, in order to test the performance of the P-DB4GL data access modules, a test harness has been used which simulates the behaviour of genuine user process modules. The User Process Test Harness ("User Harness") is capable of operating in either: interactive mode, whereby single BCU Request-Reply messages are sent to and received from the Data Access modules; or, batch mode, whereby a test run consisting of a number of transactions is performed on the Data Access modules. Each transaction is composed of a number of BCU messages, which together perform some complete database action such as storing or updating a record. The term "transaction" is not being used in the normal database sense of an indivisible collection of updates. Currently, P-DB4GL is a single user database system, concurrent processes within a P-DB4GL application do not interfere with each other and should not be able to deadlock, there is no facility to recover should a transaction fail. The decomposition of database actions (transactions) into a number of smaller "atomic" actions (each one represented by a BCU message) allows optimizations to be performed in a sequence of transactions, thus reducing the amount of data communicated between the P-DB4GL objects.

3.3 Results

The version 2 data access handlers typically give 20% to 30% improvement in execution time over the version 1 handlers for a variety of test data. The exact improvement for any given application depends both on the test data used, and the run time behaviour of the application, that is, the frequency and duration of inter-BCU and inter-transaction processing delays. The version 3 handlers are typically 40% to 50% faster than version 1 handlers. Results for version 4 handlers show the most significant improvements (see Figure 16). For an application running entirely on one processor, almost order(N) improvements are obtained. That is, as the number of coupling entities updated is increased, the improvement in execution time of v4 (concurrent update) handlers against v3 (sequential update) handlers

52

Table 1   version 4 entity handlers

Test run No 7 — a single prime entity updating N number of
                coupling entities
Filer Harness Disc Delay 64 milliseconds
Time in seconds

No of couples	0	1	3	6	9	12	15	18
ver 3 handlers	1.13	2.53	4.66	7.85	11.03	14.21	17.4	20.58
ver 4 handlers	1.14	2.55	2.63	2.74	2.86	2.99	3.13	3.27
ver 3 couple processing	—	1.4	3.53	6.72	9.9	13.08	16.27	19.45
ver 4 couple processing	—	1.41	1.49	1.6	1.72	1.85	1.99	2.13
ver3 normalised couple times	—	1	2.52	4.8	7.07	9.34	11.62	13.89
ver 4 normalised couple times	—	1.007	1.06	1.14	1.23	1.32	1.42	1.52
improvement factor	—	0.993	2.37	4.2	5.75	7.08	8.18	9.14

Figure 16 - Test results

increases proportionately. For a v3 entity handler, the time taken to update N couples is nearly N times greater than to update one couple; but, for a v4 entity handler, the time taken to update N couples is almost the same as the time to update one couple (see Figure 17).

These dramatic improvements in execution time for the concurrent coupling entity update (v4 entity handlers) have been obtained with all the data access processes running on a single processor. Tests have also been conducted with identical programs running on multi-transputer configurations, but the execution times of the test runs are practically the same as the single processor configuration. The additional available processing power of the multi-processor configurations has not effected the performance of either the concurrent or sequential version of the data access processes.

The reasons for these effects lie in the proportions of processing, idle, and communication times present in the test runs. The disc access time is orders of magnitude greater than processing and communication time. During disc access, a processor running the sequential handler algorithm is idle, thus, the total test run time is largely composed of a sequence of disc access delays. For a processor running the concurrent handler algorithm, the disc access delays occur concurrently, thereby reducing the total test run time (see Figure 18). However, as the number of coupling entities updated is increased, the ratio of processing time to idle time increases, and the improvement factor of the concurrent algorithm over the sequential algorithm declines (see Figure 19). In the test runs conducted so far, tens of coupling entities have been concurrently updated, resulting in small processing loads for a single processor. In large applications, with hundreds of concurrently executing data access processes, a single processor would become significantly loaded, and benefits of multi-processor configurations will become evident (see Figure 20).

4. Further Developments

There are several areas of work requiring further development in order to convert the prototype P-DB4GL into a fully functional P-DB4GL. It is anticipated that this work will be completed, and a final P-DB4GL product delivered, by the end of 1990. The areas of development work are:

A) A solution to the problems of mapping code to hardware and routing of messages through the transputer network. The simple database applications used for testing the prototype P-DB4GL have been very small - with five to ten processes mapped onto one to four processors. The placing of processes onto processors has been done on an ad hoc basis, with simple one-to-one mappings of channels to links. In the proper P-DB4GL system, application programs will be much larger (typically ten to a hundred processes), load balancing, multiplexing of channels over links, and routing of inter-module

<u>Graph of Normalised Coupling Entity Update Time against Number</u>
<u>of Coupling Entities Updated</u>

for an application updating a single prime entity and N number of coupling
entities, run as a PROGRAM on a single T414-20 transputer with 10 Mbit/s
link speed

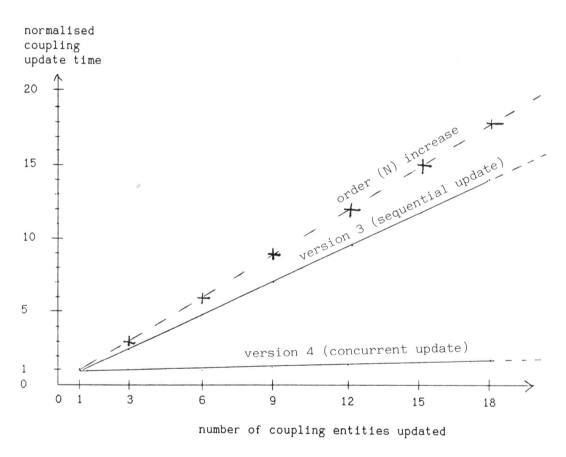

Figure 17 - Normalised coupling update times

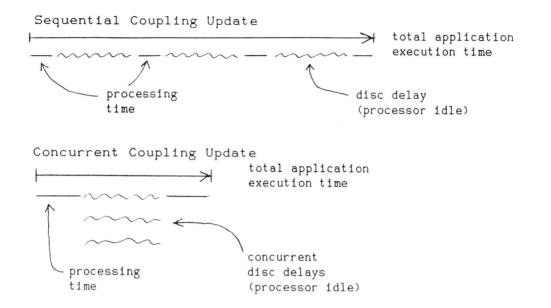

Figure 18 - Processing/disc access ratio

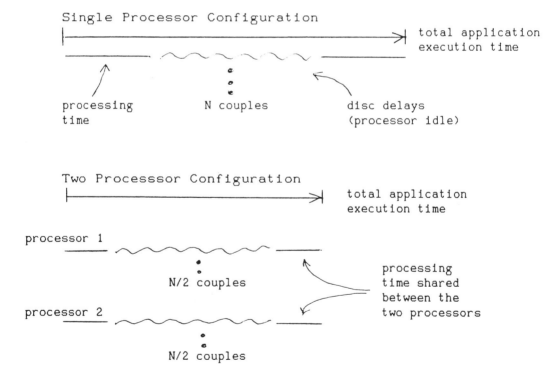

Figure 20 - Processor loading and parallel configuration

<u>Graphs of Improvement Factor and Processor Loading against</u>
<u>Number of Coupling Entities Updated</u>

for an application updating a single prime entity and N number of coupling
entities, run as a PROGRAM on a single T414-20 transputer with 10 Mbit/s
link speed, where

$$\text{improvement factor} = \frac{\text{coupling update time (sequential)}}{\text{coupling update time (concurrent)}}$$

$$\text{\% processor loading} = \frac{\text{processing time (processor busy)}}{\text{total application run time}}$$

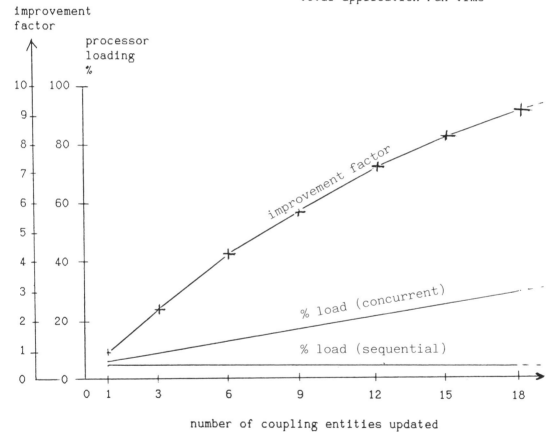

Figure 19 - Improvement factor and processor loading

messages through the network will have to be considered. A simple dedicated P-DB4GL network router using layered protocols will be developed - some initial ideas are for a three layer protocol for a ten node ring topology, with each node having a kernal process to multiplex channels, route messages, and schedule application processes (see Figure 21).

B)   Implementation of genuine User Process modules to provide a user interface and "drive" the concurrent data access modules, replacing the User Harness process used in the testing of the prototype. This will increase the number of concurrent processes in a program, causing increased processing load, and improve the opportunity for exploitation of multi-processor configurations.

C)   Replacement of the Filer Harness and Disc Process simulations with genuine filing processes and multiple transputer-controlled disc drives.

D)   Construction of an enhanced P-DB4GL data dictionary. The data dictionary schema (DDS) will be similar to the DDS of the original DB4GL [Ewin85a], but will contain additional information such as:

- the hardware configuration available to P-DB4GL;
- the mapping of entities to discs;
- the typical processing requirements and distribution of code to hardware for each application.

This information is needed for the generation of P-DB4GL database applications. When P-DB4GL is used as a database application prototype tool, this information will be updated by the system designer as new applications are defined and existing applications are improved and regenerated.

5. Conclusions

The prototype Parallel-DB4GL (P-DB4GL) system has shown that a transputer-based implementation can provide significant performance improvements for the unchanged DB4GL data model. Further development work is needed, particularly in the areas of message routing, process scheduling, and load balancing. DB4GL database applications, in common with many other database applications, tend to be disc input-ouput (I/O) bound. The main benefit of the transputer-based implementation lies in the ability to perform multiple concurrent disc I/O, thus increasing disc I/O throughput, and hence reducing overall application execution time.

An important feature of DB4GL is the reliance on indexes (coupling entities) to support pre-compiled queries with fixed access paths through the database. The maintenance of these coupling entities following an update to the prime entity to which they are coupled, produced processing delays significantly impairing the performance of the original sequential DB4GL. In P-DB4GL, the coupling entities

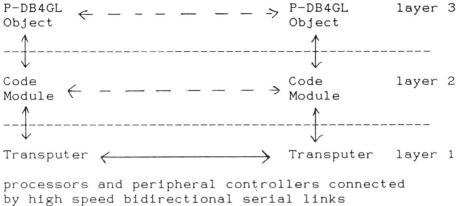

```
-----------------------------------------------------
P-DB4GL   ← — — — — — — →   P-DB4GL      layer 3
Object                      Object
  ↕                           ↕
-----------------------------------------------------
  ↕                           ↕
Code      ← — — — — — — →   Code         layer 2
Module                      Module
  ↕                           ↕
-----------------------------------------------------
  ↕                           ↕
Transputer ←————————————→  Transputer   layer 1

processors and peripheral controllers connected
by high speed bidirectional serial links
-----------------------------------------------------
```

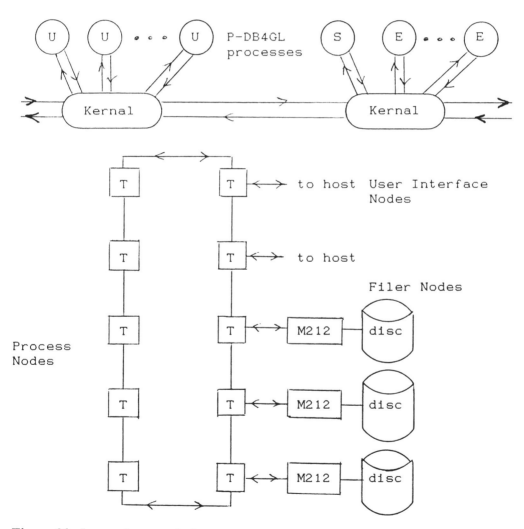

Figure 21 - Layered protocols for P-DB4GL networks

are processed in parallel, the delays associated with maintaining these coupling entities are eliminated, thus improving application execution time. Other database systems dependent on heavily indexed relations, might also benefit from a similar parallel implementation, in which index maintenance can be performed concurrently.

References

[Bakkers89]   A Bakkers (ed)
                   Applying Transputer Based Parallel Machines Proc. of 10th
                   Occam User Group Technical Meeting (OUG-10) 3-5 April
                   1989, Enschede, Netherlands, IOS, Amsterdam (1989)

[Cameron86]   J R Cameron
                   An overview of JSD' IEEE Trans. on Software Engineering Vol
                   SE-12 No 2 February (1986) 222-240

[Chen76]   P P-S Chen
                   *'The Entity-Relationship Model - Toward a Unified View of
                   Data'* ACM Trans. on Database Systems Vol 1 No 1 March
                   (1976) 9-36

[Dearnley83]   P A Dearnley and P J Mayhew
                   *'In favour of system prototypes and their integration into the
                   systems development cycle'* The Computer Journal Vol 26 No
                   1 (1983) 36-42

[Ewin84]   N A Ewin
                   *'Computer Estimating for a Speculative House Builder Using
                   4th Generation Software Tools'* Internal Research Paper
                   R/D/84/3, Dept of Building, Sheffield City Polytechnic (1984)

[Ewin85a]   N A Ewin
                   *'Advanced Application Software for Speculative Housing
                   Companies'* MPhil Thesis (CNAA), Sheffield City Polytechnic
                   (1985)

[Ewin85b]   N A Ewin, F Poole, R Oxley
                   'DB4GL: A Fourth Generation System Prototyping Tool'
                   Sheffield City Polytechnic Report, Dept. of Building Internal
                   Research Paper R/D/85/2 (1985)

[Grimsdale89]   C H R Grimsdale
                  'Distributed operating system for transputers' Microprocessors
                  and Microsystems Vol 13 No 2 March (1989) 79-87

[Hird89]   B T Hird
                  'Process Logic for an Expert Database System' PhD Thesis
                  (CNAA), Sheffield City Polytechnic (1989)

[Hoare78]   C A R Hoare
                  'Communicating sequential processes' Comms. of the ACM
                  Vol 21 No 8 August (1978) 666-677

[Horowitz85]   Horowitz and Ellis et al
                  'A Survey of Application Generators' IEEE Software Vol 2 No
                  1 January (1985) 40-54

[Howe83]   D R Howe
                  Data Analysis for Data Base Design Edward Arnold Publishers
                  Ltd (1983)

[Inmos88a]   Inmos Ltd
                  Transputer Reference Manual Prentice Hall (1988)

[Inmos88b]   Inmos Ltd
                  Occam 2 Reference Manual Prentice Hall (1988)

[Inmos88c]   Inmos Ltd
                  Transputer Development System Prentice Hall (1988)

[Inmos88d]   Inmos Ltd
                  Transputer Instruction Set; A Compiler Writer's Guide Prentice
                  Hall (1988)

[Inmos89a]   Inmos Ltd
                  Transputer Technical Notes Prentice Hall (1989)

[Inmos89b]   Inmos Ltd
                  The Transputer Databook 2nd edition (1989) Inmos Ltd, Inmos
                  Document No 72 TRN 203 01

[Jackson83]   M A Jackson
                  System Development Prentice-Hall (1983)

[Kerridge87]   J M Kerridge
                'DRAT - A Proposal for a Dynamically Reconfigurable Array of Transputers to support database applications' Proc. 7th Occam User Group Meeting Grenoble, France, 14-16 September (1987) 29-45

[Mark85]   L Mark and N Roussopoulos
                'The New Database Architecture Framework - A Progress Report' in Information Systems: Theoretical and Formal Concepts Proc. IFIP WG8.1 Working Conference on Theoretical and Formal Aspects of Information Systems, Sitges, Barcelona, Spain, 16-18 April 1985, North-Holland (1985) 3-18

[Mark86]   L Mark and N Roussopolous
                'Metadata Management' IEEE Computer Vol 19 No 12 December (1986) 26-36

[McCraken82]   D D McCraken and M A Jackson
                'Life Cycle Concept Considered Harmful' ACM SIGSOFT Software Engineering Notes Vol 7 No 2 April (1982) 29-32

[Olle78]   T W Olle
                The Codasyl Approach to Data Base Management John Wiley & Sons (1978)

[Oakley89]   H Oakley
                'Mercury: an operating system for medium-grained parallelism' Microprocessors and Microsystems Vol 13 No2 March (1989) 97-102

[Perihelion89] Perihelion Software Ltd
                The Helios Operating System Prentice-Hall (1989)

[Poole87]   F Poole
                'DB4GL - An Intelligent Database System' in Research Papers of the Conference on Automating Systems Development Leicester Polytechnic, UK, April (1987)

[Rishe89]   N Rishe, D Tal, and Q Li
                'Architecture for a Massively Parallel Database Machine' Microprocessing and Microprogramming Vol 25 (1989) 33-38

62

[Roussopoulos85] N Roussopoulos and L Mark
'Schema Manipulation in Self-Documenting Data Models'
International Journal of Computer and Information Sciences Vol 14 No 1 (1985) 1-28

[Senko73] M E Senko, E B Altman, M M Astrahan and P L Fehder
'Data Structures and Accessing in Data-base Systems' IBM Systems Journal Vol 12 No 1 (1973) 64-93

[Senko76] M E Senko
'DIAM as a Detailed Example of the ANSI SPARC Architecture'
in G M Nijssen (ed) Modelling in Data Base Management Systems North-Holland (1976)

[Storer88] R Storer
'Data-driven software design using inversion' Information and Software Technology Vol 30 No 2 March (1988) 99-107

[Stringer89] R Stringer and L C Waring
'Transputer based database organization - an example protein database implemented using pipeline and hypercube configurations' in Proc. of OUG-10 [Bakkers89] 296-300

TriStarp -
An Investigation into the
Implementation and Exploitation
of Binary Relational
Storage Structures

Peter King, Mir Derakhshan, Alexandra Poulovassilis and Carol Small

Department of Computer Science
Birkbeck College, University of London

Abstract

The motivation and objectives of TriStarp are reviewed and the overall architecture of the project presented. This architecture comprises three levels, a binary relational storage structure (BRSS) at Level 0, a computationally complete database language at Level 1, and an end-user interface at Level 2. Requirements for the BRSS are identified and methods for its implementation are discussed. Two Level 1 languages have been developed which extend the BRSS with deductive and constraint enforcement capabilities, based upon the logic and functional paradigms. We identify a common architecture for these languages and show how they can be integrated to share data. We conclude with a discussion of further research directions for TriStarp.

1. Introduction

The binary relational data model has been forcefully argued as a prime candidate for the *conceptual schema* [Tsi78] by Senko [Sen76], Nijssen et al. [Nij76] and Shave [Sha81]. The fundamental nature of binary relations was emphasised by Bracchi et al. [Bra76] who observed that any n-ary relation can be represented by n+1 binary relations. In an important position paper [Fro82], Frost reviewed the binary relational model and its implementations and formulated the definition of a *binary relational storage structure* (BRSS) which we adopt. Related approaches are described by McGregor et al. [McG87] and Lavington et al. [Lav88]. A significant practical demonstration of the effectiveness of binary relational databases for small scale end-user applications is the NDB system [Sha78].

The objective of TriStarp (*Triple Store application reseach project*) is to explore and develop the binary relational approach as a common framework through from the basic storage level to the user interface and conceptual view. It was conjectured that

(i)   with such an approach we could develop full function database systems which include deductive facilities, integrity constraints, temporal data, and provision for modelling and storing arbitrarily complex objects;

(ii)   such systems could have a higher level of data independence than hitherto achieved; and

(iii)   future increases in hardware power and improved software techniques would make such systems practically realisable for the next generation of DBMS.

One objective of TriStarp is the efficient implementation of a BRSS at Level 0 (our storage level). Such a data store consists of a set of triples over which retrieval and update operations specify their arguments by content. In this aim we have followed the work of Lavington et al. [Lav84] in subdiving the BRSS into two sub-components, a *triple store* and a *lexical token converter*. We give a description of our approach in Section 2 of the paper. It is important to appreciate that the interface provided by Level 0 to the higher levels of TriStarp is one of the fundamental aspects of the project, its use rendering the higher levels completely independent of how the BRSS is implemented.

A further objective of TriStarp is to explore the capability of a BRSS to support deductive features at Level 1 (the logical level of TriStarp). Two candidates were identified for a Level 1 model. Firstly, a binary relationship R(A,B) can be interpreted as a two-place predicate and thus an integration with logic programming is possible. Secondly, a binary relationship R(A,B) can be interpreted as a function $R:A \rightarrow set(B)$ and its inverse $R^{-1}:B \rightarrow set(A)$ and an integration with functional programming is also possible. These two approaches led respectively to the development of the logic language Exegesis [Sma88a, Sma88b] and the functional language FDL [Pou89, Pou90]. In Section 3 of the paper we address the integration of these two languages into a unified Level 1 machine.

A third objective of TriStarp is the development of user interfaces. These interfaces should provide a simple presentation of the underlying concepts of Levels 0 and 1 but with no loss of expressiveness.

The current architecture of TriStarp thus consists of three levels as illustrated in Figure 1.1 below. We describe Levels 0 and 1 in some detail in Sections 2 and 3 of the paper. We use a lazy functional language to specify the semantics of these levels : in this language, $<x_1,...,x_n>$ denotes an n-tuple, [ ] denotes the empty list, (h : t) denotes a list with head h and tail t, the construct $[e \mid p_1 \leftarrow e_1; ... p_n \leftarrow e_n]$ is a list abstraction [Pey87], and the function "map" successively applies a function $f:t1 \rightarrow t2$ to a list of elements of type t1, returning a list of elements of type t2. In Section 4 we consider briefly possible user interfaces. Finally, in Section 5 we give our concluding remarks and plans for further research.

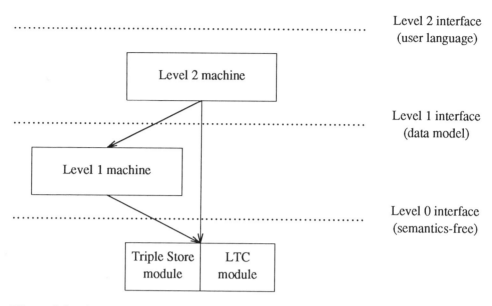

Figure 1.1 The TriStarp Architecture

2. Level 0

The Level 0 machine consists of a *triple store module* and a *lexical token converter module* (LTC). The triple store is *semantic-free* [Mar84] in the sense that it associates no meaning with the triples it stores. The triple store module supports operations for the storage and retrieval of triples of the form $<x_1, x_2, x_3>$, where each x_i is a fixed-length internal identifier generated by the LTC. An internal identifier is either associated with a unique lexical token, such as the string "P. King", the number 5, etc., or is system generated and not associated with any lexical token. A system generated identifier may, for example, be used by Levels 1 and 2 to denote an abstract entity which does not have a lexical representation. Two advantages follow from sub-dividing the Level 0 machine into a triple store and lexical token converter :

- Under the assumption that internal identifiers are shorter than the average size of a token, the use of an LTC acts as a form of data compaction.

- In our experience, deductive database systems tend to be heavily CPU bound. The use of an LTC tends to alleviate this problem since integer comparison and manipulation is normally considerably faster than comparison and manipulation of the associated lexical tokens.

The main function of the LTC is to provide two one-to-one mappings between triples of lexical tokens and their internal identifiers. The LTC module therefore supports two operations : the first, token_to_id, takes a triple of tokens and an LTC, and returns a pair comprising a triple of identifiers (corresponding to the tokens) and a new updated LTC ; the second operation, id_to_token, is the inverse of the first and takes a triple of internal identifiers and an LTC and returns the corresponding triple of tokens.

token_to_id : (token × token × token) → LTC → ((id × id × id) × LTC)
id_to_token : (id × id × id) → LTC → (token × token × token)

For example, given the triple <"held_at","BNCOD-8","york"> and an empty LTC, token_to_id will return the triple <id_1,id_2,id_3> and a new LTC which associates id_1 with the string "held_at", id_2 with "BNCOD-8", and id_3 with "york". Similarly, id_to_token when given <id_1,id_2,id_3> and the new LTC will yield <"held_at","BNCOD-8","york">.

The LTC should facilitate the maintenance of lexical tokens of type integer, floating-point, short string and long string. The need for facilities to deal with long strings arises from the realisation that many applications such as those managing text documents, images, and coded audio data often deal with strings of considerable lengths (of the order of one million characters) [Has82]. We do not consider the LTC any further here and the interested reader is referred to [Der89].

The triple store module provides operations for the insertion, deletion and retrieval of triples of internal identifiers from the triple store (TS) :

ts_insert :   id × id × id → TS → TS
ts_delete :   id × id × id → TS → TS
ts_retrieve :   id × id × id → TS → list(id × id × id)

For example,
      ts_retrieve <id_1, ?, ?> t
returns a list of all those triples in the triple store, t, which have the identifier id_1 in their first field, and
      ts_delete <id_1, ?, id_2> t
returns a new triple store obtained by removing from t all those triples with id_1 in their first field and id_2 in their third field. Either a *strict* or a *lazy* strategy may be adopted for retrieving the triples matching a given query. With a strict strategy, all the matching triples are retrieved and placed in an intermediate workspace, whereas with a lazy strategy they are retrieved one at a time upon request. A lazy strategy not only has the advantage of requiring no intermediate workspace but also can achieve a considerable reduction in computational cost when only a small subset of the matched triples are required and furthermore leads to a greater flexibility in coding tasks which require processing of inter-related queries. It should, however, be noted that an implication of adopting a lazy strategy is the need for a mechanism to resolve cases where updates and retrievals conflict, for example ts_delete <id_1, ?, id_2> t and and ts_retrieve <id_1, ?, ?> t. Such a mechanism would be required regardless of whether the environment considered is single-user or multi-user.

It follows from the above discussion that the Level 0 database consists of a triple store and an LTC, DB ≡ TS × LTC, and the operations provided by Level 0 to

67

Level 1 are :

(i)   the creation of an empty database, that is an empty triple store and LTC :

> **create** : → DB
> **create** = <[ ], [ ]>

(ii)   the insertion of a single triple of tokens :

> **insert** : token × token × token → DB → DB
> **insert** <t1,t2,t3> <ts,ltc>   =
>   `let` <<id1, id2, id3>, new_ltc> = token_to_id <t1,t2,t3> ltc `in`
>   `let` new_ts = ts_insert <id1, id2, id3> ts `in`
>   <new_ts, new_ltc>

(iii)   the deletion of a set of triples by partial specification of their three fields :

> **delete** : token × token × token → DB → DB
> **delete** <t1,t2,t3> <ts,ltc>   =
>   `let` <<id1, id2, id3>, new_ltc> = token_to_id <t1,t2,t3> ltc `in`
>   `let` new_ts = ts_delete <id1, id2, id3> ts `in`
>   <new_ts, new_ltc>

(iv)   and the retrieval of a set of triples also by partial specification :

> **retrieve** : token × token × token → DB → list(token × token × token)
> **retrieve** <t1,t2,t3> <ts,ltc>   =
>   `let` <<id1, id2, id3>, new_ltc> = token_to_id <t1,t2,t3> ltc `in`
>   map id_to_token (ts_retrieve <id1,id2,id3> ts)

In the remainder of this section we consider aspects relating to triple store implementation. Either a hardware or a software approach may be adopted for implementing such stores, although it seems that "lazy query processing" is a software
issue only. It is not the aim of this paper to discuss the relative merits of the two
approaches but rather to consider a particular approach and possible implementations for it. To this end, we consider possible software implementations and refer
the reader to [Lav88] for a discussion of hardware. The remainder of this section
is divided into two parts, Section 2.1 discussing the main issues that we believe
should be considered for a software implementation, and Section 2.2 discussing
software techniques which could take these issues into account.

2.1. Requirements for a Software Implementation of the Triple Store Module

One approach employed by software implementations of triple stores is to keep a
single copy of the triples in a master file and to build secondary indexes specific
to different types of queries [Fro82], for example an index for queries which
specify only the first field and another index for those which specify only the
third field. It is clear that such an approach is unsuitable for update-intensive

68

applications since the master file and the indexes must all be maintained. More-over, we would expect several disk page accesses to occur when using a secondary index since it is likely that the data matching the query will be scattered over the master file. Since the number of disk accesses incurred in processing a query is a dominant factor on the response time, it is more desirable to have an implementation which encourages the clustering of related data into the same disk pages.

Other software approaches can be categorised broadly into those which replicate data to improve query response times at the expense of greater storage and update costs, and those which do not replicate data but have a generally poorer query performance.

For an application which requires good performance for both updates and queries, a more suitable approach may be one which promises fast response times for updates and provides a *tuning facility* to minimise the average query response time. Such a tuning facility may be based upon information regarding the *probability distributions* of the expected queries. The need for tuning is evident as different applications in general deal with different mixes of queries and hence have different query processing requirements. For example, it may be the case that in a particular application the majority of the queries have the first and the second fields specified, whereas in another application the majority have only the second field specified. Thus, a different approach to implementing triple stores would be to use file organisation techniques which not only can take account of such differences in query processing requirements but also provide good performance for updates.

We conclude this sub-section with the observation that it is sometimes necessary to re-tune an existing system without re-organising the existing triples before further use of the triple store. This will be the case when the query processing requirements for a system already in use changes and the Database Administrator does not wish to re-organise the existing triples with respect to the new requirements but does wish the modifications resulting form updates to take the new requirements into account. Thus, the ability to re-tune gradually with future updates should be an important software consideration.

2.2. Software techniques for triple store implementation

In the discussion above we identified the following as important requirements for a software implementation of a triple store :

(i)   good performance for updates,

(ii)   clustering of related data into the same disk pages so as to improve query performance, and

(iii) a tuning (re-tuning) facility to minimise the average query response time on the basis of supplied information on the probability distributions of queries.

With respect to point (ii), we expect Level 1 to utilise any clustering facilities provided at Level 0 by assembling logically related data into a set of triples which is likely to be clustered. With respect to point (iii), we envisage that the query information is available from an analysis of application requirements, or is determined from an analysis of the triple store in operation, or by way of some appropriate operations.

Multi-dimensional file organisations facilitate maintenance and retrieval operations on records with a common format comprising a fixed number of key fields. Thus, we observe that a 3-dimensional organisation can be used to provide all the operations required on a triple store; in particular, the class of methods known as *dynamic multi-dimensional clustering methods* are particularly promising because of their characteristics, which we discuss below. These methods include grid files [Nie84, Hin85, Ouk85, Fre87], multi-dimensional extendible hashing methods [Tam81, Oto84, Oto86], and multi-dimensional tree-based methods such as the k-d-b-tree [Rob81] and the extended k-d-tree [Cha81].

The characterising features of a dynamic clustering method are :

(a) The *k-dimensional data space* (the space obtained from the cartesian product of the k key domains) is partitioned using hyper-rectangular (box-shaped) subspaces. With the exception of the Balanced and Nested Grid File (BANG) method [Fre87], the subspaces are disjoint as exemplified by the following diagram; the BANG file partitions the data space in the form of nested hyper-rectangles.

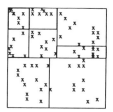

(b) Records corresponding to points in a particular partition are stored in the same disk page; hence the term "clustering". We refer to such a page as a *data page* and a partition as a *region*, and there is thus a one-to-one correspondence between regions and data pages.

(c) The *data file*, that is the set of all the data pages, grows and shrinks as the result of data page splitting and merging, the corresponding regions splitting and merging accordingly; hence the term "dynamic".

We observe from (b) above that a dynamic clustering method promises good update performance since the insertion or deletion of a record will usually require an update to a single data page only and more than one data page will be involved only when a split or merge occurs. In the remainder of this section we show that, in general, these methods also offer high potential for query performance tuning since the dynamic partitioning of the data space caused by the splitting and merging of regions can be controlled to suit given requirements. We consider only those methods which partition in the form of disjoint hyper-rectangles and thus the following discussion does not include the BANG file.

As stated in (b) above, a characterising feature of a dynamic clustering method is the growth (shrinkage) of the data file by means of splitting (merging) of data pages. When the insertion of a new record causes a data page to overflow, the page is split into two pages according to a *splitting policy*, and its corresponding region is split into two disjoint regions accordingly (so that the one-to-one correspondence between the data pages and the regions is preserved). The function of a splitting policy is to choose the dimension and point of split, that is the exact place at which the region is to be divided into two disjoint regions. Similarly, when the deletion of a record causes a data page to become undesirably under-populated, the page is considered for merging with another page. A constraint on merging is that the newly merged page must correspond to a hyper-rectangular subspace. Furthermore, with methods such as those in [Ouk85, Cha81], merging is restricted to be the exact inverse of splitting, that is two pages can merge only if their regions had been created from the same region split. The methods of [Nie84, Hin85, Oto86], however, do not impose this restriction and usually have the luxury of a choice from several candidate pages, any one of which can merge with the under-populated page. With these latter methods, a *merging policy* is used to make the choice.

With a little thought it is easily noted that the configuration of regions obtained by a splitting (merging) policy governs the number of page accesses needed to process a query. Consider for example the three different partitionings into 16 regions of the same two-dimensional data space illustrated in Figure 2.1 below. The configuration in (1) achieves symmetrical processing for queries which only specify a single field since the same number of data pages, in this case 4, will be searched for all such queries. However, the configuration shown in (2) is completely biased towards queries which only specify the field corresponding to the vertical dimension since only 1 data page will be searched as opposed to 16 for a query specifying only the horizontal dimension. Similarly, the configuration in (3) is completely biased towards queries which specify only the horizontal dimension.

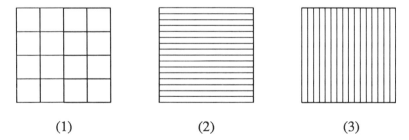

(1)   (2)   (3)

Figure 2.1. Three different partitionings of the same two-dimensional data space

In conclusion, the splitting and merging policies should be dependent on the application as different applications in general have different mixes of queries and hence different query distributions. For example, if the majority of queries in an application have the ith field specified only, then the splitting policy should select dimension i more frequently than the other dimensions.

In [Der89], the grid file method of Nievergelt *et al.* is considered as a case in point and the notions of splitting and merging are formalised to take account of the probability distributions of queries. In particular, the PDS (Parameter Driven Splitting) policy and the PDM (Parameter Driven Merging) policy are introduced, each of which is parameterised with respect to the probability distributions regarding both the expected form of, and the expected specified values in, queries. By "form" of a query, we mean the combination of the specified and unspecified fields in the query. In the remainder of this section, we briefly describe the PDS splitting policy. The reader is referred to [Der89] for more details including the PDM merging policy and some performance figures.

Let us consider a 3-dimensional data space and denote by Δ_i the domain of dimension i (i=1,2,3), where each Δ_i is assumed to be linearly ordered. Let us also denote the form of a query as a subset of {1,2,3} the elements of which define the fields specified in the query, and let us use Q as a variable ranging over the different query forms. Thus, denoting a specified field by * and an unspecified field by ?, Q may take one of the six query forms :

$$\{1\} = <*, ?, ?>, \qquad \{2\} = <?, *, ?>, \qquad \{3\} = <?, ?, *>,$$
$$\{1,2\} = <*, *, ?>, \qquad \{1,3\} = <*, ?, *>, \qquad \{2,3\} = <?, *, *>.$$

We not consider the query form <?, ?, ?> as it represents the entire triple store. Also, we do not consider the query form <*, *, *> as it will always result in a search through a single data page irrespective of the configuration of the regions over the data space.

Now, let P_Q be the probability that a query is of form Q, and $pr(x_i \in R_i)$ the probability that the specified value in a query of form {i} lies in the interval $R_i \subseteq \Delta_i$. Similarly, let $pr((x_i, x_j) \in R_i \times R_j)$ be the probability that the pair of specified values in a query of form {i,j} belongs to $R_i \times R_j$, where $R_i \subseteq \Delta_i$ and $R_j \subseteq \Delta_j$. Suppose that a page requires splitting and denote by $R = R_1 \times R_2 \times R_3$ the region corresponding to this page, where R_i is the interval obtained from projecting region R in dimension i and hence $R_i \subseteq \Delta_i$. In [Der89], it is proved that if the region R splits in dimension i, then the consequent increase in the average number of page accesses needed to process a query, denoted by C_i, is :

$$C_i = P_{\{j\}} \cdot pr(x_j \in R_j) + P_{\{k\}} \cdot pr(x_k \in R_k) + P_{\{j,k\}} \cdot pr((x_j, x_k) \in R_j \times R_k)$$
where $j \neq k \neq i$.

This result is used by the PDS splitting policy to choose the dimension of split to be the dimension k such that C_k is the minimum of C_1, C_2 and C_3. The PDS splitting policy thus generalises the notion of splitting as it takes account of the probability distributions of queries. For example, it can be easily seen that a configuration similar to any one of the three shown in Figure 2.1 can be obtained by supplying the appropriate probability distributions.

2.3. Summary

In this section we have discussed how the sub-division of Level 0 into triple store and lexical token converter modules provides both a form of data compaction and a method of reducing the CPU cost of applications developed at Level 1, how the adoption of a lazy retrieval strategy by the Level 0 machine results in a reduction of intermediate workspace and considerable savings when only a small subset of the triples matching a query are required, and how multi-dimensional file organisations can be adapted to take into consideration expected query distributions to provide better retrieval performance.

In the next section we discuss how Level 0 can be utilised by Level 1 for the storage and retrieval of its persistent data structures.

3. Level 1

The aim of Level 1 is to enhance the underlying Level 0 machine by providing integrity constraints and rules for the deduction of implied and default information. So far, two Level 1 languages have been developed : the logic language Exegesis, which is described in [Sma88a, Sma88b], and the functional language FDL, which is described in [Pou89, Pou90]. Although Exegesis and FDL were developed independently, a major aim is their ultimate integration in order to remove redundant functionality while retaining the expressive power of both approaches. As the first step towards this integration, we address the problem of defining a uniform representation for the storage of functional and logic rules. As will become apparent below, this representation allows the two Level 1 languages to share a number of common modules; more importantly, applications developed using the two languages will be able to access the majority of each other's data (the fact base).

We begin this section by defining two simplified declarative languages, a logic language, L, and a functional language, F, in Sections 3.1 and 3.2 respectively. We then introduce an abstract syntax which unifies both L and F in Section 3.3. In Section 3.4 we describe the integrated Level 1 architecture. Finally, in Sections 3.5 and 3.6 we describe in detail two key components of this architecture.

3.1. The Logic Language

The syntax for L, our archetypal logic language at Level 1, is given below, where {$construct$} represents 0 or more occurrences of a construct :

statement :	Insert_L eqn | Delete_L eqn | Query_L exp
eqn :	atom | atom "←" exp
exp :	atom {"&" atom}
atom :	pred "(" term {"," term} ")"
term :	var | fun-symbol | fun-symbol "(" term {"," term} ")"

We note that an equation in the above syntax corresponds to a Horn clause and an exp(ression) corresponds to a goal (or query) clause. We have not given productions for pred(icates), var(iables), or function symbols since we assume that they are primitive syntactic constructs. Thus, for example, clauses to determine the length of a list are given by the following L statements :

Insert$_L$ length(nil,0)
Insert$_L$ length(cons(X,Y),+(1,Z)) ← length(Y,Z)

Of course, the language L is rather simplistic lacking, for example, list notation, negation as failure [Cla78], default rules [Rei80] and integrity constraints [Nic82], but it will suffice to demonstrate the salient points of our Level 1 architecture.

3.2. The Functional Language

The syntax for F, our archetypal functional language at Level 1, is given below. For simplicity we have assumed that F is untyped (cf. FP [Bac78]) and we leave for future research the problem of typing a unified functional and logic language.

statement :	Insert$_F$ eqn I Delete$_F$ eqn I Query$_F$ exp
eqn :	fun {pattern} "=" exp {"," exp}
exp :	var I fun I const I exp exp I "(" exp ")"
pattern :	var I const {pattern} I "(" pattern ")"

The functions of F can return *multi-sets*, that is lists whose elements appear in a non-deterministic order. For example, the following equation records the authors of this paper :

authors "TriStarp ..." =   "M.Derakhshan", "P.King", "C.Small",
                          "A.Poulovassilis"

We have not given productions for fun(ctions), var(iables), or const(ructors) above since we assume that they are primitive syntactic constructs. Also, we regard built-in constants (numbers, booleans and characters) as constructors of zero arity. Thus, for example, we may define a function which determines the length of a list by the following F statements, where "cons" and "nil" are the usual list constructors :

Insert$_F$ length nil = 0
Insert$_F$ length (cons X Y) = + 1 (length Y)

Again, the language F is simple lacking, for example, local definitions and list abstractions [Pey87] but it will suffice for our present purposes.

3.3.   The Abstract Syntax

Statements in both L and F can be converted into the following unifying *abstract syntax expressions* (AEs), where [AE] represents a list of AEs :

AE :   Insert [AE] I Delete [AE] I Query$_F$ AE I Query$_L$ [AE] I
        Var num I Op string [AE] I Con string [AE]

In this abstract syntax, the predicates of L and the functions of F are represented by Op(erators), and the function symbols of L and constructors of F by Con(stants). For example, the two L statements defining "length" in Section 3.1

are represented by

       Insert [Op "length" [Con "nil" [ ], Con "0" [ ]]]

and

       Insert [Op "length"
              [Con "cons" [Var "X", Var "Y"], Con "+" [Con "1" [ ], Var "Z"]],
              Op "length" [Var "Y", Var "Z"]]]

We distinguish between the *facts* and *rules* in our two languages, L and F. An equation of L with no right hand side (RHS) is a fact, otherwise it is a rule. An equation of F with no operators on its RHS is a fact, otherwise it is a rule. Thus, L and F can share the same fact base if any functional equation

       $f\ p_1\ ...\ p_n = E_1, E_2,..., E_m$

is represented as m logic equations with no RHS :

      $f\ (p_1,...,p_n,E_1)$
      $f\ (p_1,...,p_n,E_2)$

      ...

      $f\ (p_1,...,p_n,E_m)$

For example, the functional equation

      length nil = 0

is represented by the same abstract syntax as the logic equation

      length(nil,0)

and can thus be shared by both L and F. Similarly, the functional equation

      authors "TriStarp ..." = "M.Derakhshan", "P.King", "C.Small",
                         "A.Poulovassilis"

is represented by the same abstract syntax as the four logic equations below and can be shared by both L and F :

      authors("TriStarp ...","M.Derakhshan")
      authors("TriStarp ...","P.King")
      authors("TriStarp ...","C.Small")
      authors("TriStarp ...","A.Poulovassilis")

We note that, in general, equations of F and L which are rules will not be sharable. For example, the second F statement defining "length" in Section 3.2 is represented by

      Insert [Op "length"   [Con "cons" [Var "X", Var "Y"],
                         Con "+" [Con "1" [ ], Op "length" [Var "Y"]]]]

which differs from the representation given above for the second L statement for "length".

3.4.   The Level 1 Architecture

The Level 1 architecture falls into two parts : the *update architecture*, illustrated in Figure 3.1 below, handles the insertion and removal of information while the *query architecture*, illustrated in Figure 3.2, handles the evaluation of queries.

3.4.1. The Update Architecture

Updates at Level 1 consist of the insertion and deletion of equations. An equation (of L or F) to be inserted or deleted is converted by the *translator* into an AE. The equation is then passed to the *assembler* which constructs a series of triple insertion or deletion requests to be passed to Level 0. We describe the assembly of equations in Section 3.5 below.

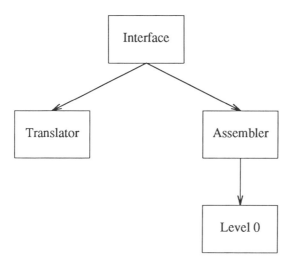

Figure 3.1. Update Architecture

3.4.2. The Query Architecture

Queries are also converted into the form of an AE by the translator, before being passed to the appropriate *evaluator* for evaluation.

In the case of a logic query, the evaluator simulates *SLD-Resolution* [Llo88] by taking a list of AEs (representing the atoms of a goal clause), and repeatedly transforming the list until an empty list (representing the empty clause) is derived. At each transformation step, the evaluator selects an atom from the goal and retrieves from Level 0 all the equations whose left hand side (LHS) unifies with the atom. For each of these equations, the selected atom is replaced in the goal by the atoms on the RHS of the equation, and the evaluator calls itself recursively with the new list.

In the case of a functional query, the evaluator transforms the AE into a *normal form* [Fie88] by repeatedly selecting and simplifying reducible sub-expressions (*redexes*), where a redex is a function applied to the correct number of arguments. The evaluator retrieves from Level 0 the equation whose LHS is the most specific match for the given function and arguments, instantiates the variables in the RHS of this equation to their corresponding arguments, and replaces the redex by the resulting RHS. For functions returning multi-sets there may be a number of equations with the same, most specific, LHS in which case the redex is replaced by a list constructed from their RHSs.

76

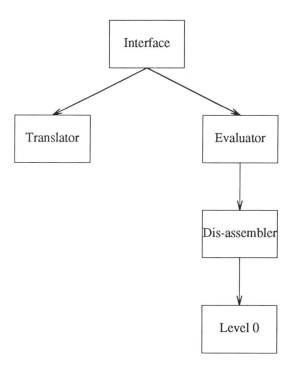

Figure 3.2. Query Architecture

3.5. The Assembler/Dis-Assembler

We now turn our attention to the two key components of our unified Level 1 architecture : in this section we consider the assembler/dis-assembler, and in section 3.6 below we consider the evaluator.

The assembler takes the list of AEs representing an equation to be inserted or deleted and assembles a series of triples to be inserted or deleted by Level 0. For the purposes of the unified Level 1 machine, we assume that Level 0 stores triples of the form <token,token,token> where a token has the syntax :

      token : Var num | Op string | Con string | Node num | Arg | Empty

For each operator, p, a set of triples

    <Node EqnRoot, Op p, Node n_1>, <Node EqnRoot, Op p, Node n_2>, ...,
    <Node EqnRoot, Op p, Node n_m>

are stored in the database, where Node EqnRoot is a unique, system-reserved, token and each Node n_i is a token uniquely identifying a further set of triples representing one equation for p. The triples representing an equation take the form of an S-expression and all have the same token Node n_i in their first field. For example, we can visualise the second L equation of "length" in Section 3.3 as the S-expression shown in Figure 3.3.

77

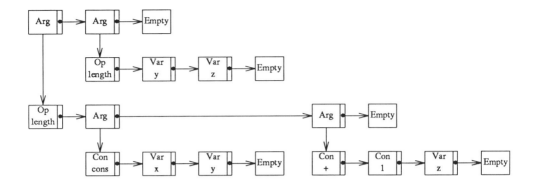

Figure 3.3. S-expression representation of an equation

Each cell of the S-expression has three components : an address given by an in-order traversal of the S-expression, a value and an implicit pointer to the next cell. Consequently, the decomposition of such an S-expression into a set of triples each with the same first field is straight-forward. For example, the S-expression of Figure 3.3 is represented by the following triples, where Node n_k is the unique token identifying the second L equation of "length" :

<Node n_k, Node 1, Arg>,	<Node n_k, Node 2, Op "length">,
<Node n_k, Node 3, Arg>,	<Node n_k, Node 4, Con "cons">,
<Node n_k, Node 5, Var "X">,	<Node n_k, Node 6, Var "Y">,
<Node n_k, Node 7, Empty>,	<Node n_k, Node 8, Arg>,
<Node n_k, Node 9, Con "+">,	<Node n_k, Node 10, Con "1">,
<Node n_k, Node 11, Var "Z">,	<Node n_k, Node 12, Empty>,
<Node n_k, Node 13, Empty>,	<Node n_k, Node 14, Arg>,
<Node n_k, Node 15, Op "length">,	<Node n_k, Node 16, Var "Y">,
<Node n_k, Node 17, Var "Z">,	<Node n_k, Node 18, Empty>,
<Node n_k, Node 19, Empty>	

The dis-assembler takes a database and the token identifying an equation and reverses the process undertaken by the assembler. Thus, for example, the following call to the dis-assembler reconstructs the AE for the second L equation of "length" :

$\qquad$ **dis-assemble** db (Node n_k)

3.6. The Evaluator

The evaluator is the only module of the proposed architecture which requires two versions, one for each of the languages L and F. Thus, in Sections 3.6.1 and 3.6.2 below we describe the evaluators for L and F respectively. In Section 3.6.1 we assume the reader has some familiarity with SLD-resolution (definitions for any italicised terms can be found in [Llo88]).

3.6.1. The Evaluator for L

Our evaluator for the logic language regards a query (or goal) as a list of atoms, $[A_1, ..., A_n]$, and attempts to construct a list of all possible substitutions σ for the variables in the atoms such that $(A_1 \& ... \& A_n)\sigma$ is implied by the database. In our definition of the evaluator below, we represent a substitution as a list of pairs of AEs, and use the synonym sub $\equiv$ list(AE $\times$ AE). In a substitution [<Var k_1, AE_1>, ..., <Var k_n, AE_n>] each Var k_i represents a variable and each AE_i a term. If $\sigma = [v_1/t_1, ..., v_n/t_n]$ is a substitution and A is an AE then $A\sigma$ is the AE obtained by simultaneously replacing each occurrence of v_i in A by t_i. A substitution σ is a *unifier* of two AEs A_1 and A_2 if $A_1\sigma = A_2\sigma$, and a *most general unifier* (*mgu*) if for any other unifier, τ, there exists a substitution ψ such that $(A_1\sigma)\psi = A_1\tau$ and $(A_2\sigma)\psi = A_2\tau$.

The evaluator, defined below, requires a function "unify" which takes two atoms, a_1 and a_2, and a current substitution, ψ, and returns <True,σ> if $a_1\psi$ and $a_2\psi$ are unifiable with mgu σ, and <False,[ ]> otherwise. The notion of a *derived* goal can be couched in terms of "unify" : from <$[a_1, ..., a_n]$,ϕ> we can derive the goal <$[b_1, ..., b_m, a_2, ..., a_n]$,$\sigma$> if there is an equation $[lhs, b_1, ..., b_m]$ such that
      unify a_1 lhs ϕ = <True,σ>

The evaluator, **eval$_L$**, simulates the construction of all *SLD-refutations* of a goal. **eval$_L$** takes a pair comprising a list of AEs representing a goal clause together with an empty substitution, and gives the list of all substitutions, σ, such that there is a finite sequence <goal,[ ]> $\equiv$ <g_1,σ_1>, <g_2,σ_2>, ..., <g_n,σ_n> $\equiv$ <[ ],σ> where each <g_i,σ_i> is derived from <g_{i-1},σ_{i-1}>. If such a σ can be constructed then gσ is implied by the rules and shared facts.

```
eval_L : DB → (list(AE) × sub) → list(sub)
eval_L db <[ ],s>          = [s]
eval_L db <(Op p args) : t, old-sub> =
  concatenate
  [eval_L db <append t rhs,compose old-sub new-sub> |
    (lhs:rhs) ← [dis-assemble db id |
                      <n1,n2,id> ← retrieve <Node EqnRoot,Op p,?> db];
      <True,new-sub> ← [unify (Op p args) lhs old-sub]
  ]
```

We note that the above evaluator undertakes a breadth-first search of the SLD-tree for our logic and shared equations, and that consequently all SLD-refutations of the goal will be found. A depth-first search would be obtained by changing the head of the list abstraction to :

    eval$_L$ db <*append rhs t*,compose old-sub new-sub>

This would then be equivalent to a Prolog evaluator provided the database returns equations in the order in which they were inserted.

3.6.2. The Evaluator for F

The functional evaluator **eval**$_F$ takes an AE and transforms it to a normal form AE, that is an AE containing no redexes. We observe that our definition of **eval**$_F$ below is similar to that of **eval**$_L$, the main differences being that

(i)   the arguments of the operator are evaluated before the redex is unified against the equations (hence, the functions of F are evaluated *strictly* [Pey87]);

(ii) each equation defining the operator consists of a single AE (since, from our discussion in Section 3.3, F equations are represented as L equations with no RHS);

(iii) the unused variable Var 0 is appended to the argument list of the operator to unify with the last term in the LHS (which represents the RHS of the original F equation);

(iv) the substitutions constructed by "unify" for equations which unify with the redex are passed to the operation

> select : token → list(sub) → AE

which chooses a single substitution, σ, and returns the instantiation of (Var 0) with respect to σ. The choice of substitution is governed by a *pattern matching strategy* adopted for F, for example "best-fit" pattern matching as used by HOPE+ [Fie88] or "left-to-right" pattern-matching as used by FDL [Pou89, 90]. For a multi-valued function, there may be a number of substitutions which are identical for all variables apart from Var 0 (and are thus equally eligible to be chosen by the pattern matching strategy). In this case the instantiations of Var 0 are formed into a list (in an arbitrary order) and this is the AE returned by "select".

```
evalF : DB → AE → AE
evalF db (Con c args)    = Con c (map (evalF db) args)
evalF db (Op p args)     =
  let args´ = append (map (evalF db) args) [Var 0] in
  evalF db
    (select (Op p)
    [new_sub |
    [lhs] ← [dis-assemble db id |
                    <n1,n2,id> ← retrieve <Node EqnRoot,Op p,?> db];
     <True,new_sub> ← [unify (Op p args´) lhs [ ] ]
    ])
```

3.7.   Summary

In this section we have described a unified architecture for two declarative languages L and F both of which enhance the underlying Level 0 machine with rules for the derivation of implied information. This common architecture allows the two Level 1 languages to share a number of common modules and to access a large proportion of each other's data (the fact base).

We have seen how L and F equations can be assembled into sets of triples for storage by the Level 0 machine. We have utilised the clustering facility provided by Level 0 by giving the triples representing an equation the same unique identifier in their first field. We observe that the evaluators for L and F call **retrieve** with the query form <*, *, ?> while the dis-assembler calls **retrieve** with the query form <*, ?, ?> (to obtain all the triples constituting an S-expression before reconstructing the AE in memory). Thus, the PDS splitting policy can be utilised to bias query processing in favour of these two query forms.

Two aspects of the integrated architecture require further work. Firstly, the evaluators should be optimised to retrieve equations *lazily* according to the unifiability of their LHS with the selected atom, as opposed to retrieving them fully and then unifying with the select atom. Secondly, a more compact method of storing facts is required; in particular, a binary relationship should occupy no more than one triple.

4.   Level 2

The objective of the Level 2 machine is to deliver at the user interface the facilities provided by Levels 0 and 1 in a way that is not only ergonomically acceptable but also aids conceptualisation and, where necessary, the process of database design. Hitherto, work at Level 2 has been under-resourced relative to Levels 0 and 1, although arguably concrete results at these levels are needed before extensive Level 2 work can proceed.

To date only a single experimental user interface has been developed, the Fluent system [Nic88], which attempts to provide a pseudo-natural language utilising the facilities provided by Exegesis at Level 1. Fluent aims to free the user from the need to model the world explicitly in terms of objects identified as non-lexical entities, and instead to capture the implicit modelling which occurs in the natural use of natural language. The implementation was limited by being confined to interfacing with the user via a simple text terminal rather than a more general workstation. As yet no user interfaces have been constructed over FDL.

The importance of research at the end user interface has been emphasised in the Laguna Beach Report [Lag89] which states that "there are virtually no researchers investigating better end user interfaces to data bases", that "there was a universal consensus that this was an extremely important area", and that in order to investigate such interfaces "a mammoth amount of low level code must be constructed before the actual interface can be built." It is indeed our experience that the user interface is inherently more difficult than we had hitherto supposed and it is now clear that more research effort must be devoted to it if the long-term goals of TriStarp are to be realised.

5. Conclusions and Future Work

Work on TriStarp commenced in October 1984 by the first author (PK) and a group of three full time research students, including MD and CS; the third author

81

(AP) joined the project in 1986. The architecture of Figure 1.1 was soon established and investigations were made into a suitable approach for Level 0.

A development of Nievergelt's grid file was fixed on for Level 0, a new form of directory for the grid file was devised and methods for optimisation were developed to take account of query distributions. A robust implementation was made which is now used in the project's operational software. We have identified areas for further improvement, including the need to deal with interval queries. Performance comparisons of our Level 0 with the hardware BRSS of Lavington would be of interest.

The major effort of the project to date has been at Level 1 with the design and implementation of two independent systems, the logic based Exegesis and the functional FDL. Exegesis included facilities for default rules, essentially following the work of Reiter [Rei80], and new theoretical results were obtained on conditions which a set of default rules must satisfy to avoid the derivation of conflicting assumptions. FDL extended the functional data model to computational completeness, thus obtaining a uniform approach to factual, procedural and default data. The implementations of Exegesis and FDL are both based upon the architecture of Section 3.4. Initial work aimed at unifying these languages has been summarised in this paper and is described in greater detail in [Sma90].

A major thrust of the project from October 1989 has been in the area of the Level 2 user interface upon which two full time and one part time students are working. This development aims to take account of the workstation developments using windowing (cf. Smalltalk). A further theme being investigated by one full time research student is the introduction of temporal facilities with the object, in particular, of establishing at which level the time dimension should be introduced into the TriStarp architecture.

Acknowledgements

The authors are grateful for the financial support of the SERC and of IBM United Kingdom Laboratories Ltd. Alexandra Poulovassilis currently holds a Postdoctoral Fellowship from the SERC at the Department of Computer Science, University College London. The authors are particularly grateful to Dr G.C.H Sharman of IBM for his continued interest in and encouragement of the project, to Norman Winterbottom (also of IBM) and to Nigel Nicholson.

References

[Bra76]   Bracchi, G. Paolini, P. and Pelagatti, G. *Binary Logical Associations in Data Modelling*, in [Nij76].

[Cha81]   Chang, J.M. and Fu, K.S. *A Dynamic Clustering Technique for Physical Database Design*, IEEE Trans. on Softw. Eng. 7(3) 1981.

[Cla78]   Clark, K. *Negation as Failure*, in Logic and Databases (Eds Gallaire, H. Minker, J.), Plenum Press, 1978.

[Der89]   Derakhshan, M. *A Development of the Grid File for the Storage of Binary Relations*, Ph.D. Thesis, Birkbeck College, Univ. of London, 1989.

[Fie88]   Field, A.J. and Harrison, P.G. *Functional Programming*, Addison-Wesley, 1988.

[Fre87]   Freeston, M. *The BANG File : a new kind of Grid File*, Proc. ACM SIGMOD 1987.

[Fro82]   Frost, R.A. *Binary-Relational Storage Structures*, The Computer Journal, 25(3) 1982.

[Has82]   Haskin, R.L. and Lorie, R.A. *On Extending the Functions of a Relational Database System*, Proc. ACM SIGMOD 1982.

[Hin85]   Hinrichs, K.H. *The Grid File System : Implementation and Case Studies of Applications*, Doctor of Technical Sciences Dissertation, Swiss Federal Institute of Technology, Zurich, 1985.

[Lag89]   *The Laguna Beach Report*, SIGMOD Record, 18(1) 1989.

[Lav84]   Lavington, S.H. and Wang, C. *A Lexical Token Converter for the IFS*, Internal Report IFS/5/84, Department of Computer Science, Univ. of Manchester.

[Lav88]   Lavington, S.H. *Technical Overview of the Intelligent File Store*, Knowledge Based Systems, 1(3) 1988.

[Llo88]   Lloyd, J.W. *Foundations of Logic Programming (2nd Edition)*, Springer-Verlag, 1988.

[Mar84]   Martin, N.J. *The Construction of Interfaces to Triple Based Machines*, 3rd BNCOD, Cambridge University Press, 1984.

[McG87]   McGregor, D. McInnes, S. and Henning, M. *An Architecture for Associative Processing of Large Knowledge Bases*, Computer Journal, 30(5) 1987.

[Mil78]   Milner, R. *A Theory of Type Polymorphism in Programming*, Journal of Computer and System Science, 17 1978.

[Nic82]   Nicolas, J.M. *Logic for Improving Integrity Checking in Relational Databases*, Acta Informatica, 18 1982.

[Nic88]   Nicholson, N. *The Design of a User-Interface to a Deductive Database : A Sentence Based Approach*, Ph.D. Thesis, Birkbeck College, Univ. of London, 1988.

[Nie84]   Nievergelt, J., Hinterberger, H. and Sevcik, K.C. *The Grid File : An Adaptable, Symmetric Multikey File Structure*, ACM Trans. on Database Systems, 9(1) 1984.

[Nij76]   Nijssen, G.M. *Modelling in Data Base Management Systems*, Proc. IFIP TC-2, North Holland, 1976.

[Oto84]   Otoo, E.J. *A Mapping Function for the Directory of a Multidimensional Extendible Hashing*, Proc. ACM SIGMOD 1985.

[Oto86] Otoo, E.J. *Balanced Multidimensional Extendible Hash Tree*, Proc. ACM SIGACT-SIGMOD PoDS 1986.

[Ouk85] Ouksel, M. *The Interpolation-Based Grid File*, Proc. ACM SIGACT-SIGMOD PoDS 1985.

[Pey87] Peyton Jones, S.L. *The Implementation of Functional Programming Languages*, Prentice-Hall, 1987.

[Pou89] Poulovassilis, A. *The Design and Implementation of FDL, a Functional Database Language*, Ph.D. Thesis, Birkbeck College, Univ. of London, 1989.

[Pou90] Poulovassilis, A. and King, P. *Extending the Functional Data Model to Computational Completeness*, To appear in Proc. EDBT-90, March 1990, Springer-Verlag.

[Rei80] Reiter, R. *A Logic for Default Reasoning*, Artificial Intelligence, 13 1980.

[Rob81] Robinson, J.T. "The K-D-B-Tree: A Search Structure for Large Multidimensional Dynamic Indexes, Proc. ACM SIGMOD 1981.

[Sen76] Senko, M.E. *DIAM as a Detailed Example of the ANSI/SPARC Architecture* in [Nij76].

[Sha78] Sharman, G.C.H. and Winterbottom, N. *The Data Dictionary Facilities of NDB*, Proc. 4th VLDB 1978.

[Sha81] Shave, M.J.R. *Entities, functions and binary relations : steps to a conceptual schema*, Computer Journal, 24(1) 1981.

[Shi81] Shipman, D.W. *The Functional Data Model and the Data Language DAPLEX*, A.C.M. Transactions on Database Systems, 6(1) 1981.

[Sma88a] Small, C. *Guarded Default Databases : an approach to the control of Incomplete Information*, Ph.D. Thesis, Birkbeck College, Univ. of London, 1988.

[Sma88b] Small, C. *Guarded Default Databases : A Prototype Implementation*, in "Prolog and Databases : Implementations and New Directions" (Eds. Gray, P.M.D. and Lucas, R.J.), Ellis Horwood, 1988.

[Sma90] Small, C. and Poulovassilis, A. *On the coupling of logic and functional databases*, submitted for publication.

[Tam81] Tamminen, M. *Order Preserving Extendible Hashing and Bucket Tries*, BIT, 21 1981.

[Tsi78] Tsichritzis, D.C. and Klug, A. *The ANSI/X3/SPARC DBMS Framework : Report of the Study Group on Database Management Systems*, Information Systems, 3 1978.

Compilation of Complex DATALOG with Stratified Negation

Thomas Ludwig *

Fachbereich 4   University of Trier

Postfach 3825   5500 Trier   FRG

Abstract

We describe a two-phase compiler for queries of non-flat DATALOG with stratified negation. The compiler maps them to operator-trees of *EFTA*, the database-retrieval algebra of our experimental database-system *LILOG-DB* which we are currently implementing for database-support of knowledge-based systems.

The compiler works in two phases. The query-independent phase 1 translates DATALOG-programs into a network of *EFTA-templates*, i.e. incomplete EFTA-expressions. The query-dependent phase 2 works on these *EFTA*-templates: For a given query, it fetches the relevant templates and inserts the constants of the query at the right places. Phase 1 can be seen as a *precompilation* of DATALOG-programs, while phase 2 is the kernel *query-compilation*.

The basic principle of the compiler is to minimize the effort of query-compilation by doing as much as possible at precompilation-time, avoiding duplicate work by performing the query-independent part only once instead of repeating it for each new query.

1   Introduction

In *LILOG-DB* ([8,9]), we research techniques for the database support of knowledge-based systems, especially in the context of natural-language processing given by our embedding project *LILOG*.

Our current prototype implementation incorporates the language *FLL*, which is a DATALOG successor allowing stratified negation and set-grouping, and supporting the complex objects and the strong typing of our so-called *Feature Term Data Model* (*FTDM*). *FLL*-queries are compiled to our database-retrieval algebra *EFTA*, which is the language of the *LILOG-DB*-query-processor.

Although *FLL* has some interesting features (e.g. order-sortedness or support of the open-world assumption, see [5]), we restrict our presentation of the two-phase compilation approach to the compilation of DATALOG with function symbols and stratified negation (DATALOG^{cn}, c for complex objects, n for negation), instead of describing it for *FLL*, which is upwards compatible to DATALOG^{cn}: A presentation of the full query compiler would require a full description of *FLL*, which would overload the paper without contributing much technical substance.

---

*The work reported here was carried out within the LILOG-project of IBM Germany

85

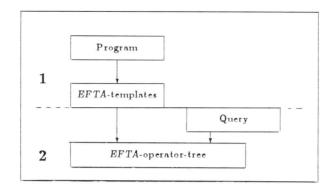

Figure 1: Schema of Two-Phase Compilation

Orientation of the Paper

In this paper, we sketch a two-phase compilation algorithm which is better suited to first-order databases than standard one-phase compilation, and thereby demonstrate the adequacy of our *Extended Feature-Term Algebra (EFTA)* as a target language for a query-compiler.

Although much about the theoretical possibilities of compilation of deductive database programs is known, there is little work published on the structure and construction of such compilers.

In this paper, we focus on the main engineering principles of the compiler we have implemented for LILOG-DB, and their manifestation on the level of algorithms and data-structures.

Especially, we advocate a two-phase approach to query-compilation, the embedding of the kernel-compiler into a global source-level optimizer and a local object-code optimizer and the use of a graph-structure as an intermediate language, providing the potential for incremental (and, thus, module-wise) compilation.

The Compiler

Our query-compiler from $DATALOG^{cn}$ to $EFTA$ will use a two-phase approach: in a first phase, we will compile the $DATALOG^{cn}$-program as a whole to a set of query-independent *EFTA-templates*; the second phase only consists of searching the relevant templates for a query and pushing the constants into them.

Only the second phase has to be performed at runtime, i.e. it is query-dependent. That means that we do as much as possible only once at compile-time of the $DATALOG^{cn}$-programs (instead of doing it again for every query) and as less as possible at query-evaluation-time. Thus, when a query is read, only two operations will have to be performed in the second phase of our algorithm:

- The relevant parts of the *EFTA*-templates have to be fetched.
- The constants of the query have to be pushed into the template to obtain a plan for *efficient* query evaluation.

A schema of compilation can be visualized as in Fig. 1. The precompilation-phase reads a $DATALOG^{cn}$-program, and translates it into an *EFTA-template-graph*. The second phase uses this graph and a given query to construct an *EFTA-operator-tree*.

Programs		
Layers		
Partitions		
Clauses		
Heads	Bodies	
	pos. Subgoals	neg. Subgoals
	Pairs of Subgoals	
	single Subgoals	

Figure 2: Components of a Program

Decomposition of Programs

The notion of *stratification* of first-order programs with negation has been introduced to describe when the use of negation in programs is safe, i.e. produces predictable and unique results. The stratification restriction basically states that negation should only be used to refer to an "already known" relation. A consequence is that *no negation can be used through recursion* (see [1]). For a stratified program, there always exists at least one *layering* that assigns levels to the predicates so that for each rule

$p :- \ldots not\, q \ldots$

it is guaranteed that the level of q is lower then the level of p, i.e. negation always accesses lower levels of the layering.

Since our system compiles stratified programs, we can thus see (see Fig. 2) a DATALOG^{cn}-program as a set of *layers*, where each layer is a set of one or more partitions (a *partition* is the set of clauses with the same name and arity defining a predicate). A clause consists of a *head* and a possibly empty set of *subgoals*, the *body*. A *clause* is said to be a *rule* if the subgoal-set is non-empty, else we call it a *fact*. According to their *sign*, we divide the set of subgoals of a rule into the *positive* and the *negative* ones. For reasons that will become clear later, we want to separate a set of equally signed (positive or negative) subgoals into pairs of single subgoals.

By this decomposition-hierarchy of stratified programs, we have isolated the units of compilation, i.e. in the rest of this paper, we will describe the compilation of these units separately.

An Example

Throughout our presentation, we will use a well-known DATALOG^{cn}-program that describes some grades of personal relativity (*par* stands for *parent*, *sg* for *same-generation*, *mother* and *father* are base-predicates) to give examples for single compilation steps.

87

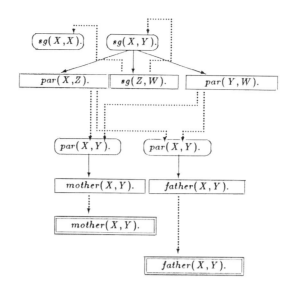

Figure 3: RGG for the Generation-Program

$$
\begin{array}{ll}
father(b,a). & mother(f,g). \\
father(a,c). & mother(g,h). \\
father(d,c). & mother(i,h). \\
father(f,d). & \\
father(j,i). & \\
\end{array}
$$

$par(X,Y) :- mother(X,Y).$
$par(X,Y) :- father(X,Y).$

$sg(X,X).$
$sg(X,Y) :- par(X,Z), sg(Z,W), par(Y,W).$

Fig. 3 depicts the representation of this program as a *Rule-Goal-Graph* (*RGG*), where oval nodes stand for the head of a clause, square boxes represent subgoals of a rule and the base-predicates are highlighted. The full lines go from the head of a rule to its subgoals, the dotted lines from subgoals to possibly matching heads of clauses. In our implementation, *RGGs* are the input-structure of the compiler (see below).

In section 2, we will give a brief description of our database algebra *EFTA*, the target language of the compiler. In section 3, we describe the query-independent precompilation of programs to *EFTA*-template-graphs, section 4 copes with the query-compilation phase. Section 5 gives an illustrated example, section 6 some concluding remarks.

2   EFTA

EFTA (*Extended Feature Term Algebra*, see [6]) is the language of the *LILOG-DB* query-processor. It is based on the *Feature Term Data Model* (*FTDM*).

The term universe of the *FTDM* consists of atomic terms (integers, reals, atoms), complex terms (functors and lists, sets and feature-tuples) and variables. Examples for *FTDM*-terms are

2	an integer	2.0	a real
two	an atom	$f(2)$	a functor
$[2, two]$	a list	$\langle a : 1, b : 2 \rangle$	a feature-tuple
$\{1, 2\}$	a set	*TWO*	a variable

Functors and lists are the complex objects of *EFTA* as well as of DATALOG^{cn}, sets and feature-tuples do not occur in DATALOG^{cn}-programs and are not further discussed here (see [5]).

Basic Operations on Terms

In contrast to Relational Algebra (*RA*,[4]), *EFTA* copes with arbitrarily complex objects. So, we have to generalize the relational concept of an attribute by the concept of the application t/p of **paths** p (of arbitrary length) to terms t. A path is a sequence of names and position-numbers, finished by a □. E.g.

$$f(\langle age : 20 \rangle)) / 1.age.\square = 20$$

The **conditions** that can be checked for terms in *EFTA* extend *RA* in that they allow type- and structure-inspection of terms (see [6]).

To compose arbitrary complex objects, we have to replace the tuple-aggregation by the application $cons(c, t)$ of **constructors** c to terms t. E.g.

$$cons(\ f(\langle age : \square \rangle),\ 20\ )$$

constructs the term $f(\langle age : 20 \rangle)$.

In addition, we allow the application $apply(cc, t)$ of **conditional constructors** cc which perform construction-operations dependent on the evaluation of conditions, so that e.g. the application of

$$if\ 2.\square < 30\ then\ person(1.\square, young)\ else\ person(1.\square, middle - aged)$$

to $person(john, 20)$ yields $person(john, young)$.
RA has no equivalent for this.

Sets instead of Relations

Feature-term sets (*ft-sets*), the data-containers of *EFTA*, are (potentially heterogeneous) sets of (arbitrary) terms instead of relations structured by columns as in *RA*. Because *EFTA* is designed for (deductive) **retrieval** of feature-terms, we disallow the occurence of variables. The decision for sets instead of relations is based on the insight that in the general case of knowledge bases with incomplete information it is not appropriate to force the information into relations by flattening. This requires too much effort for decomposition and produces too many small "intermediate" and "secondary" relations which are expensive to update.

We then regard the database as a collection of named sets too.

Cross Product, Union and Difference

The cross-product $A \times B$ of two sets $A = \{a_1, \ldots, a_n\}$ and $B = \{b_1, \ldots, b_m\}$ in *EFTA* is the set of all binary tuples [1] $\{\langle a_1, b_1 \rangle, \ldots, \langle a_n, b_m \rangle\}$. Note that it is neither commutative nor associative. In contrast to the union-compatibility-restrictions of *RA*, we can define union $A \cup B$ and difference $A \setminus B$ in a pure set-theoretic

---

[1] The attribute-names are omitted in this example

manner.

The γ-Operator

The γ-operator $\gamma_{cc}\, S$ allows the application of the basic term-level operators of *EFTA* to sets of terms. It comprises the capabilities of *EFTA* for single scans of sets: a conditional constructor cc can be applied to each element of a given set S, the set of the resulting terms is the result of the γ-application.

We can now write "selections" and "projections" informally as [2]

(i) $\quad \sigma_c\, R \quad = \quad \gamma_{if\ c\ then\ \square}\, R$

(ii) $\quad \pi_p\, R \quad = \quad \gamma_{if\ true\ then\ p}\, R \;=\; \gamma_p\, R$

Thus the γ-operator is an abstraction of selection and projection in RA, including constructive capabilities as they are needed for deductive retrieval.

For instance the evaluation of

$$\gamma_{if\ 1.\square>5\ then\ f(1.\square,2.\square)\ else\ f(5.2.\square)}\ \{g(3,4),g(4,5),g(9,6),g(7,2)\}$$

yields the result

$$\{f(5,4),f(5,5),f(9,6),f(7,2)\}.$$

Nesting and Unnesting

nest and *unnest* are needed for (dis-)aggregation of ft-sets. The *unnest*-operator $unnest_p\, F$ decomposes an element of F with a set-valued attribute s at path p into a set of terms with the elements of s at position p:

$$unnest_{1.\square}\ \{\, f(\{1,2\}),\ f(\{2,3\})\,\} = \{f(1),f(2),f(3)\}$$

nest works in the opposite direction:

$$nest_{1.\square}\ \{\, f(1),\ f(2),\ f(3)\,\} \;=\; \{\, f(\{1,2,3\})\,\}$$

As can be seen in the example, *nest* and *unnest* are not inverse to each other!

In the absence of the *set-grouping* facilities of *FLL*, nesting and unnesting are not used by our compiler.

The Closure-Operator

By the operators given so far, we do not yet have enough power to cope with recursive queries. Thus we include a closure-operator Φ. This enables us to process an arbitrary (recursive) query in our data-model.

Seen from an operational point of view, the closure-operator mimics what is called in the literature a *naive machine* ([2], [3]): When evaluating $\Phi_{\langle e_1,\ldots,e_n\rangle}\,\langle I_1,\ldots,I_n\rangle$, a vector (syntactically represented as a tuple) $\langle e_1,\ldots,e_n\rangle$ of n *EFTA*-expressions is iteratively applied to a vector $\langle I_1,\ldots,I_n\rangle$ of n initializing arguments until no more terms are generated. The terms generated in each iteration are added to the intermediate result. The example

$$\Phi_{\langle\gamma_{if\ (1.2.\square=2.1.\square)\ then\ anc(1.1.\square,2.2.\square)}\rangle}\ (1\times 1))\ \langle R\rangle \qquad (1)$$

with $n = 1$ shows that the intermediate results can be accessed via *position-numbers*, as in the cross-product 1×1.

The evaluation-schema for $\Phi_{\langle e_1,\ldots,e_n\rangle}\,\langle I_1,\ldots,I_n\rangle$ is the following (*imr* stands for "intermediate result"):

---

[2] Note that we abbreviate $\gamma_{if\ true\ then\ p}\, R$ by $\gamma_p\, R$

```
   for j = 1 to n
     imr[0, j] := I_j
   i := 1
   repeat
     for j = 1 to n
       /* apply expression to the vector imr[i-1] of intermediate results */
       imr[i, j] := e_j(imr[i - 1]) ∪ imr[i - 1, j]
       nothing_changed := (∀j = 1 ... n : imr[i, j] = imr[i - 1, j])
       i := i + 1
   until nothing_changed
```

For
$$R = \{\ anc(0, 01), anc(01, 011), anc(01, 012), anc(012, 0121)\ \}$$
the sample query (1) yields

$$
\begin{aligned}
imr_0 \quad &= \quad \langle\ \{\ anc(0, 01), anc(01, 011), anc(01, 012), anc(012, 0121)\}\ \rangle \\
imr_1 \quad &= \quad \langle\ \{\ anc(0, 011), anc(0, 012), anc(01, 0121)\}\ \cup imr_0\ \rangle \\
imr_2 \quad &= \quad \langle\ \{\ anc(0, 0121)\}\ \cup imr_1\ \rangle \\
RESULT \quad &= \quad \{\ imr_2\ \}
\end{aligned}
$$

i.e. it computes the transitive closure of the anc-relation.

3   Phase 1: Precompilation

3.1   Data-Structure Considerations

LPRGGs

Assuming a representation $term$ for literals of the language, we can give a data-structure for $DATALOG^{cn}$-programs (see Fig. 4) which can be considered as a specialization of RGGs better suited to our approach of $DATALOG^{cn}$-compilation.

When compiling a program, we decompose it in $layers$. For stratified programs this can be normally done in many ways. We choose a topological sorting of the recursive cliques along the order described above, so that we obtain a level-mapping which only contains one layer per level. We thus see a $DATALOG^{cn}$-program as an array of layers.

Layers are represented as arrays of $partitions$, which themselves are arrays of $clauses$.[3]

A clause is modeled as a record with components for the head (a positive literal) and the positive and negative subgoal-sets of the body, each represented as an array of $literals$.

A $literal$ is a record containing the literal itself and a reference to the partition by which it is defined. This $partition$-ID consists of an index for the level of the partition and the number of the partition in the array of partitions building the level.

For our sample program we can give a graphic representation of this structure as a $layered$ $partitioned$ $rule$-$goal$-$graph$ ($LPRGG$). In the $LPRGG$ the $partition$-IDs are visualized as pointers from subgoals to partitions (see Fig. 5).

---

[3] We use arrays instead of sets for modeling programs because we will need and excessively use an indexing-facility for layers, partitions and clauses during compilation. We assume our arrays to be of variable length.

```
        program =    array of layer
          layer =    array of partition
      partition =    array of clause
         clause =    record
                       head : literal
                       body : record
                                pos : subgoals
                                neg : subgoals
                              end
                     end
       subgoals =    array of literal
         literal =   record
                       lit :      term
                       respect : partition-ID
                     end
    partition-ID =   record
                       level : integer
                       part : integer
                     end
```

Figure 4: Data-Structure of DATALOG^{cn}-Programs

EFTA-Templates

Fig. 6 gives our representation of *EFTA-program-templates* which are the result of phase 1 of *DATALOG^{cn}*-compilation.

As for literals of *DATALOG^{cn}* in the corresponding data-structure of Fig. 4, we here assume the representation of *EFTA-expressions* (i.e. operator trees) to be given. It can be seen that the structure of *LPRGG* for *DATALOG^{cn}* is mostly preserved by pass *1*, except that **DATALOG^{cn}-clauses are transformed to EFTA-templates.**

The *expr*-part of these *EFTA-templates* basically is the same as an *EFTA-expression*, but it may contain a *partition-id* where an *EFTA-expression* contains an argument. E.g. if the partition where R is defined has the *partition-ID (1,3)* then for

$\gamma_c R$

the corresponding *EFTA*-template-*expr* is

$\gamma_c (1,3)$

The omitted arguments will be inserted into these expressions (which will then possibly be modified) in pass 2. After pass *1* of our algorithm they are represented by the *respect*-reference to the (compiled) *EFTA-partition* which supplies the argument.

3.2   Structure-Compilation: Programs, Layers, Partitions

The precompilation of an *LPRGG* to the corresponding *EFTA*-template structure translates each *Clause* in the *LPRGG* independently to an *EFTA*-template, so that the structure of the *LPRGG* is preserved in the *EFTA*-template-graph.

In a bottom-up manner we compile each layer separately, beginning with level 1:

```
for i = 1 to ♯layers do
   for j = 1 to ♯partitions of layer_i do
      comp-partition(partition_j of layer_j)
```

92

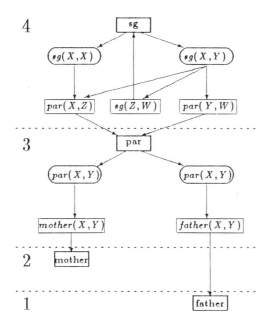

Figure 5: LPRGG for the Generation-Program

EFTA-Program =	**array of** *EFTA-Layer*
EFTA-Layer =	**array of** *EFTA-Partition*
EFTA-Partition =	**array of** *EFTA-Clause*
EFTA-Template =	**record**
	expr : *EFTA-Expr*
	respect : PId-List
	end
PId-List =	**array of** *Partition-Id*

Figure 6: Data-Structure of EFTA-Template-Graphs

A *layer* is a set of partitions *pi* which are compiled separately. In the compilation of partitions, we distinguish two cases. If the partition stands for a base-predicate (whose extension is stored in the external database), we have nothing to do. Otherwise, we compile each clause separately, distinguishing three cases: A clause can be a rule, a ground fact (containing no variables), or a non-ground fact.

The procedure *comp-partition* translates all ground facts of the partition "as is" into a single set *ground-set*, which is stored into the last field of the (array representing the) *EFTA*-partition which is the result of *comp-partition*.

Non-ground facts and rules are compiled separately, and each generated *EFTA*-template is stored in a separate field of the resulting array. E.g. for

$sg(a, b)$.
$sg(b, c)$.
$sg(X, X)$.
$sg(X, Y) :\text{-} par(X, Z), sg(Z, W), par(Y, W)$.

the resulting array *efta-part* would have three fields, the first component containing the result of the compilation of $sg(X, X)$ and the second the compiled rule, while

93

efta-part$_3$ contains the set-constant $\{sg(a,b), sg(b,c)\}$.

```
Procedure:  comp-partition
Input:      a DATALOG^cn-Partition fll-part
Output:     an EFTA-Partition efta-part
begin
    ground-set:= { }
    len  := 0
    for i := 0 to ♯clauses of fll-part do
       if clause_i is Ground-Fact
            ground-set := ground-set ∪ clause_i
       if clause_i is Non-Ground-Fact
            efta-part[len] := comp-ngf(clause_i)
            len := len + 1
       if clause_i is Rule
            efta-part[len] := comp-rule(clause_i)
            len := len + 1
    efta-part[len] := make-expr-objects-efta(ground-set)
    return (efta-part)
end
```

Till now we have considered programs, layers and partitions. In their compilation, we assumed the *EFTA*-templates for clauses to be computed and our only job was to structure them adequately. This is why we call that task *structure-compilation*. Let's now come to the hard kernel of compilation where *EFTA*-templates are generated: the clause-compilation.

3.3 Clause-Compilation

Rules

Let $G = \{g_1, .., g_n\}$ be a set of goals (i.e. literals), $V = \{v_1, .., v_m\}$ the set of variables occuring in G.

Let for each goal $g_i (1 \leq i \leq n)$ $e_i = e_i(g_i)$ be the corresponding EFTA-template, $E = E(G) = \{e_1, .., e_n\}$.

When compiling a rule with a subgoal-set G, these e_i can be assumed to be soon computed because of our stratification-assumption coupled with our bottom-up approach to program-compilation.

Then we call the set $GE = \{(g_1, e_1), .., (g_n, e_n)\}$ of pairs of goals and their corresponding EFTA-templates the *compiled-goal-set* of the goal-set G.

If we want to compile the body $sg_1, .., sg_n$ of a rule $r = (head :- sg_1, .., sg_n)$, we cannot only consider the set $G(r)$ of goals in the body of r, compile each of them to EFTA and return something like $e_1, .., e_n$ as a result.

Instead, we have to return one EFTA-template for the body as a whole, and when constructing it, we have to capture the semantics of the interconnections between the single subgoals which are realized by the variables in the body.

In other words: to catch the meaning of what is normally called *sideways informa-tion passing*, that is to correctly compile the cross-references between two or more subgoals, we have to give the normal answer of database-people to cross-references and construct a *join* of the corresponding EFTA-templates *ei* which computes these cross-references.

This join [4] might look like

$$e_1 \bowtie_{jc_1} \ldots \bowtie_{jc_{n-1}} e_n$$

---

[4] A formal definition of the join will be given below.

with the join-conditions $jc_i(1 \leq i < n)$. The join-conditions capture the cross-references by specifying which paths in the arguments of the join have to agree, i.e. it looks like

$$path_1 = path_2 \text{ and } \ldots \text{ and } path_{n-1} = path_n$$

Example: For the subgoals

$$p(X, Y), p(Y, Z)$$

if the EFTA-template for $p(V1, V2)$ were

$$\gamma_{p(1.\square,2.\square)} \, PAR$$

(PAR is the partition-ID corresponding to the predicate p) we would construct

$$\gamma_{p(1.\square,2.\square)} \, PAR \bowtie_{2.\square=1.\square} \gamma_{p(1.\square,2.\square)} \, PAR$$

In the following, we will specify a process which for n subgoals successively constructs the at most $n - 1$ joins which are needed to completely compile the whole body b of a rule r.

We will do that by successively taking two pairs (sg_i, e_i) and (sg_j, e_j) from the compiled-goal-set $G(B) = (sg_1, e_1), .., (sg_n, e_n)$ and replacing them by a new pair $((sg_i, sg_j), (e_i \bowtie e_j))$ which denotes the *compiled conjunction* of them. The process will stop when the resulting compiled-goal-set is a singleton-set: then we have compiled an equivalent EFTA-template for the body as a whole.

During this process, at each step we have to keep track of which logical variable corresponds to which pathes in the EFTA-templates so far constructed.

Therefore we introduce the *variable-path-tableau* $VPT(GE, V)$ for a compiled-goal-set GE and a corresponding variable-set $V = V(GE)$. For each logic variable v this tableau contains all elements $ge = (sg, e)$ of GE in which it occurs, and for each such occurence the path to which it corresponds in the compiled subexpression e.

Definition : A *variable-path-tableau* $VPT(GE, V)$ is a subset of $V \times GE \times P^5$.

Example(continued): For the subgoals $p(X, Y), p(Y, Z)$ of our example and their compiled-goal-set

$$\{ (p(X, Y), \gamma_{p(1.\square,2.\square)} \, PAR), \; (p(Y, Z), \gamma_{p(1.\square,2.\square)} \, PAR)\}$$

we obtain

Variable	Compiled-Goal	Path
X	$(p(X, Y), \gamma_{p(1.\square,2.\square)} \, PAR)$	$1.\square$
Y	$(p(X, Y), \gamma_{p(1.\square,2.\square)} \, PAR)$	$2.\square$
Y	$(p(Y, Z), \gamma_{p(1.\square,2.\square)} \, PAR)$	$1.\square$
Z	$(p(Y, Z), \gamma_{p(1.\square,2.\square)} \, PAR)$	$2.\square$

In the following we assume to have a function $path(x, sg)$ which returns a path p for which a triple of the form $(x, (sg, e), p)$ is in VPT, so that this function determines a "position" of x in the compiled equivalent e of sg. Note that more than one such entry can exist!

Our sketch of body-compilation works only for subgoals with equal signs, i.e. all subgoals have to be positive or all subgoals have to be negative literals. Since we allow definite clauses with stratified negation, we have to cope with bodies of the form [6]

$$sg_1, \ldots, sg_n, \text{ not } sg_{n+1}, \ldots, \text{ not } sg_m$$

That means that we have to use our VPT-method of successively generating an EFTA-equivalent for a subgoal-conjunction with equal signs twice: once for the

---

[5] We here assume the variables of each two clauses to be distinct.

[6] Because of the declarative semantics of DATALOG^{cn} we can w.l.o.g. assume all the negated literals at the end of the body.

positive subgoals and once for the negative ones. Finally we have to compute the "difference" (see below) and produce an expression for the clause as a whole (that basically means that we have to "link" the head to the compiled body).

Resuming our considerations so far, we can give an implementation of rule-compilation below. Therein we assume a global *rule-vpt* for later use in the sub-procedures of *comp-rule*. The subtasks in which we have to split it will be described in detail in the following subsections.

The set-valued variables *posvars*, *negvars* and *shared* and the *vpt*-variable *rule-vpt* defined in *comp-rule* are assumed to be global for its sub-procedures.

```
Procedure: comp-rule
Input:        a DATALOGᶜⁿ-Clause of the form
   head(headlist) :- body
Output:       equivalent EFTA-Template result
begin
    headvars    := { V | V variable in headlist }
    posvars     := { V | V variable in body → pos }
    negvars     := { V | V variable in body → neg }
    shared      := posvars ∩ negvars

    vptpos      := init-vpt(body → pos)
    vptneg      := init-vpt(body → neg)

    possg       := comp-subgoals(body → pos)
    negsg       := comp-subgoals(body → neg)
    diff        := comp-body(possg, negsg, shared)
    result      := comp-head(head, diff)
    return (result)
end
```

From the point of view of database-retrieval, a subgoal of a rule is nothing more than a reference or view on data that are defined elsewhere, i.e. in other partitions.

Before we can generate access-statements (EFTA-expressions) for these data, we have to know their format. That means that we have to know how the EFTA-template looks which is a result of a partition-compilation, because we refer to it as a subgoal in the currently compiled rule which we do need to compile the current partition, which is accessed by other subgoals and so on ..: A normal-form has to be defined! Let us use the example

r_1 : $p(X, Y)$.
r_2 : $s(X, Z)$:- $p(X, Y), \ldots, q(Y, Z)$.

to illustrate that we do not need to construct anything else than a **proper image of the data-flow** or information-passing induced by the variables. We do this by translating variables to paths of *EFTA*. So when compiling $r1$, we produce an expression

$$\gamma_{p(path_1, \ldots, path_n)}$$

During the compilation of the subgoal $p(X, Y)$ in $r2$ we can thus assume this normal-form for p. The algorithm derived from these considerations is

```
Procedure: comp-sg
Input:        a DATALOG^cn-Literal sg(arguments)
Output:       a EFTA-γ-Operation
   γ if (Cond.) then sg(Path-List) SUBGOAL
begin
    cond := true
    SG := partition-ID(sg)
    copy arguments in an Object-List arglist
    ♯elements := ♯elements of Object-List
    for i := 0 to ♯elements do
        if arglist_i = Variable
            replace arglist_i by its path i.□
            for j := i + 1 to ♯elements do
                if arglist_i = arglist_j
                    cond := cond and (i.□ = j.□)
    return (γ if (cond) then sg(1.□, ..., n.□) SG)
end
```

Based on *comp-sg*, the procedure *comp-subgoals* compiles a sequence $sg_1, \ldots, sg_n$ of subgoals with equal sign to a singleton compiled-goal-set by starting with *compiled-goal-set* initialized to the results $\{(sg_1, comp\text{-}sg(sg_1)), \ldots, (sg_n, comp\text{-}sg(sg_n))\}$ of the compilations of the single subgoals and then successively eliminating the two elements with the most variables in common and replacing them by the result of compiling the join of them (*comp-join*), until all subgoals are compiled to a single expression.

```
Procedure: comp-subgoals
Input:        a subgoal-conjunction sg_1, ..., sg_m
    with equal signs
Output:       a unique Compiled-Goal-Set
    compiled-goal-set
begin
    initialize compiled-goal-set
    with {(sg_1, comp-sg(sg_1)),...,
            (sg_m, comp-sg(sg_m))}
    while || compiled-goal-set || > 1
        search the two elements
        elem_i = (sg_i, expr_i) and
        elem_j = (sg_j, expr_j)
        with the most variables in common
        elem_new := comp-join(elem_i, elem_j)
        compiled-goal-set := compiled-goal-set
            - {elem_i, elem_j} + elem_new
    return (compiled-goal-set)
end
```

The procedure *comp-join* required by *comp-subgoals* uses the following definition of equi-joins for *EFTA*:

$$A \bowtie_{p=q} B :\Leftrightarrow \sigma_{1.p = 2.q} (A \times B)$$

Supposing two compiled goals $(sg_1, expr_1)$ and $(sg_2, expr_2)$ as input, it takes every common variable of sg_1 and sg_2 and generates an equality-condition *cond* for them. The resulting join-expression is

$$join = expr_1 \bowtie_{cond} expr_2$$

Then the *variable-path-table* (*VPT*) is updated by appending a 1 to each path of $expr_1$ and a 2 to each path of $expr_2$; the paths created this way are the valid ones for the new join-expression.

Example (continued) : If we had compiled the subgoals

97

$p(X, Y), p(Y, Z)$.

to the singleton set

$$R = \{ \, ((p(X,Y), p(Y,Z)), \ (\gamma_{\Gamma(1.\Box,2.\Box)} PAR \bowtie_{2.\Box=1.\Box} \gamma_{\Gamma(1.\Box,2.\Box)} PAR)) \, \},$$

VPT were

$$VPT = \{ \, (X, R, 1.1.\Box), (Y, R, 1.2.\Box), (Y, R, 2.1.\Box), (Z, R, 2.2.\Box), \}$$

Finally, a *tuplelist* containing the correct path of each variable is constructed, and the expression

$$\gamma_{if\ true\ then\ (tuplelist)} join$$

is returned.

```
Procedure: comp-join
Input:      two Compiled-Goals (sg₁, expr₁)
  and (sg₂, expr₂)
Output:     an EFTA-γ-Operation
  γ if (true) then (pathlist) join
begin
    cond := true
    for every Variable V in sg₁ and sg₂ do
        path₁   := path(V, expr₁)
        path₂   := path(V, expr₂)
        cond    := cond and (path₁ = path₂)
    join := expr₁ ⋈_cond expr₂
    for every Variable V in sg₁ do
        replace every entry (V, sg₁, expr₁, path)
        in the VPT
        by (V, (sg₁, sg₂), join, 1.path)
    for every Variable V in sg₂ do
        replace every entry (V, sg₂, expr₂, path)
        in the VPT
        by (V, (sg₁, sg₂), join, 2.path)
    tuplelist := { }
    for every Variable V in sg₁ do
        path         := path(V, join)
        tuplelist    := tuplelist & path
    for every Variable V in sg₂ / sg₁ do
        path         := path(V, join)
        tuplelist    := tuplelist & path
    return ( γ if (true) then (tuplelist) join )
end
```

Compiling Head and Body

The compilation of the rule-body as a whole makes use of the non-primitive *EFTA*-operator *modified difference*

$$A \ -_{p=q} B :\Leftrightarrow A \ - \ \pi_1 (A \bowtie_{p=q} B)$$

which is a generalization of the ordinary set difference since

$$A \ - \ B = A \ -_{\Box=\Box} B$$

The modified difference is especially supported by the *EFTA*-query-processor. The body-compilation simply constructs an equality-condition *cond* over the paths of all variables that occur in positive (*posexpr*) and negative (*negexpr*) subgoals of the body, and returns the modified difference

$$posexpr \ -_{cond} negexpr$$

```
Procedure: comp-body
Input:        EFTA-expressions posexpr, negexpr and
a list shared of their common variables
Output:       an EFTA-expression
  posexpr −condition negexpr
begin
    for every Variable V in shared do
        path₁  := path( V, posexpr )
        path₂  := path( V, negexpr )
        cond   := cond and (path₁ = path₂)
    return ( posexpr −cond negexpr)
end
```

The connection between head and body is simply compiled by generating a γ-expression

$$\gamma_{if\ cond\ then\ head(arglist)}\ bodyexpr$$

which, similar to the construction in *comp-join*, fetches the right paths for the variables of the head, encodes them in a tuple $(arglist)$, and puts the arising equality-conditions into *cond*.

```
Procedure: comp-head
Input:        a DATALOG^{cn}-Literal head( headlist )
and an EFTA-expression bodyexpr
Output:       an EFTA-expression bodyexpr
   γ if (Condition) then head( Path − List) bodyexpr
begin
    cond := true
    copy headlist in an Object-List arglist
    for i := 0 to ♯elements of Object-List do
    if arglistᵢ = Variable V
        arglistᵢ := path(V, bodyexpr)
        for j := i + 1 to ♯elements of arglist do
            if arglistᵢ = arglistⱼ
                pathⱼ  := path of arglistⱼ
                cond   := cond and (pathᵢ = pathⱼ)
    return (γ if (cond) then head(arglist) bodyexpr)
end
```

Compilation of Non-Ground Facts

The precompilation of non-ground facts is a simple restriction of rule-compilation where no *body* has to be analyzed and only equality-conditions for the paths corresponding to the variables of the fact have to be inserted into the resulting γ-expression. E.g., if PID were the partition-ID corresponding to the recursive predicate sg of our example, *comp-ngf* would translate the non-ground fact

$$sg(X, X).$$

to

$$\gamma_{if\ (1.\square=2.\square)\ then\ sg(1.\square,2.\square)} PID$$

The algorithm of *comp-ngf* shall not be explicitly given here.

4   Query-Compilation

While the first phase of compilation is performed only once for a $DATALOG^{cn}$-program, the second phase is activated for each new query. From the *EFTA-template-graph* constructed in phase 1 and the query, phase 2 constructs an *EFTA-*

99

operator-tree.

This construction basically cuts the parts which are irrelevant for the query out of the *EFTA*-template-graph and inserts the constants of the query into the remaining templates. Roughly speaking, a template is *irrelevant* for a query iff it belongs to a partition that is never reached during the traversal of the *EFTA*-template-graph which is initiated by the query, or if it has a constant at a position where the query has a different constant.

So, constants are inserted if they agree with the constants in the templates, or if the templates contain variables.

For a given query, the *EFTA*-template-graph is traversed top-down as follows: At first, the layer of the *LPRGG* is determined where the $DATALOG^{cn}$-clauses corresponding to the query are stored. Then, the clauses of this layer and all clauses transitively referred to via subgoals are considered.

To give an example, we extend our *generation*-program by the ground facts

$sg(k, l).$
$sg(a, l).$

Now suppose the following query to be given:

$? - sg(a, Y).$

The corresponding clauses are

$sg(k, l).$
$sg(a, l).$
$sg(X, X).$
$sg(X, Y) :- par(X, Z), sg(Z, W), par(Y, W).$

They are located in partition 1 of layer 4 of the *LPRGG* (see Fig. 5). The subgoals of the predicate *par*/2 have the partition-ID 3|1 and thereby refer to partition 1 of layer 3, in which the *parent*-clauses are stored. These clauses themselves refer to partition 1 of layer 1 and partition 1 of layer 2, in which the base-predicates *father* and *mother* are stored.

The clauses of layer 4/partition 1 of the *LPRGG* correspond to the templates of layer 4/partition 1 in the *EFTA*-template-graph, which are now successively examined.

If the *EFTA*-expression of a template is a set-constant, it is simply left "as is". In the example, there is a set-constant in partition 1 of layer 4, which is

$\{sg(k, l), sg(a, l)\}$

which will later be included into the *EFTA*-operator-tree.

The *EFTA*-templates which are no set-constants receive the constants of the query if they contain variables or agreeing constants at the corresponding positions. E.g., the *EFTA*-templates for the clauses

$sg(X, X)$
$sg(X, Y) :- par(X, Z), sg(Z, W), par(Y, W).$

looked like

$\gamma_{if\ (1.\square=2.\square)\ then\ sg(1.\square,2.\square)}\ SG$
$\gamma_{if\ true\ then\ sg(1.\square,2.\square)}\ (\cdots)$

They are now modified by pushing the constants in [7]:

$\{sg(a, a)\}$
$\gamma_{if\ 1.\square=a\ then\ sg(a,2.\square)}\ (EOT)$

where *EOT* is the *EFTA*-operator-tree generated for the subgoals of the recursive rule.

---

[7]Note that the template generated for a non-ground fact is now translated to a ground fact.

```
Procedure: comp-query
Input:       an LPRGG lprgg,
    an EFTA-Template-Graph etg and
    a Query query
Output:      an EFTA-Operator-Tree expr
begin
respect := search-in-lprgg(query, lprgg)
♯parts := ♯partitions of layer[respect → level]
for i := 0 to ♯parts do
    for j := 0 to ♯templates temp of partition_i do
        if temp_j is a set-constant
            unrec_i := unrec_i ∪ temp_j
        else if temp_j is a ngf
            expr := push(temp_j, query)
            unrec_i := unrec_i ∪ expr
        else if temp_j is a rule
            for k := 0 to ♯entries pid of PID-list do
                tree_2 := build-tree(etg, pid_k)
                tree_1 := tree_1 ∪ tree_2
            temp_j → expr := tree_1
            if temp_j is recursive
                expr := push(temp_j, query)
                rec_i := rec_i ∪ expr
                cycle := 1
            else
                expr := push(temp_j, query)
                unrec_i := unrec_i ∪ expr
if cycle != 0
    expr := Φ_(unrec) ⟨rec⟩
    expr := γ_{if true then (respect → part)} expr
else
    expr := unrec_0
return (expr)
end
```

Figure 7: Algorithm for Query-Compilation

If sg were a non-recursive partition, we could now complete phase 2 of $DATALOG^{cn}$-compilation by simply constructing the union $e_1 \cup \ldots \cup e_n$ of the $EFTA$-expressions $e_1, \ldots, e_n$ generated for the single clauses. This union-construction corresponds to the disjunctive semantics of single clauses in $DATALOG^{cn}$-programs.

But our example sg is recursive, and so we have to compute the transitive closure of the union-expressions. So, we generate an expression

$$\Phi_{(e_1 \cup \ldots \cup e_n)} \langle I_1 \cup \ldots \cup I_m \rangle$$

where $e_1 \cup \ldots \cup e_n$ are the $EFTA$-expressions recursively accessing the intermediate results, and the expressions $I_1 \cup \ldots \cup I_n$ generated for non-recursive clauses are taken as the initialization of the closure.

The complete $EFTA$-expression generated for our program and the query

$$? - sg(a, Y).$$

is given in Fig. 8[8].

The $EFTA$-expression generated here is far from optimal. E.g., subexpressions like $\gamma_{\ldots} \{mother \ldots\}$ could be directly evaluated. But note that the result of our

---

[8]Note that $MOTHER$ and $FATHER$ are the names of the ft-sets representing the base-predicates $mother$ and $father$ of our sample-program.

101

$$\gamma_{if\ 1.\square=a\ then\ 2.\square}\ ($$
$$\gamma_{1.\square}\ ($$
$$\Phi$$
$$(\gamma_{sg(1.\square,4.\square)}\ ($$
$$\gamma_{(1.1.\square,1.2.\square,1.3.\square,2.3.\square)}\ ($$
$$\gamma_{(1.1.\square,1.2.\square,3.\square)}\ ($$
$$\gamma_{(1.\square,2.\square)}\ ($$
$$\gamma_{par(1.\square,2.\square)}\ MOTHER$$
$$\cup\ \gamma_{par(1.\square,2.\square)}\ FATHER$$
$$)$$
$$\bowtie_{2.\square=1.\square}$$
$$\gamma_{(1.\square,2.\square)}\ 1$$
$$)$$
$$\bowtie_{3.\square=2.\square}$$
$$\gamma_{(1.\square,2.\square)}\ ($$
$$\gamma_{par(1.\square,2.\square)}\ MOTHER$$
$$\cup\ \gamma_{par(1.\square,2.\square)}\ FATHER$$
$$)\ )\qquad)$$
$$)$$
$$(\ \{sg(k,l),sg(a,l)\}\ \cup\ \{sg(a,a)\}\ )$$
$$)\ )$$

Figure 8: EFTA-Expression generated for ?- $sg(a, X)$.

$$\gamma_{if\ 1.1.\square=a\ then\ 1.2.\square}\ ($$
$$\Phi$$
$$(\gamma_{sg(1.1.1.\square,2.1.\square)}\ ($$
$$\gamma_{(1.\square,2.\square)}\ MOTHER\cup FATHER$$
$$\bowtie_{2.\square=1.\square}$$
$$\gamma_{(1.\square,2.\square)}\ 1$$
$$\bowtie_{2.2.\square=2.\square}$$
$$\gamma_{(1.\square,2.\square)}\ MOTHER\cup FATHER$$
$$)$$
$$)$$
$$(\{sg(a,l),sg(k,l),sg(a,a)\})$$
$$)$$

Figure 9: EFTA-Expression for ?- $sg(a, X)$., optimized

compiler is processed by an *EFTA*-optimizer (see [7]) before submission to the query-processor. Since the optimizer performs tasks like the pre-evaluation of trivial subexpressions, they need not be integrated into the compiler. See Fig. 9 for the optimized version of our sample query.

We want to resume this section with some comments on the algorithm given in Fig. 7. *comp-query* first determines the *partition-ID* of the goal matching the query ($respect:=\ldots$).

Then for all partitions of the template-graph and for all templates of these partitions three cases are distinguished.

1. If the template is a **set-constant**, it is simply included into the non-recursive part of the result.

   (For a layer with n partitions the n-ary arrays rec and $unrec$ are stored, rec_i ($unrec_i$) contains the union of all subexpressions generated for recursive (non-recursive) clauses of the partition i)

2. If it is a **non-ground fact**, the constants of the query are pushed into the

102

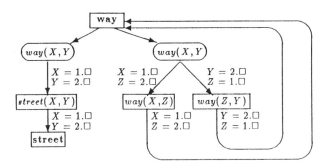

Figure 10: An LPRGG with variable-path equations

corresponding template (procedure $push$ [9]) and the resulting subexpression is included into the union of non-recursive subexpressions for the partition.

3. If the template stands for a **rule**, the procedure $build\text{-}tree$ (a variant of $comp\text{-}query$ not especially presented here) is used to build an operator-tree from the part of the $EFTA$-template-graph to which the rule refers to (without pushing constants, i.e. $build\text{-}tree$ behaves like $comp\text{-}query$ in the absence of constants). Then constants are pushed in as usual and the result is included either in the recursive or non-recursive part of the result.

Finally, if a recursive cycle has occured, we generate a Φ-expression as discussed above, while in the non-recursive case our work is finished.

5   An Illustrated Example

In this section, we want to visualize the main steps of compilation using the sample program

$way(X, Y) :\!\text{-} street(X, Y).$
$way(X, Y) :\!\text{-} way(X, Z), way(Z, Y).$

In Fig. 10, we have depicted the $LPRGG$ for the program. Since we do not want to augment each picture by a difficult-to-read $Variable\text{-}Path\text{-}Table$, we have labeled the edges with equations encoding which variable in the source of the edge corresponds to which path in the referenced target. E.g. X in $street(X, Y)$ refers to the first argument in the base-relation street.

Fig. 11 shows the state of compilation after all single subgoals in the bodies of rules have been compiled: All subgoals have been replaced by $EFTA\text{-}templates$ encoding γ-expressions in which the variables of the subgoals are replaced by their corresponding paths.

In Fig. 12, the body of the recursive rule has been compiled, i.e. the head of the rule now refers to a single join-expression whose join-condition reflects the equality of the second variable of the left subgoal and the first variable of the right subgoal in the body.

---

[9] The lack of space forbids us a deeper discussion of strategies for the pushing of constants into the $EFTA$-operator-tree generated by the compiler. In the restricted version presented here, we only push constants into the γ-conditions on the top of each subtree compiled from a rule. In reality, we do a little better

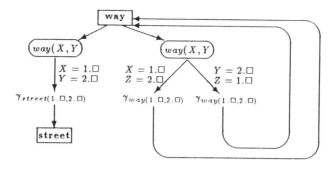

Figure 11: After the compilation of the single subgoals

The *EFTA-template-graph* resulting from phase 1 of compilation is depicted in Fig. 13: the γ-expressions normalizing the templates for the clauses to the forms of the heads have been generated.

Assuming the query ?- $way(X, Y)$, the operator-tree resulting from the query-dependent phase 2 of compilation is given in Fig. 14. Note that the non-recursive part is put in the initialization of the closure (the left arc under the Φ-node), and that another γ-expression had to be generated to normalize the result of the closure.

6 Conclusion

We described a two-phase compiler which translates queries of complex DATALOG with stratified negation to our database algebra EFTA, the language of the LILOG-DB query-processor.

The first phase of the compiler is a query-independent precompilation of the program to a graph-structure of EFTA-templates. This pass retains the structure of the layered-partitioned Rule-Goal-Graph (LPRGG) representing the program, but replaces each clause by a corresponding EFTA-template.

Variables in the DATALOG-programs are transformed to paths in the EFTA-templates, the compiler keeps track of the correspondence of variables and paths in a variable-path-tableau (VPT). The second pass, called query-compilation, selects

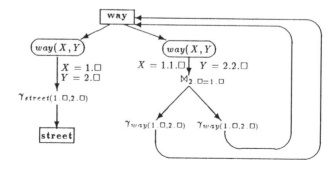

Figure 12: After the join of the subgoals in the rule

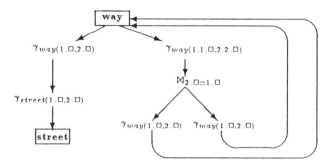

Figure 13: The resulting EFTA-template-graph

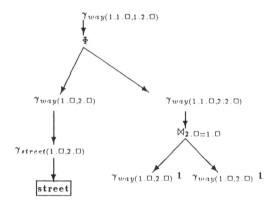

Figure 14: The resulting EFTA-operator-tree for the query $way(X, Y)$

105

the relevant templates for a query, inserts the constants and composes the templates to an EFTA-operator-tree, which can then be evaluated against the database by the LILOG-DB query processor. Recursive predicates are translated using the closure-operator Φ of EFTA.

For reasons of lack of space, we restricted our attention to DATALOG ^{cn} instead of presenting the full compiler for our deductive database language FLL, which is an upwards-compatible extension of DATALOG ^{cn} including order-sorting and the additional aggregations set and feature tuple.

But the full compiler is still not complete, the two most important extensions to be implemented are the inclusion of built-in predicates like $=$, $<$ etc. into the compilation and the incorporation of a safety-check. While the first task is relatively simple, the second one will require some more conceptual work.

The compiler does not perform any optimization. The reason is that the compiler is embedded into two optimizers. On the top-level, a Rule-Rewriting Component performs the global semantic optimization (see [11]), including pushing of constants into recursive cliques and the generation of specially tuned versions of programs for query-forms which shall be most efficiently supported, while conventional local optimization is performed on EFTA-operator-trees.

Our approach has two major advantages: A speed-up of query-processing can be achieved by performing the query-independent part of compilation only once and minimizing the work that has to be done at runtime for a given query.

The other basic advantage is that the splitting of the precompilation- phase into structure- and clause-precompilation allows for incremental compilation. In other words: there is a very simple correspondence between Rule-Goal-Graphs (the input of precompilation) and EFTA-Template-Graphs, so that updates of the input-program can be easily translated to updates of the ETG.

So, we hope to have achieved the two goals of this paper: to present a convincing concept for the compilation of first-order deductive database languages, and to show that our database algebra EFTA is an adequate target language for the resulting compilers.

Acknowledgements

An implementation of the FLL-compiler has been worked out by Armin Schmidt. I want to thank him and Martina Effertz, who prepared parts of the manuscript.

Thanks too to my colleagues at the University of Trier for many fruitful discussions.

References

[1] K.Apt, H.Blair, A.Walker:
   Towards a Theory of Declarative Knowledge
   in: Foundations of Deductive Databases and Logic Programming, ed. J.Minker, Morgan Kaufmann, 1988

[2] F. Bancilhon:
   Naive Evaluation of Recursively Defined Relations
   in: On Knowledge Base Management Systems, eds. M.Brodie, J. Mylopoulos, Springer, 1986, pp. 165-178

[3] F. Bancilhon, R. Ramakrishnan:

An Amateur's Introduction to Recursive Query Processing Strategies
SIGMOD, Washington, 1986, pp. 16-52

[4] E.F. Codd:
A Relational Model for Large Shared Data Banks
CACM 13:6, pp. 377-387

[5] T. Ludwig:
FLL: A First-Order Language for Deductive Retrieval of Feature Terms
LILOG-Report 57, 1988

[6] T. Ludwig:
EFTA: An Algebra for Deductive Retrieval of Feature Terms
LILOG-Report 58, 1988

[7] T. Ludwig:
Algebraic Optimization of EFTA-Expressions
LILOG-Report 59, 1988

[8] T. Ludwig:
A Brief Overview of LILOG-DB
Proceedings Data Engineering, Feb. 1990, Los Angeles

[9] T. Ludwig, B.Walter, M.Ley, A.Maier, E.Gehlen:
LILOG-DB: Database-Support for Knowledge-Based Systems
Proceedings BTW, March 1989, Springer

[10] C. Zaniolo:
Safety and Compilation of Non-Recursive Horn Clauses
Proc. 1st Int. Conf. on Expert Database Systems, Charleston, 1986

[11] C. Zaniolo and D. Sacca:
Rule Rewriting Methods for Efficient Implementations of Horn Logic
MCC Technical Report DB-084-87, 1987

Semantic Transaction Optimization in Relational Databases

X.Y. Wang
W.A. Gray
N.J. Fiddian

Department of Computing Mathematics
University of Wales College of Cardiff

Abstract

In this paper, we investigate the feasibility of using semantic
information to optimize transactions in relational databases, where a
transaction is a sequence of elementary update operations. A sound
but not complete method is proposed for optimizing transactions by
utilizing a very important type of semantic information : integrity
constraints. Three heuristic rules are identified. These enable us to
replace expensive update operations with cheaper but semantically
equivalent operations, or to remove those update operations which
have no effect on the database state or leave the database state
intact. No database access is needed during this optimization
process.

1. Introduction

In a relational database, a database transaction is a logical unit of work consisting
of one or a sequence of elementary database update operations. It transforms a
consistent state of the database into another consistent state, without necessarily
preserving consistency at all intermediate points [9]. The elementary database
update operations act on a single relation and are of one of the following three
types:

(1).   Insertion: which inserts a tuple or a set of tuples into a relation;

(2).   Deletion: which deletes from a relation all tuples satisfying a given
        qualification;

(3).   Modification: which modifies in a relation all tuples satisfying a
        given qualification.

Database transactions have been extensively studied in the literature. However, most previous work has focused on solving problems associated with concurrency or recovery [10,16,17,18]. Investigation of transaction optimization has attracted less attention. Even though there are earlier papers discussing transaction optimization, they mainly concentrate on finding an efficient execution strategy, based on the costs associated with accessing and processing data, and the effects of concurrency controls in a multi-user environment [19,20]. This strategy is developed before any data is accessed in the database, by the optimizer using information held in the schema and examining the current processing state of the database. An available source of useful information for optimization at this stage has been ignored, namely the semantics held in the integrity constraints. These can be examined to identify update operations within a transaction which are redundant, or can be replaced by cheaper but semantically equivalent operations.

Transaction optimization proves important, as the nature of transactions makes them vital in determining the overall performance of database applications. Most existing DBMSs support concurrent transaction execution in order to enhance the system's throughput. This requires a protection overhead. A commonly used concurrency control mechanism is locking. While locking ensures that concurrent transactions do not interfere with each other, it also degrades the overall performance by forcing other transactions to wait for certain data items to be unlocked (the protection overhead). A higher degree of concurrency with its associated reduction in the protection overhead can be achieved by reducing the number of locks (either exclusive or shared) , or the locking time on data items. It will be seen in section 3 that our method optimizes a transaction containing redundant operations so that the protection overhead is reduced.

We believe that transaction optimization can be enhanced by dividing it into two stages. The first stage aims at eliminating redundant operations and at replacing expensive operations with cheaper but semantically equivalent operations (these terms are defined in section 3), while the second (conventional) stage aims at finding the "most optimal" transaction execution plan. This first stage of optimization is the focus of this paper.

The first stage of transaction optimization can be approached either syntactically or semantically. Previous work has only taken the syntactic approach [6], and we know of no past attempts to optimize transactions via semantic transformations as described in this paper.

[6] is an early work which formally investigates database transactions. It shows how an equivalent optimal transaction can be obtained from each given transaction. Three optimization criteria are proposed. However, all of them are based on high-level syntactic transformation.

In this paper, we investigate the feasibility of optimizing transactions by using semantic information in the form of the integrity constraints. A scheme is proposed which optimizes a given transaction in the following respects:

(1). eliminating redundant elementary update operations ;

(2). replacing elementary update operations with cheaper but semantically equivalent operations.

The paper is organized as follows. Section 2 describes the types of integrity constraint used for transaction optimization in this paper. Section 3 describes three heuristic rules and shows how a transaction can be optimized using them. A Prolog-based implementation of the method is described in section 4. Section 5 draws conclusions and identifies promising lines of future research.

2. Integrity constraints

A very important means of specifying the semantics of certain application domains is via integrity constraints, which are rules derived from the application domain which the database is modelling. Integrity constraints describe the properties that must be satisfied by the database contents. It is possible to distinguish between integrity constraints that must hold at all times and those that describe allowable changes in database contents. The former type are referred to as **state constraints** and the latter as **transition constraints** [16]. Furthermore, each type of constraint can be classified into two subtypes : aggregate-free constraints and aggregate constraints. Examples of these types of constraint are given in figure 1:

> *employee's age is less than 65* (aggregate-free state constraint)
> *the number of employees in the sales department is less than 50* (aggregate state constraint)
> *when the age value is updated, the new age value must be greater than the old* (aggregate-free transition constraint)
> *when the salary value is updated, the new salary value must be less than the old if the average of all employee's salaries is greater than 20,000* (aggregate transition constraint)

Fig 1. Example integrity constraints

Our discussion is based upon first-order predicate calculus. Since all types of transition constraints and aggregate state constraints are not (one-sorted) first-order expressible, our discussion is confined to aggregate-free state constraints. Among aggregate-free state constraints, two subclasses are distinguished. They are **attribute constraints** and **tuple constraints**.

Attribute constraints either restrict the value of an attribute to some range, such as *employee's age is less than 65*, or specify the relationships that must exist between attributes in the same or different relations. For instance, the following attribute constraint relates two attributes in the same relation : *if the rank is clerk, salary must be less than 25,000.*

Tuple constraints represent relationships between tuples in the same or different relations. They express the following semantics : if some tuples fulfilling certain conditions exist in the database, then other tuples (possibly with unknown values), fulfilling certain conditions, must also (or must not) exist in the database. Examples of tuple constraints are given in figure 2 below :

if a company supplies nuts, then it must also supply bolts ("must")
if a person is in relation Application (meaning that he is applying for a job),
then he must not be in relation Replacements (meaning that he has a job) ("must not")

Fig 2. Tuple constraints

To maintain the generality of our method, we admit integrity constraints as arbitrary, function-free first order formulas in prenex form. However, the price we must pay for such generality is that our method is only sound but not complete. This problem will be discussed in the next section. We also require that each integrity constraint be domain independent so that during our optimization process, only those integrity constraints which refer to the updated relation are considered [13].

The example database and integrity constraints used in the subsequent discussion are given in figures 3 and 4. This database is self-explanatory , so no further comment is necessary. The first four integrity constraints IC-1, IC-2, IC-3 and IC-4 are attribute constraints, while IC-5 and IC-6 are tuple constraints.

supplier(sno,sname,city)
part(pno,pname,weight)
shipment(sno,pno,qty)

Fig 3. Relational schema

IC-1: All London suppliers have sno which is less than 500
  $\forall x \forall y \forall z((supplier(x,y,z) \land z='London') \Rightarrow x<500)$
IC-2: Part p2 has standard weight of 17
  $\forall x \forall y \forall z ((part(x,y,z) \land x=p2) \Rightarrow z=17)$
IC-3: No supplier ships any part in quantity exceeding 500
  $\forall x \forall y \forall z(shipment(x,y,z) \Rightarrow z<=500)$
IC-4: Only London suppliers ship parts in quantity exceeding 300
  $\forall x \forall y \forall z \exists u \exists v((shipment(x,y,z) \land z>300) \Rightarrow (supplier(x,u,v) \land v='London'))$
IC-5: Any supplier shipping part p1 also ships the same quantity of part p2.
  $\forall x \forall y \forall z((shipment(x,y,z) \land y=p1) \Rightarrow shipment(x,p2,z))$
IC-6: Any supplier shipping part p2 also ships the same quantity of part p3.
  $\forall x \forall y \forall z((shipment(x,y,z) \land y=p2) \Rightarrow shipment(x,p3,z))$

Fig 4. Integrity constraints

3. Semantic transaction optimization

In section 1, we claimed that our method optimizes a given transaction by

(1). eliminating redundant elementary update operations ;

(2). replacing certain elementary update operations with semantically equivalent, but cheaper operations.

The first of these can reduce the number of locks (either exclusive or shared) which would otherwise be required by those redundant elementary update operations, while the second can reduce the locking time so permitting a potentially higher degree of concurrency.

Integrity constraints serve as the resource for our optimization. We assume that ordinary users may not update the integrity constraint set. Thus, the only allowed operation on the integrity constraint set is retrieval, and retrieval can be shared by all users. The optimization process is expected to be rapid, as the set of integrity constraints is much smaller than the data relations. The gain will be more conspicuous if the detected redundant elementary operations require exclusive locks either

(1). on a large portion of a relational database, such as when the selection of updated tuples involves joins, or

(2). for relatively long periods of time, such as when the updated tuples are selected by identifying the values or range of values of some attributes which have no fast access paths.

3.1 Preliminaries

The following definitions and assumptions are necessary in the subsequent discussion.

3.1.1 Definitions

Definition-1: A target relation is a relation referred to by an elementary update operation.

Definition-2: An insert operation is redundant if the tuple(s) to be inserted is(are) already in the target relation.

Definition-3: A delete operation is redundant if no tuple in the target relation satisfies the given qualification.

Definition-4: A modify operation is redundant if (a) no tuple in the target relation satisfies the given qualification or (b) the target relation remains unchanged after the modification.

Definition-5: Two elementary update operations are semantically equivalent if they refer to the same target relation and have the same effect on it.

Definition-6:   An elementary update operation A can be a replacement of another elementary update operation B (A and B are different) if A and B are semantically equivalent.

Definition-7:   An elementary update operation A is said to be cheaper than another elementary update operation B (A and B are different) if A is less complicated than B.

We follow the same increasing order of complexity among elementary operations as proposed in [6]: Insertion Deletion Modification. This implies that insertion is the cheapest, deletion is more expensive and modification is the most expensive. Thus, if a delete operation is semantically equivalent to a modify operation, it will replace the modify operation in the transaction, and a cheaper (more optimal) transaction will result.

3.1.2 Assumptions

Assumption-1: The set of integrity constraints is consistent.

Assumption-2: No two tuples in any relation are identical.

Assumption-3: The current database state (the database state prior to the start of the transaction) satisfies all the integrity constraints.

Assumption 3 needs further explanation. In this paper, we take a proof-theoretic view of databases [1,13]. Furthermore, the theory T, which admits an instance of the database as a unique model, is complete (i.e. for any closed formula W, either T |- W or T |- ¬W). Therefore, if we use IC-set to represent the set of all integrity constraints, then the database obeys the integrity constraints in IC-set iff T∪IC-set is consistent [1].

3.2 Heuristic rules and their applications

All the heuristic rules identified in this paper aim at detecting redundant elementary update operations or discovering cheaper replacements for elementary update operations. We have the following three heuristic rules :

Rule-1:   Redundant delete operation elimination

Rule-2:   Redundant modify operation elimination

Rule-3:   Complexity reduction

Note that insert operation optimization is ignored, because no integrity constraint validates that the tuple(s) to be inserted is(are) already in the target relation (we do not admit an integrity constraint of the form : $\exists x\ P(a,x)$, as it will evaluate to false when the database is empty).

Our method applies to arbitrary database transactions. These consist of sequences of insertions, deletions and modifications where the tuples to be deleted or modified are selected by specifying the values or the range of values of some attributes of the target relation using arithmetic comparison operators ($=, \neq$, $>, >=, <, <=$). Therefore, the language of theory T needs to be extended to include those operators.

In the following illustration, we use a Quel-like language [15] to express elementary update operations so as to demonstrate these applications of the three heuristic rules.

3.2.1 Rule-1 : Redundant delete operation elimination

The observation behind the proposal of Rule-1 is as follows: According to assumption-3, the current database state obeys all the integrity constraints. In other words, no tuple exists whose attributes contain values that violate certain integrity constraints. Therefore, any attempt to delete tuples of this type is redundant, as there will be no tuple in the target relation that satisfies the given qualification.

The following examples illustrate the application of Rule-1.

Delete-operation-1:
Supplier whose sno is 340 no longer ships parts in quantity equal to 600.

Quel-form:
delete shipment
where shipment.sno=340 and shipment.qty=600
From IC-3 and assumption-3, we know that no tuple in shipment satisfies *shipment.qty=600*. Therefore, this delete operation is redundant.

Delete-operation-2:
Suppliers whose sno is greater than 600 no longer ship parts in quantity exceeding 300.

Quel-form:
delete shipment
where shipment.sno > 600 and shipment.qty > 300
IC-1 tells us that suppliers whose sno is greater than 600 are not in London , and IC-4 tells us that only a London supplier can ship in quantities exceeding 300. Based on assumption-3, we know that no tuple in shipment satisfies both *shipment.sno > 600* and *shipment.qty > 300*. Therefore, this delete operation is redundant.

Delete-operation-3:
Remove supplier whose sno is 650 and based in 'London'.

Quel-form:
delete supplier
where supplier.sno=650 and supplier.city='London'
From IC-1 and assumption-3, we know that no tuple in supplier satisfies both *supplier.sno=650* and *supplier.city='London'*. Therefore, this delete operation is redundant.

3.2.2 Rule-2 : Redundant modify operation elimination

Definition-4 in 3.1.1 is derived from the semantics of the modify operation. Rule-2 aims at detecting redundant modify operations of type (a) (no tuple in the target relation satisfying the given qualification) or (b) (the target relation remains unchanged after the modification). The method in 3.2.1 can be used to detect redundancy of type (a), while the proof of redundancy of type (b) is based on the following observations:

(1). Certain attribute constraints express the following semantics: if some attributes fulfilling certain conditions exist in the database, then some other attributes fulfilling certain conditions must also exist in the database.

(2). The tuples to be modified are selected by specifying the values or range of values of some attributes of the target relation.

Thus, from the attribute constraints and the specified values or range of values of certain attributes of the target relation, we can obtain a more instantiated tuple, which means that the values of some other attributes not specified are also known. If we can prove that those attributes to be modified are all instantiated in this way, and furthermore, that the modified values are the same as the instantiated values, then we know that the target relation will remain unchanged after the modification. Modify-operation-2 and modify-operation-3 serve as illustrations.

An example of type (a) redundancy is:

Modify-operation-1:
   Supplier whose sno is 550 reduces its shipping of any part from 400 to 200.

Quel-form:
   replace shipment(qty=200)
   where shipment.sno=550 and shipment.qty=400

IC-1 tells us that supplier whose sno is 550 is not in London , and IC-4 tells us that only a London supplier can ship in quantity equalling 400. Based on assumption-3, we know that no tuple in shipment satisfies both *shipment.sno=550* and *shipment.qty=400*. Therefore, this modify operation is redundant.

Examples of type (b) redundancy are as follows :

Modify-operation-2:
   Modify the weight of part p2 to 17.

Quel-form:
   replace part(weight=17)
   where part.pno=p2

From IC-2, the specified value *pno=p2* and assumption-3, we get a more instantiated tuple (p2,_,17), where "_" signifies that the value of the second attribute is unknown. Since only attribute "weight" is modified and the modified value 17 happens to be the same as the instantiated value 17, we know that relation part remains the same after this modification. Therefore, this modify operation is redundant.

Modify-operation-3:
Modify the cities of all suppliers who ship in quantity exceeding 300 to 'London'.

Quel-form:
replace supplier(city="London")
where supplier.sno=shipment.sno and shipment.qty > 300
IC-4 tells us that all suppliers who ship in quantity exceeding 300 are in London. Therefore, we know that relation supplier remains the same after this modification, and that consequently this modify operation is redundant.

3.2.3 Rule-3 : Complexity reduction

A modify operation, if practically executed, can be viewed as a small transaction which contains two elementary update operations : first deletion and then insertion. If we fail to establish either *no tuple in the target relation satisfying the given qualification* or *the target relation remains unchanged after the modification* using rule-2, we assume that there are tuples in the target relation that satisfy the qualification. We then attempt to prove that the modified tuples are already in the target relation. If we can prove this, then the insertion part of the modify operation is redundant, which means the modify operation is semantically equivalent to a delete operation. Therefore, we can replace the modify operation with a delete operation, and the complexity of the transaction is reduced. The above observation motivates the proposal of rule-3.

Tuple constraints serve as the source of this type of optimization. The following examples illustrate this.

Modify-operation-4:
All suppliers of part p1 stop shipping p1 and begin to ship p2.

Quel-form:
replace shipment(pno=p2)
where shipment.pno=p1
IC-5 tells us that if supplier s1 ships part p1 in quantity q1, then s1 also ships part p2 in quantity q1. Therefore, after the modification, there will be two identical tuples (s1,p2, q1) in shipment. In accordance with assumption-2 , one must be deleted. Therefore, the overall effect of this modify operation is the same as that of a delete operation. Since a delete operation is cheaper , it can replace the modify operation, thus resulting in an optimal transaction.
The delete operation is: *delete shipment where shipment.pno=p1.*

Modify-operation-5:
All suppliers of part p1 stop shipping p1 and begin to ship p3.

Quel-form:

      replace shipment(pno=p3)

      where shipment.pno=p1

According to IC-5, any supplier who ships part p1 also ships part p2 in the same quantity. Furthermore, IC-6 tells us that any supplier who ships part p2 also ships part p3 in the same quantity, therefore, any supplier who ships part p1 also ships part p3 in the same quantity. In accordance with the discussion in modify-operation-4, the modify operation can be replaced by a delete operation, resulting in an optimal transaction.

      The delete operation is: *delete shipment where shipment.pno=p1.*

4. Implementation considerations

All three heuristic rules have been implemented using Prolog, which is part of POPLOG available on a Sun workstation.

      Each n-ary relation R is represented by an n-place predicate symbol R. The integrity constraints are transformed into clausal forms first, and then each clause is represented as a list whose elements are the literals in the clause. A list L is stored in a Prolog database as integrity(L), where "integrity" is a special predicate symbol representing integrity constraints. The following 2-place predicate symbols have been defined to represent arithmetic comparison operators : eq (=), not_eq (≠), gt (>), gt_or_eq (>=), lt (<) and lt_or_eq (<=). As negated literals will be introduced when converting formulas into clausal forms, another special predicate symbol "not" is defined which represents negation. Note that "not" here is only a symbol (sign), not a logical operator.

      When transforming the integrity constraints into internal forms, the following two valid formulas are used as simplification rules :

(1). $\forall$ x (x≠a ∨ P(x)) ⟺ P(a)

(2). $\exists$ x (x=a ∧ P(x)) ⟺ P(a)

      In addition, universally or existentially quantified variables which appear only once in a clause are replaced with the anonymous symbol "_" for concise representation and efficient unification. That is because they are not used elsewhere in the clause, and hence their instantiations are meaningless. Thus they will not contribute in our search for proof .

      The internal forms of the integrity constraints defined in figure 4 are given in figure 5.

IC-1: integrity ([not(supplier(X,_,'London')) , lt(X,500)])

IC-2: integrity ([not(part(p2,_,Z)), eq(Z,17)])

IC-3: integrity ([not(shipment(_,_,Z)), lt_or_eq(Z,500)])

IC-4: integrity ([not(shipment(X,_,Z)), lt_or_eq(Z,300), supplier(X,_,'London')])

IC-5: integrity ([not(shipment(X,p1,Z)), shipment(X,p2,Z)])

Fig 5. Internal forms of integrity constraints

Each elementary update operation is also transformed into a Prolog clause of the following form : operation(Operation-type,Template), where Operation-type is one of : insert, delete or modify. Template is an n-place predicate symbol representing the n-ary target relation. For insertion, each argument of the template is substituted with the value of its corresponding attribute in the tuple(s) to be inserted. For deletion, those arguments whose corresponding attributes are mentioned in the qualification of the deletion are replaced with the specified values or range of values. The rest of the arguments are replaced by the anonymous symbol "_". For modification, two templates are needed, the first represents the tuples to be modified and the second represents the new values. The replacement of arguments in both templates follows the method used for deletion. For instance, **delete-operation-1** is expressed as:

operation(delete, shipment(340,_,600));

and **modify-operation-1** is expressed as:

operation(modify, [shipment(550,_,400), shipment(_,_,200)]).

(The transformations of elementary update operations into internal forms can be very complicated because of the complexity of their qualifications. For example, the qualification can be derived from several relations, such as that of **modify-operation-3**. Due to space limitations, we will not give further description of these transformations).

In the following sub-sections, the implemented algorithms are given in pseudo-English for clarity of presentation, and not in their Prolog format.

4.1 Algorithm for Rule-1.

We use a template Temp to represent the set of tuples to be deleted from the target relation. We then assume that the tuples represented by Temp exist in the target relation and we attempt to prove IC-set∪Temp is inconsistent. If we succeed, then we have proved that our assumption is wrong, which means the tuples represented by Temp do not exist in the target relation. Thus, the delete operation is redundant.

However, as we put no restriction on the forms of the prefix of the integrity constraints, the problem of proving the consistency of IC-set∪Temp is only semi-decidable [4,5,8]. This means that if Temp represents tuples that do not violate any integrity constraint (IC-set∪Temp is consistent), no proving procedure is guaranteed to terminate. To overcome this problem, we introduce a limitation on the number of iterations in our search for proof. If the empty clause cannot be derived after a number of iterations (10 in our implementation, as our examples are relatively simple), then the integrity constraint involved is said to be not violated. The program then moves to the next relevant integrity constraint in the IC-set. (An integrity constraint is said to be relevant if it can resolve with

Temp).

We propose an algorithm which is based on binary resolution governed by set of support [12]. This algorithm is sound and complete for a template representing tuples violating certain integrity constraints. The following theorem substantiates this statement:

Set-of-support theorem: If S is an unsatisfiable set of clauses, and if S1 is a subset of S such that S-S1 is satisfiable, then with S1 being the set of support, the imposition of the set of support strategy on the combination of binary resolution and factoring preserves the property of refutation completeness for that combination [12].

In our case, S is IC-set∪Temp, and S1 is Temp. Therefore, S-S1 is IC-set, which is satisfiable(consistent) according to assumption-1.

We have the following recursive algorithm for rule-1.

```
(1).construct Temp from the qualification
(2).counter=0
(3).call procedure A(Temp,counter,flag)
    if flag=redundant
      remove this delete operation
    endif

Procedure A ( Temp,counter, flag)
(1). if counter = 10
        flag=valid; return
      else
        goto (2)
      endif
(2).get the next integrity constraint C from IC-set
      if IC-set is empty
      flag=valid ; return
      else
        goto (3)
      endif
(3). if C is irrelevant
        goto (2)
      else
        if resolvent of Temp and C is reduced to null
          flag=redundant; return
        else
          goto (4)
        endif
      endif
(4). if the resolvant  R of Temp and C is reduced to true or unknown
        goto (2)
      else
        goto (5)
```

endif
(5).get a literal L from R
    if R is empty
     flag=redundant; return
    else
     goto (6)
    endif
(6).counter=counter+1
    call procedure A(L,counter,flag)
    if flag=redundant
     goto (5)
    else
     return
    endif

4.2 Algorithm for Rule-2.

A template Temp is used to represent the set of tuples to be modified in the target relation. We first attempt to prove that the set of tuples to be modified is not in the target relation by calling the algorithm for rule-1. If we fail, we then attempt to prove that the target relation remains unchanged after the modification.

A second template Temp1 is built from both Temp and the integrity constraints such that Temp1 is like Temp, but more arguments are instantiated.

The following algorithm implements Rule-2:

(1). construct Temp from the qualification
(2). counter=0
(3). call procedure A(Temp,counter,flag)
    if flag=redundant
     goto (5)
    else
     goto (4)
    endif
(4). construct Temp1 from Temp and integrity constraints (attribute constraints)
    if the target relation remains unchanged
    flag=redundant;goto (5)
    else
    flag=valid; goto (5)
    endif
(5). if flag=redundant
    remove this modify operation
    endif

Note that a side-effect of this algorithm is that it can detect the violation of certain integrity constraints. For instance, according to IC-2, part p2 has a standard weight of 17. If a modify operation modifies the weight of p2 to a new value which is not 17, then IC-2 is violated and the modified value cannot be inserted into the target relation. In this case, an error message is signalled and the optimization process stops.

4.3 Algorithm for Rule-3.

This algorithm is called when the algorithm for rule-2 fails to prove either *no tuple in the target relation satisfies the given qualification* or *the target relation remains unchanged after the modification.* It is assumed that the set of tuples to be modified exists in the target relation. Then an attempt is made to generate other tuples whose existence is required by the existence of tuples represented by Temp1 (as in 4.2).

We use a new template Temp2 to represent the newly-generated tuples. We start from step (5) ((1)-(4) are carried out in the algorithm of rule-2).

```
(5). construct Temp2 from Temp1 and integrity constraints (tuple constraints)
        if one of Temp2 is the same as the modified tuples
        flag=redundant;goto (6)
        else
        flag=valid; goto (6)
        endif
(6). if flag=redundant
         replace this modify operation with a delete operation which
         deletes the tuples represented by Temp
         endif
```

Note that this algorithm supports forward-chaining. Each generated tuple may in turn generate other new tuples (c.f. modify-operation-5).

5. Conclusion

A method for optimizing transactions in relational databases using semantic information has been proposed in this paper. It has been shown that "improved" or "optimal" transactions can be obtained from the original transactions by using the three heuristic rules identified. The underlying principles of our method are an extension of those of semantic query optimization [2]. A small overhead is introduced by checking the integrity constraint set, but the potential gain can be large.

The technique presented in this paper could be useful in situations where users are likely to issue redundant update operations because they are unaware of the integrity constraints. This can happen when the database has a large number of integrity constraints, there is a large number of casual users of the database or the integrity constraints are complex.

There are many ways in which this work can be extended. We have observed that all the other types of integrity constraint can be utilized in semantic transaction optimization as described in this paper. For example, if an aggregate state constraint says that no course has more than 30 students, then a modify operation: *assign those courses which have more than 30 students to lecture room 1* can be detected as redundant. We plan to extend the current method to include such facilities as integrity constraint checking and optimization using high-level syntactic transformation.

References

1. H. Gaillaire, J. Minker and J-M. Nicolas. Logic and Databases: A Deductive Approach. *ACM Computing Surveys* (1984), Vol.16,No.2,pp.153-185.

2. S. T. Shenoy and Z. M. Ozsoyoglu. A System for Semantic Query Optimization. *Proceedings ACM SIGMOD Conference 1987*, pp. 181-195.

3. K. G. Jeffrey, J. Lay and T. Curtis. Logic Programming and Database Technology used for Validation within Transactions. *Proceedings of the Seventh British National Conference On Databases*, Cambridge,1989, pp. 71-84.

4. Z. Manna. *Mathematical Theory of Computation*. McGraw-Hill Book Co. 1974.

5. R.A. Frost. *Introduction to Knowledge Base Systems*. Collins Professional & Technical Books, 1986.

6. S. Abiteboul and V. Vianu. Transactions in Relational Databases (Preliminary Report). *Proceedings of the 10th VLDB Conference*, Singapore, Aug. 1984, pp.46-56.

7. R.C.Goldstein. *Database: Technology and Management.* John Wiley&Sons, Inc. 1985.

8. W.H. Joyner jr. Resolution Strategies as Decision Procedures. *Journal of the ACM*, Vol.23, No.3, July 1976, pp. 398-417.

9. C.J.Date. *An Introduction to Database Systems*. Vol. 1, Fourth Edition, Addison-Wesley Publishing Company, 1986.

10. J.D.Ullman. *Principles of Database Systems*. Second Edition, PITMAN, 1982.

11. J.M.Nicolas and K.Yazdanian. Integrity checking in deductive databases, in *H.Gallaire, J.Minker (eds.): Logic and Databases*, Plenum Press, New York, 1978, pp. 325-344.

12. L.Wos, R.Overbeek, E.Lusk and J.Boyle. *Automated Reasoning: Introduction and Applications*. Prentice-Hall , Inc. 1984.

13. W.W.McCune, L.J.Henschen. Maintaining State Constraints in Relational Databases: A Proof Theoretic Basis. *JACM*, Vol.36, No.1, Jan. 1989, pp. 46-68.

14. W.F.Clocksin and C.S.Mellish. *Programming in Prolog*. Second Edition, Springer-Verlag, 1984.

15. M.R.Stonbraker, E. Wong, P.Kreps and G.Held. The design and implementation of INGRES. *ACM TODS* ,Sept. 1976, pp. 189-222.

16. C.J.Date. *An Introduction to Database Systems*. Vol. II. Addison-Wesley Publishing Company, 1985.

17. H.F.Korth and G.D.Speegle. Formal method of correctness without serializability, *Proceedings ACM SIGMOD Conference 1988*, pp. 379-386.

18. P.Franciszek and J.T.Robinson. Limitations of Concurrency in Transaction Processing. *ACM TODS*, Vol. 10, No. 1, Mar. 1985 ,pp. 1-28.

19. P.A.Dwyer and A.R.Hevner. Transaction Optimization in A Distributed Database Testbed System. *The Proceedings of COMPSAC 1983*, pp. 564-570.

20. R.Unland, U.Praedel and G.Schlageter. Design alternatives for optimistic concurrency control schemes. *Proceedings of Second International Conference on Databases*, Sept. 1983, pp. 288-297.

Graph Views and Recursive Query Languages

P.T. Wood

Department of Computer Science
University of Cape Town

Abstract

Much recent research has been directed towards providing a mechanism for formulating recursive queries on relational databases. For applications where this is appropriate, it seems that the data can very often be represented naturally by a graph structure, while the queries themselves can be viewed as asking about the existence of paths in such a graph that satisfy certain properties. In this paper, we describe a means for defining graph views on relational databases along with two languages for querying these views. The first language, Grasp, is itself graph-based, thus providing a natural correspondence between the queries and the data structure being queried. Users famílar with SQL may prefer the second language, called Resql, since it extends SQL with the ability to specify path traversals and computations. The use of regular expressions to specify path properties in both Grasp and Resql results in languages that are both powerful and concise.

1 Introduction

The desirability for query languages to be able to express recursive queries has been recognized for some time now [2], mostly with regard to domains other than traditional business applications [9]. A number of authors have noted that many of these applications share the characteristic that their data can be viewed most naturally in terms of a directed, labelled graph or network [4, 9]. Typical examples include different forms of routing networks, bill-of-materials applications, project scheduling charts, as well as any form of hierarchical data (whether representing ancestors, managers or property inheritance). In this paper, we make this correspondence explicit firstly by allowing users to define graph-based views of relations, and secondly by providing query languages containing constructs for graph traversal.

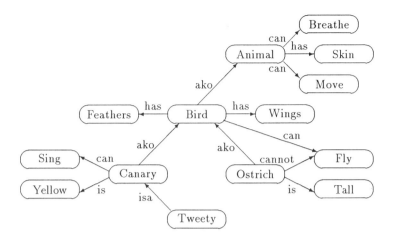

Fig 1. Part of a semantic network

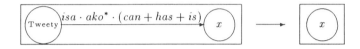

Fig 2. Query to find all properties Tweety inherits

The first query language, called Grasp, is a graphical language well suited to pictorial implementation using a bit-mapped display, and is essentially the language described in [7, 8] with different semantics. Graph view definitions can be displayed pictorially, while both a Grasp query and its output are labelled graphs. For users who prefer keyword-based languages, an extended version of SQL, called Resql, is provided. This language shares some features with the query language described in [4]. In both Grasp and Resql, a typical query asks about nodes in a graph view that are connected by a path satisfying some property. The particular property is specified by means of a regular expression, which states that only those paths in the graph whose concatenation of edge labels is in the language denoted by the given regular expression are to be considered. Examples of queries in each language follow.

Example 1 Various forms of semantic network have been found to be useful in knowledge representation. An example of such a network is given in Figure 1, where *ako* represents generalisation (subset relationships) and *isa* represents classification (membership relation). The regular expression $isa \cdot ako^* \cdot (can + has + is)$ can be used to determine all the properties that Tweety inherits. The corresponding query expressed in Grasp is shown in Figure 2. The left-hand box in Figure 2 contains the pattern graph, while the right-hand box contains the summary graph which specifies how the output is to be presented to the user. In this case, the output is simply the set of

125

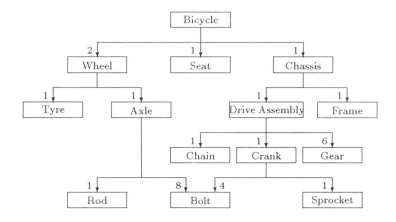

Fig 3. Parts explosion of a bicycle

nodes that can be reached in the semantic network by following paths that start from the node labelled Tweety and whose concatenation of edge labels satisfy the regular expression in the pattern graph. This turns out to be all the property nodes except that labelled Tall in Figure 1. □

Of course, the above query can be expressed in any language that has the power to compute the transitive closure of a relation. The additional power of our languages is gained when regular expressions are used in conjunction with variables rather than constants as discussed in Section 3. Coupling this with the ability to perform computations over paths (such as shortest path) as well as to integrate with existing languages in the case of Resql results in a powerful, yet easy-to-use query facility.

Example 2 Consider a bill-of-materials application in which we have a hierarchy of parts, along with quantities of each subpart required to assemble a superpart. A possible hierarchy for a bicycle (modified from [15]) is shown in Figure 3. The following query in the language Resql finds the total quantities of each part required to assemble a bicycle.

```
SELECT FINAL part, SUM(total)
FROM PATHS IN part_hierarchy
WITH total = TIMES(quantity)
WHERE INITIAL part = 'Bicycle'
GROUP BY FINAL part;
```

The syntax of Resql is sufficiently similar to that of SQL so as not to require too much explanation. The above query computes over paths in the graph view *part_hierarchy*, starting from the initial part 'Bicycle'. Attribute *total* is derived by multiplying all quantity values along each path from 'Bicycle' to every other part. The final quantities are given by adding all the path totals for each such part. Figure 4 lists the output of the query. □

126

part	sum		part	sum
Wheel	2		Chain	1
Seat	1		Crank	1
Chassis	1		Gear	6
Tyre	2		Rod	2
Axle	2		Bolt	20
Drive Assembly	1		Sprocket	1
Frame	1			

Fig 4. Total quantities of parts required to assemble a bicycle

The outline of the rest of the paper is as follows. In the next section, we present the mechanism for defining graph views, mostly by means of a number of examples. Section 3 is devoted to a description of our recursive query languages. First we introduce regular expressions as a query language primitive over graph views, emphasizing the conciseness that they provide compared to other approaches. The remainder of Section 3 describes the query languages Grasp and Resql, both of which are based on the use of regular expressions. Query evaluation algorithms and implementation details are covered in Section 4, while Section 5 contains conclusions and topics for future work.

2 Graph Views

We have already provided two example applications where graph views might be appropriate. In this section we demonstrate the syntax of graph view definitions by means of a number of examples that will be useful later in the paper.

When constructing a graph view G from a relation r over scheme R, each tuple in r is represented as a directed edge in G. Values from two attributes of R are used to label nodes in G, one for the head of edges and the other for the tail of edges in G. There are essentially two ways in which the edges of G can be labelled. In the first, a number of relations can be represented as a graph G by labelling the edges of G with the names of the relations themselves. This is the case in Example 1 above. In the second, an edge e of G representing tuple t of r is labelled with the values of some subset of the attributes of R appearing in tuple t other than those labelling nodes. Example 2 above demonstrates this.

Example 3 Consider Example 1 above and assume that the semantic network is stored in a relational database comprising six relation schemes as follows.

> *ako (subClass, superClass)*
> *isa (instance, class)*
> *can (class, property)*

127

cannot (class, property)
has (class, property)
is (class, property)

The graph view shown in Figure 1 could be constructed by the following view definition.

```
CREATE GRAPH VIEW semantic_network AS
    EDGES BETWEEN class NODES LABELLED subClass
        AND class NODES LABELLED superClass
    FROM RELATION ako
UNION
    EDGES BETWEEN instance NODES LABELLED instance
        AND class NODES LABELLED class
    FROM RELATION isa
UNION
    ⋮
UNION
    EDGES BETWEEN class NODES LABELLED class
        AND property NODES LABELLED property
    FROM RELATION is
```

In this view there are three types of nodes, namely *class*, *instance* and *property*. By default, edges are labelled with the relation names from which they are derived, giving rise to the structure of Figure 1. The case of labelling edges explicitly is demonstrated by the graph view definition for Example 2. Assume that the components comprising a bicycle are stored in a single relation with scheme *component (subPart, superPart, quantity)*. The view definition for Figure 3 is given below.

```
CREATE GRAPH VIEW part_hierarchy AS
    EDGES LABELLED quantity BETWEEN part NODES
        LABELLED superPart AND part NODES LABELLED subPart
    FROM RELATION component
```

In the resulting graph, edges are labelled with the corresponding values of the attribute *quantity* from the *component* relation. Since the above graph definition facility is rather verbose, various shortened forms and defaults are available. □

Although neither of the above examples show it, both nodes and edges in graph views can be labelled with *tuples* of values rather than single values. The following example of a graph view will be used later in order to introduce a number of features of the query languages.

Example 4 Consider a relation *flights* with attributes *flight-no, source, dest, airline,* and *plane*. A tuple in *flights* is interpreted as representing that flight *flight-no* flies from the *source* city to the *dest* city using the given *airline* and *plane* type. One graph view definition is as follows.

```
CREATE GRAPH VIEW flight_network AS
    EDGES LABELLED airline, plane BETWEEN city NODES
        LABELLED source AND city NODES LABELLED dest
    FROM RELATION flights
```

In this case, each edge between a source city node and a destination city node is labelled with the corresponding airline name and plane type. □

In order to simplify query formulation, various defaults exist so that defining a graph view is not always even necessary. For example, assume that *flights* is an n-ary relation defined over attributes $A_1, A_2, \ldots, A_n$. Then attributes A_1 and A_2 are assumed to label nodes in the graph G of *flights*, while $A_3, \ldots, A_n$ label the edges; that is, a tuple $(a_1, a_2, \ldots, a_n)$ in *flights* corresponds to an edge from node a_1 to node a_2 labelled $(a_3, \ldots, a_n)$ in G. Of course, a binary relation is modelled as a graph with edges labelled by the relation name itself. Nodes in a query can be referred to by either attribute A_1 or A_2.

Example 5 Using the defaults described above, the query of Example 2 could be formulated directly on the relation *component* as follows.

```
SELECT FINAL subPart, SUM(total)
FROM PATHS IN component
WITH total = TIMES(quantity)
WHERE INITIAL superPart = 'Bicycle'
GROUP BY FINAL subPart;
```

□

The graph view definitions are stored in special relations in the database in a straightforward way. On receipt of a Grasp or Resql query, the system uses the appropriate definition to determine the correspondence between the graph view and the underlying relations. The manner in which graph-based queries are translated into embedded SQL is the subject of Section 5.

3 Recursive Query Languages

We now turn our attention to the languages for querying graph views. Because of the central role played by regular expressions in these languages, we begin in Section 3.1 by introducing our form of regular expressions which allow the use of variables as well as constants. This gives rise to a conciseness of notation that does not seem to be shared by similar query languages. The definition of the language Grasp is given in Section 3.2, while Resql is described in Section 3.3.

3.1 Regular expressions

We begin by defining the syntax of our regular expressions. Let Σ be a finite alphabet disjoint from $\{\epsilon, \emptyset, (,)\}$. A *regular expression* over Σ is defined recursively as follows.

1. The empty string ϵ, the empty set $\emptyset$, and each $a \in \Sigma$ are regular expressions.

2. If A and B are regular expressions, then $(A + B)$, $(A \cdot B)$ and $(A)^*$ are regular expressions.

3. Nothing else is a regular expression.

The expression $(A + B)$ is called the *alternation* of A and B, $(A \cdot B)$ is called the *concatenation* of A and B, and $(A)^*$ is called the *closure* of A. We use the question mark (?) as shorthand for the alternation of all elements of Σ. Also, $(A)^+$ denotes $A \cdot A^*$, the *positive closure* of A. The language $L(R)$ denoted by a regular expression R is defined in the usual way [10].

A significant departure from traditional regular expressions is in the partitioning of Σ into two disjoint sets, a set V of *variables* (usually denoted by the letters x, y, z) and a set U of *constants* (usually denoted by the letters a, b, c)[1]. Our use of variables is more restricted than that provided by some Unix[2] pattern matching utilities, where regular expressions with "back-referencing" are allowed [1]. Within such an expression R, *strings* matching arbitrary regular expressions can be assigned to variables and referred to subsequently in R. This assignment can occur inside the scope of a closure operator, for example, thereby permitting local binding of variables. These features increase the expressive power of such expressions considerably, allowing even non-context-free languages to be denoted [1]. In contrast, only *constants* can be assigned to variables in our regular expressions, and all binding of variables is global.

Example 6 Consider the regular expression $R = x^*$, where the set U of constants in Σ is $\{a_1, \ldots, a_n\}$. Then R is equivalent to the expression $R' = a_1^* + \cdots + a_n^*$, and is more concise. Other examples of regular expressions with variables are $(x \cdot x)^*$, which matches strings of even length comprising single symbols from U, and $(x + y)^*$, which matches strings of arbitrary length comprising at most two symbols from U. □

In our query languages, a regular expression R is used to match edge labels along paths in a (virtual) graph G defined by a graph view. Let us call these graphs *database graphs* (or *db-graphs*, for short). The alphabet Σ of R comprises the constants and variables appearing in R as well as the constants (which will often be strings) labelling edges in G. A *valuation* ρ of R is an assignment of constants to all the alphabet symbols in R, such that ρ is the identity mapping on constants. We let $\rho(R)$ denote the result of applying ρ to each symbol in R. We say that a path p in G *satisfies* R if there is a valuation ρ such that the string comprising the concatenation of edge labels

---

[1] In Grasp and Resql, this disjointness is enforced by enclosing constants in quotes.
[2] Unix is a trademark of AT&T.

along p is in the language $L(\rho(R))$. The valuation ρ is called a *satisfying valuation* for p and R.

Example 7 Referring back to Example 1 (the semantic network), we can see why the regular expression $isa \cdot ako^* \cdot (can + has + is)$ will match the paths from Tweety to Sing, Yellow, Feathers, Wings, Fly, Breathe, Skin and Move. For an example involving variables, consider the *flight_network* view of Example 4, assuming that edges are labelled with *airline* values alone. Then the regular expression $(x + y)^*$ of the previous example will match only those flight paths that use at most two airlines. □

3.2   Grasp

As stated earlier, Grasp is based on the language $\mathbf{G}^+$ which was introduced in [8]. In the Introduction, we presented an example of a Grasp query (Figure 2) and provided some intuition into the meaning of such queries. In this section, we review the syntax of Grasp briefly and comment on our choice of semantics, mostly by means of examples.

The simplest form of Grasp query Q consists of a *pattern graph P* and a *summary graph S*. The pattern graph specifies the patterns which are to be matched in the db-graph being queried, while the summary graph specifies the form of the output. A pattern graph is similar to a db-graph (being a directed, labelled multigraph), but its nodes and edges, instead of being labelled with constant values, may be labelled with variables, or, in the case of edges, regular expressions. A summary graph is simply a graph with at most two nodes and one edge, labelled by constants and variables taken from those occurring in the pattern graph.

In order to define the meaning of Grasp queries, we can extend the notion of a valuation for a regular expression to a valuation for a pattern graph P, which is an assignment of constants to *all* symbols occurring in P, including those labelling nodes. Similarly, we can extend the concept of a path satisfying a regular expression. We say that a subgraph H of a db-graph G *satisfies* pattern graph P if there is a valuation ρ of the symbols in P such that (1) there is a one-to-one mapping ν from the nodes of $\rho(P)$ to the nodes of H that preserves their labels, and (2) for each edge e in P from node x to node y labelled with regular expression R_e, there is a path p from $\nu(x)$ to $\nu(y)$ in H such that ρ is a satisfying valuation for p and R_e.

Let Q be a Grasp query comprising pattern graph P and summary graph S, and G be the db-graph to which Q is applied. The *answer* of Q applied to G is the union of all graphs obtained by applying a satisfying valuation for P and G to the summary graph S.

Example 8 Consider once again the db-graph G representing the semantic network of Figure 1, along with the Grasp query Q depicted in Figure 5 which finds pairs of classes that might have properties in common by virtue

Fig 5. Query to find pairs of classes that might have properties in common

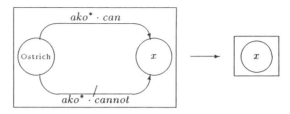

Fig 6. Query to find out the capabilities of Ostriches

of inheriting them from a common ancestor. Query Q has three variables in its pattern graph P, while its summary graph S comprises a single edge rather than a single node as before. One satisfying valuation for P and G is given by mapping x to Canary, y to Bird, and z to Animal, since there is a path labelled $ako \cdot ako$ from Canary to Animal, and a path labelled ako from Bird to Animal. Hence, nodes Canary and Bird appear in the answer with an edge from Canary to Bird. □

In the definition of query answers for the language $\mathbf{G^+}$, edges in a pattern graph are mapped to *simple* paths in a db-graph G. This obviously changes the meaning of queries only when cyclic db-graphs are being queried. However, it also turns out to affect the complexity of evaluating queries adversely in that the evaluation problem for certain queries becomes NP-complete [12]. Without the restriction to simple paths, all queries can be evaluated in polynomial time, hence our definition above.

Grasp queries can be considerably more extensive than those given above. Both disjunction and composition can be expressed, while functions can be applied to path labels in the spirit of Example 2. For a description of these features, the reader is referred to [8]. It is also possible to express a certain form of negation in the language by means of crossed-out edges in pattern graphs.

Example 9 In our semantic network of Example 1, we might be interested in the capabilities of ostriches (in terms of properties inherited through *ako* and *can* edges). However, we would like to take into account the possibility that properties can be overridden by edges labelled *cannot*. The Grasp query of Figure 6 finds the correct set of inherited properties. In this case a property p will appear in the answer of the query only if there is a path satisfying $ako^* \cdot can$ from Ostrich to p and no path from Ostrich to p satisfying $ako^* \cdot cannot$. Thus, property Fly, for example, will not be in the answer. □

In order to interpret crossed-out edges in a pattern graph P, it is necessary to extend the notion of a subgraph H of a db-graph G satisfying P. Let us call an edge in P that is not crossed out an *ordinary* edge. Condition (2) above is then altered to read: for each edge e in P from node x to node y labelled with regular expression R_e, (i) if e is ordinary, there is a path p from $\nu(x)$ to $\nu(y)$ in H such that ρ is a satisfying valuation for p and R_e, or (ii) if e is crossed out, there is *no* path from $\nu(x)$ to $\nu(y)$ in H for which ρ is a satisfying valuation.

3.3 Resql

While there have been many proposals for recursive query languages, very few papers have considered extending existing query languages, such as SQL and QUEL, to allow the formulation of recursive queries [4, 11, 15]. In this section, we extend SQL along the lines advocated in [4]. The resulting language is called Resql in recognition of the central role played by regular expressions in query formulation. Once again, we introduce language features mostly through examples, although the semantics of Resql queries on graph views can be defined analagously to the semantics of Grasp given in the previous section.

A subset of Resql syntax, dealing mosting with applying functions to paths in a graph view, was introduced in Example 2. It is quite possible that typical users of SQL may not be familiar or comfortable with the concept of regular expressions. We believe, however, that the keyword syntax we have chosen provides for a natural interpretation that is easy to understand. The following example demonstrates this keyword syntax.

Example 10 Consider the *flight_network* graph view defined in Example 4. The following Resql query finds those destination cities that can be reached from London using any number of flights such that the only airlines used are British Airways or American Airlines, and the only planes used are Boeings or Concordes.

```
SELECT FINAL city
FROM PATHS IN flight_network
WHERE airline PATH IS ('BA' OR 'AA') REPEATED
AND plane PATH IS ('Boeing' OR 'Concorde') REPEATED
AND INITIAL city IS 'London';
```

The keywords PATHS IN signify that this is a query on a graph view rather than on conventional relations or views. Recall that in the *flight_network* view nodes are labelled with *city* values, while edges are labelled with *airline* and *plane* values. The keywords INITIAL and FINAL are used to denote the starting and ending nodes, respectively, of paths in the graph. Conditions are placed on the edge attribute values of paths by means of regular expressions in the WHERE clause. For those users who find the above syntax too verbose, the usual regular expression operators can substituted for the keywords OR and REPEATED. □

It is instructive to see how the above query could be formulated in the similar languages of [11, 15], as well as in Datalog [16], one of the most extensively researched recursive query languages.

Example 11 The previous query is expressed as follows in QUEL* [11].

```
RANGE OF f IS flights
RETRIEVE INTO tclose (f.dest)
WHERE (f.source = 'London'
AND (f.airline = 'BA' OR f.airline = 'AA')
AND (f.plane = 'Boeing' OR f.plane = 'Concorde'))
APPEND* TO tclose (f.dest)
WHERE (tclose.dest = f.source
AND (f.airline = 'BA' OR f.airline = 'AA')
AND (f.plane = 'Boeing' OR f.plane = 'Concorde'))
```

Here, the RETRIEVE operation returns an initial set of destinations, while the APPEND* operation repeats until no new tuples are added to *tclose*. The same query could be expressed as follows in the language of [15].

```
RANGE OF f IS flights
RETRIEVE (f.dest BY TCLOSE(f.source, f.dest))
WHERE (f.source = 'London'
AND (f.airline = 'BA' OR f.airline = 'AA')
AND (f.plane = 'Boeing' OR f.plane = 'Concorde'))
```

Note that here TCLOSE is part of the language. It is not clear from [15] whether the conditions in the WHERE clause are applied at each stage of the transitive closure (presumably they would not be for *f.source*), or only initially. If the latter is the case, then extra conditions would have to be added to the above query. In Datalog, this query could be expressed by the following program.

```
airline_ok(X,Y) :- flight(X,Y,'BA',_).
airline_ok(X,Y) :- flight(X,Y,'AA',_).
plane_ok(X,Y) :- flight(X,Y,_,'Boeing').
plane_ok(X,Y) :- flight(X,Y,_,'Concorde').
flight_ok(X,Y) :- airline_ok(X,Y) & plane_ok(X,Y).
tclose(X,Y) :- flight_ok(X,Y).
tclose(X,Y) :- flight_ok(X,Z) & tclose(Z,Y).
answer(Y) :- tclose('London',Y).
```

□

Example 12 The following query asks for all cities reachable from London such that at least one flight is with British Airways.

```
SELECT FINAL city
FROM PATHS IN flight_network
WHERE airline PATH IS ? REPEATED FOLLOWED BY 'BA'
FOLLOWED BY ? REPEATED AND initial CITY = 'London';
```

Recall that the question mark is a wildcard that, in this query, matches any airline name. The keywords FOLLOWED BY correspond to the usual concatenation operator in regular expressions. □

In the next example, we introduce the Resql syntax for regular expressions containing variables. A variable is introduced in the WHERE clause by means of the keyword EXISTS, the intension being to maintain readability.

Example 13 The following query asks for those cities that are connected by sequences of flights with the same airline.

```
SELECT INITIAL city, FINAL city, company
FROM PATHS IN flight_network
WHERE EXISTS company (airline PATH IS company REPEATED);
```

□

The above query is not expressible in standard relational query languages augmented with only a transitive closure operator [17]. It can be expressed in QUEL* by adding another column to the transitive closure relation being computed and another condition to the join for the APPEND* operation, principles which can be applied when expressing the query in Datalog as well. This is essentially the method we use to evaluate the above query (see the next section), although of course the details are all decided automatically by the query processor rather than having to be specified by the user. It is not clear, however, whether the above query can be expressed in the language of [15].

Of course path conditions specified by means of regular expressions and path computations using operators (as in Example 2) can be combined, as demonstrated in the following example.

Example 14 Assuming the existence of an attribute *duration* in the view *flight_network*, the following query finds the sequence of flights of shortest duration between London and Hong Kong such that at most two different airline companies are used.

```
SELECT city PATH WITH MIN(total_time)
FROM PATHS IN flight_network WITH total_time = SUM(duration)
WHERE INITIAL city IS 'London' AND FINAL city IS 'Hong Kong'
AND EXISTS A1, A2 (airline PATH IS (A1 OR A2) REPEATED);
```

Since standard Datalog does not have operators such as MIN, let us simplify the above query for comparative purposes. Assume that we are interested in finding all cities reachable from London using at most two different airline companies. Once again this can be expressed in Datalog by adding components to the transitive closure relation being computed.

135

```
tc(X,Y,Z,W) :- flight(X,Y,Z) & flight(_,_,W).
tc(X,Y,Z,W) :- flight(X,Y,W) & flight(_,_,Z).
tc(X,Y,Z,W) :- flight(X,U,Z) & tc(U,Y,Z,W).
tc(X,Y,Z,W) :- flight(X,U,W) & tc(U,Y,Z,W).
answer(Y) :- tc('London',Y,Z,W).
```

As we describe in the following section, this is in essence the transformation our query processor performs automatically. □

4   Algorithms and Implementation

A prototype implementation of the precursor to Grasp has been developed at the University of Toronto [6]. This implementation is for a stand-alone graph-based language, with all processing being performed in main memory using Smalltalk on a Sun workstation. Our intension is to offer both Grasp and Resql as query interfaces to a conventional relational database system. To this end, we have developed a prototype implementation of Resql using embedded C on top of the Oracle database system [14]. We will restrict the discussion to this implementation since the basic evaluation algorithms for Resql and Grasp with respect to regular expressions are the same.

There are essentially two language features that need to be addressed in the Resql implementation, as reflected in the following two subsections. In the first, we cover the evaluation of queries comprising only regular expressions, while in Section 4.2 we discuss how queries using operators to compute functions such as shortest path are evaluated.

4.1   Basic evaluation algorithm

In this subsection, we are concerned only with Resql queries that contain regular expressions, possibly with initial and final conditions (that is, constants) for the endpoints of paths. To begin with, we will also assume that any query contains only a single regular expression.

The evaluation algorithm used by the query processor is effectively the semi-naive, bottom-up evaluation algorithm used to evaluate recursive Datalog programs [3, 16]. Although the processor does not actually construct a Datalog program equivalent to the given Resql query, the corresponding program does indicate how evaluation proceeds. For this reason, we will provide the programs in the following examples.

When constants are present in a query (either Resql or Datalog), it is crucial for performance that the program be optimized so that selections to appropriate attributes are performed as early as possible in the evaluation process. Another optimization in the presence of constants is the reduction in degree of recursive predicates through a process of *factoring*, thereby leading to more efficient evaluation [13].

Given a Resql query Q containing regular expression R, the query processor constructs a deterministic finite-state automaton M accepting $L(R)$ [10]. This automaton is used to control the evaluation of Q on a given graph view. In effect, the evaluation mimics the bottom-up evaluation of a Datalog program P generated from the regular grammar corresponding to M. The evaluation process is efficient since it has been shown recently that program P is always factorable in the presence of constants [18].

Example 15 Let us assume that we are required to evaluate the query of Example 1 expressed in Resql rather than Grasp. Recall that the regular expression in the query is $isa \cdot ako^* \cdot (can + has + is)$. The query processor's translation of a Resql query depends on whether the edge labels in the graph view correspond to relation names or attribute values in the underlying relational database. In this example, the edge labels in the semantic network correspond to relation names. The Datalog program P that reflects the evaluation process for this query is as follows.

```
t(Y) :- isa('Tweety',Y).
t(Y) :- t(X), ako(X,Y).
answer(Y) :- t(X), can(X,Y).
answer(Y) :- t(X), has(X,Y).
answer(Y) :- t(X), is(X,Y).
```

Bottom-up evaluation of P leads to the following sequence of SQL queries. Firstly, the set of classes of which 'Tweety' is an instance is selected from the *isa* relation. This tempory relation t is then joined repeatedly with *ako* until a fixed point is reached (using loop constructs in C). Finally, the resulting relation is joined with the union of *can*, *has* and *is* to obtain the answer. It should be noted that the selection (for 'Tweety') has been performed as early as possible, and that the recursive predicate t is unary rather than binary which should benefit evaluation efficiency. □

Example 16 Consider the query of Example 10 which asked for destinations reachable from London using airlines British Airways or American Airlines and flying on Boeings or Concordes. In this case, edges in the *flight_network* view are labelled with attribute values from the *flights* relation. Also, there are two regular expressions in the query, one relating to airlines and the other to planes. Our prototype processor evaluates such a query simply by evaluating each of the regular expressions independently and then taking the intersection of the corresponding answer relations. This time, however, selections for the appropriate airline or plane must be applied to the relation *flights* beforehand, since edge labels correspond to attribute values. □

We now turn our attention to Resql queries in which the regular expressions contain variables. To simplify the evaluation process, we disallow such queries on graph views in which edge labels are relation names rather than

137

attribute values. We already hinted in the previous section as to how queries with variables could be evaluated by adding attributes to the relations being computed. Rather than giving the general scheme here, we will discuss how the evaluation proceeds for a specific example.

Example 17 Consider again the restricted version of Example 14 in which we are interested in the pairs of cities reachable from London using at most two airlines. The corresponding regular expression might be $(z+w)^*$, where z and w are variables. In this case, we extend the transitive closure relation being computed, call it t, with the attributes Z and W. Once again, the evaluation scheme is essentially given by the semi-naive evaluation of the following Datalog program P.

```
t(Y,Z,W) :- flight('London',Y,Z) & flight(_,_,W).
t(Y,Z,W) :- flight('London',Y,W) & flight(_,_,Z).
t(Y,Z,W) :- t(X,Z,W) & flight(X,Y,Z).
t(Y,Z,W) :- t(X,Z,W) & flight(X,Y,W).
answer(Y) :- t(Y,Z,W).
```

It is instructive to compare P with the Datalog program presented in Example 14. Note how in P the selection for 'London' has been moved to the *flight* relation, and the degree of the recursive predicate t has been reduced from four to three. □

The above examples serve to demonstrate the basic principles for evaluating Resql queries containing only regular expressions. The details of how to derive the evaluation schemes as well as the proofs that the resulting Datalog programs are always factorable are given in [18].

4.2 Operators

Queries with operators are those such as in Examples 2 and 14 where one is computing either total numbers of components (using TIMES and SUM) or shortest paths (using SUM and MIN). (Other useful examples are given in [9].) The basic principle for evaluating such queries is similar to that for evaluating queries with variables in regular expressions, as described in the previous subsection.

Assume that the WITH clause in a Resql query is as follows.

```
WITH A1 = OP(A2)
```

Initially, the attribute *A1* is added to the answer relation to be computed. Then, at each iteration of the semi-naive evaluation, the operator OP is applied to *A1* and the attribute *A2* from the relation defining the graph view. If there is also an operator in the SELECT clause along with an appropriate GROUP BY clause, then this operator can be applied at each iteration to the relevant sets of tuples in the usual way using SQL.

Example 18 Consider the Resql query of Example 2 where the total number of each component required to assemble a bicycle is to be computed. The corresponding `WITH` clause is

```
WITH total = TIMES(quantity).
```

The relation *tc* used to produce the final answer has attributes *subPart* and *total*. At each iteration of the algorithm the first SQL statement applied is as follows.

```
SELECT component.subPart, tc.total * component.quantity
FROM tc, component
WHERE tc.subPart = component.superPart;
```

Since `SUM(total)` appears in the `SELECT` clause where these totals are to be grouped by `FINAL part`, the following SQL statement is also executed after the above statement at each iteration.

```
SELECT subPart, SUM(total)
FROM tc
GROUP BY subPart;
```

In this way, the final answer shown in Figure 4 is computed. □

In the above example, it is safe to apply the second SQL statement at each iteration since `SUM` distributes over `TIMES`. In general, this can be done if the semiring comprising the operators is absorptive or the graph view itself is absorptive [5]. Also, there are no problems with termination as the corresponding graph view is acyclic. More care has to be exercised with queries on views like that of Example 14 (the *flight_network*), which no doubt is cyclic.

The full treatment of query evaluation in the presence of operators, as well as evaluation of Grasp queries including crossed-out edges is deferred to subsequent papers.

5   Conclusions

We have argued in favour of the utility of graph views for relational databases by presenting a number of applications in which data seems to be represented most naturally in graph form. Not only is a graph view a more appropriate modelling tool in these cases, but we have also developed two powerful and concise query languages for extracting information from graph views.

The query language Grasp is itself graph-based and is suitable for implementation on bit-mapped displays. On the other hand, Resql is a more conventional keyword-based extension of the language SQL. A novel feature of Grasp and Resql is their use of regular expressions for formulating recursive queries. In particular, the availablility of variables in regular expressions leads to additional power and conciseness when compared to similar languages. To support this claim, we compared our languages to those of [11, 15, 16], mostly by means of example.

Prototype implementations of both Grasp and Resql have been undertaken. The intension is to provide support for both languages on top of a conventional relational database system. To this end, we have implemented a subset of Resql on top of Oracle. The fact that the queries in this subset correspond to factorable Datalog programs means that they can be evaluated efficiently using the semi-naive algorithm [16]. Efficient implementation of the full set of Resql queries as well as those Grasp queries involving negation is the next step.

References

1   A.V. Aho, Pattern Matching in Strings, in *Formal Language Theory: Perspectives and Open Problems*, R.V. Book (Ed.), Academic Press (1980).

2   A.V. Aho and J.D. Ullman, Universality of Data Retrieval Languages, in *Proc. 6th ACM Symp. on Principles of Programming Languages* (1979).

3   F. Bancilhon, Naive Evaluation of Recursively Defined Relations, in *On Knowledge Base Management Systems: Integrating Artificial Intelligence and Database Technologies*, M.L. Brodie and J. Mylopoulos (Eds.), Springer-Verlag (1986).

4   J. Biskup, U. Räsch and H. Stiefeling, An Extended Relational Query Language for Knowledgebase Support, Tech. Report 4/87, Hochschule Hildesheim (1987).

5   B. Carré, *Graphs and Networks*, Oxford University Press (1979).

6   M. Consens, Graphlog: "Real Life" Recursive Queries Using Graphs, M.Sc. Thesis, Dept. of Computer Science, Univ. of Toronto (1989).

7   I.F. Cruz, A.O. Mendelzon and P.T. Wood, A Graphical Query Language Supporting Recursion, in *Proc. ACM SIGMOD Conf. on Management of Data* (1987).

8   I.F. Cruz, A.O. Mendelzon and P.T. Wood, $\mathbf{G^+}$: Recursive Queries Without Recursion, in *Proc. 2nd Int. Conf. on Expert Database Systems* (1988).

9   U. Dayal and J.M. Smith, PROBE: A Knowledge-Oriented Database Management System, in *On Knowledge Base Management Systems: Integrating Artificial Intelligence and Database Technologies*, M.L. Brodie and J. Mylopoulos (Eds.), Springer-Verlag (1986).

10   J.E. Hopcroft and J.D. Ullman, *Introduction to Automata Theory, Languages, and Computation*, Addison-Wesley (1979).

11   R.-M. Kung, E. Hanson, Y. Ioannidis, T. Sellis, L. Shapiro, and M. Stonebraker, Heuristic Search in Data Base Systems, in *Proc. 1st Int. Workshop on Expert Database Systems* (1984).

12   A.O. Mendelzon and P.T. Wood, Finding Regular Simple Paths in Graph Databases, in *Proc. 15th Int. Conf. on Very Large Data Bases* (1989).

13   J.F. Naughton, R. Ramakrishnan, Y. Sagiv and J.D. Ullman, Argument Reduction by Factoring, in *Proc. 15th Int. Conf. on Very Large Data Bases* (1989).

14   Oracle Corporation, Oracle Relational Database Management System (1985).

15   J. Tillquist and F.-Y. Kuo, An Approach to the Recursive Retrieval Problem in the Relational Database, *Commun. ACM*, Vol. 32, No. 2 (Feb. 1989).

16   J.D. Ullman, *Principles of Database and Knowledge-Base Systems, Vol. I*, Computer Science Press (1988).

17   M.Y. Vardi, The Complexity of Relational Query Languages, in *Proc. 14th Ann. ACM Symp. on Theory of Computing* (1982).

18   P.T. Wood, Factoring Augmented Regular Chain Programs, Tech. Report CS-90-02-00, Univ. of Cape Town (Feb. 1990).

Implementing the emerging ISO Standard STEP into a relational database

Deborah Thomas

Informatics Department
SERC, Rutherford Appleton Laboratory

Abstract

STEP is the emerging International Standard for exchange of product model data. This standard will cover all areas of engineering data throughout the life-cycle of a product. The methodology being used in its creation is based on separating the logical view of the data from the physical exchange file. The logical data model which forms the basis of STEP can also be used to generate database schemas which could aid applications integration. This paper presents the work done at the Rutherford Appleton Laboratory in implementing STEP into a relational database.

1. Introduction

In database applications, engineering data has lagged behind areas such as finance and administration. Any implementations which have been done have been specific to a certain engineering application area. There are many engineering packages on the market some of which have their own database but more which use flat files in a native format to store data between runs. These work well when the package is used in isolation but more and more there is a need for these to communicate both between the same type of package.g.. CAD (Computer Aided Design) systems at a company and its subcontractor, and between different types of package e.g. CAD and CAM (Computer Aided Manufacture).

Data exchange standards which specify neutral files go some way to solving this problem but a better solution would be a neutral database. This could be accessed by all the different applications packages. If the database conformed to a neutral schema then each package would have just one interface to read from the database and one to write to it. It would be easier to archive data and to find what data is available. Each package could obtain just the information it needed from the database.

There is an emerging International Standard for exchange of engineering data known as STEP. This paper presents the work done at the Rutherford Appleton Laboratory to determine whether this standard can be used as a basis for a neutral database for integration of engineering applications.

2. The STEP Methodology

The STandard for Exchange of Product model data, known colloquially as STEP, is being developed by the ISO committee TC184/SC4/WG1. STEP was issued as an ISO Draft Proposal in December 1988 and a second issue is expected early in 1990. This standard is intended to cover exchange of all data which completely define an engineering product for all applications over its expected life cycle. STEP includes areas of general use, e.g. geometry, topology, presentation and features, and specific application areas, e.g. AEC (Architecture, Engineering and Construction), finite element analysis (FEA), electrical and drafting.

The development of this standard has used a methodology which includes the use of reference models, formal definition languages and a three layer architecture (application, logical and physical). Many application area models have been developed by specialised committees, using a variety of modelling languages. These collectively form the applications layer. Once a data model is believed, by the relevant committee, to be complete and correct, it is integrated into the single Integrated Product Information Model (IPIM). In the process of integration, entities which represent the same idea in different application areas are removed from any single area, placed in a part called resources and made available to all areas. This IPIM forms the logical layer and is the core of the standard.

At present, the neutral file for data exchange is the only physical implementation layer in STEP. This neutral file is not defined as an absolute thing but is defined by a mapping from the IPIM. This methodology of separating the logical data model from the physical implementation means that other physical implementations may be created simply by defining a new mapping from the logical layer.

3. Applications Integration

Applications integration requires the ability for different engineering packages, e.g. CAD, FEA, CAM, to communicate. At the user level this involves design environments and UIMS (User Interface Management Systems). However, these are not sufficient; they present a common interface to the user but the packages may still not be able to share data. At present STEP can achieve a limited degree of application integration through the use of neutral files.

The software to interface between the application packages and the neutral file can be split into two parts. First there is general software for reading and writing the neutral file; this takes care of such things as checking that the neutral file conforms to the syntax, that each entity exists in the data model and has the correct number and type of attributes. Also required is software specific to an application. This will take care of transforming entities and attributes from the form required by the neutral file to that specified by the application and vice versa. For example, converting the specification of a circle from three points on the circumference to a centre point and a radius. Figure 1 illustrates this exchange of data.

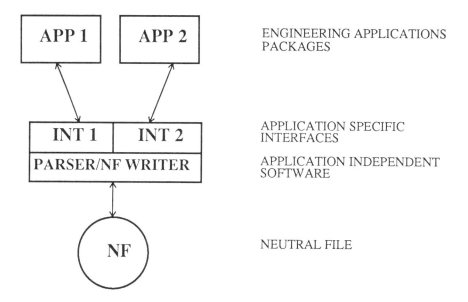

Figure 1. Exchange of data between applications and neutral file

A better method of integration would be to enable data sharing by using a common database. However, having one database which several applications use for their data storage does not help applications integration if each package uses the database in its own way. It is necessary to impose a standard database schema so that each package knows in exactly what form it has to store its data and in what form it may find the data it requires. Of course, each enterprise could write their own data model for their business and achieve integration within the enterprise. However, more interfaces are then needed to deal with exchange formats when it comes to exchanging data with contractors and customers.

STEP is on the way to becoming an International Standard and is being encouraged by the US DoD, so if the STEP data model is used for both applications integration and data exchange then software requirements become much simpler. Figure 2 shows how a database based on a standard schema could work.

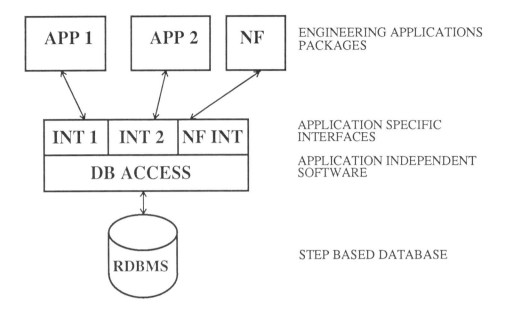

Figure 2. Exchange of data between applications and neutral database

In this method the Neutral File can be just like another application. When a neutral file is received it may be read directly into the database and any of the applications may then access the data as normal. It can be seen that this is very similar to figure 1, with specific interfaces for each application and general software for accessing the database.

4. EXPRESS

EXPRESS [2] is an information modelling language which is being used to describe the logical content of STEP. It is a formal language which describes entities, attributes, relationships and constraints.

Each entity is described in turn together with its set of attributes and their types. The STEP information model is written in EXPRESS and the current physical layer describes a mapping from EXPRESS to a neutral file syntax. Although the work described here is directed at STEP it would apply to any data model written in EXPRESS. Example 1 shows a small part of an EXPRESS schema.

```
ENTITY point;
        x : REAL;
        y : REAL;
        z : OPTIONAL REAL;
END_ENTITY;

ENTITY line;
        p0 : point;
        p1 : point;
END_ENTITY;

ENTITY curve;
        points : LIST [ 1:# ] OF point;
END_ENTITY
```

Example 1. Part of an EXPRESS Schema

It can be seen in the example that an entity is represented by a name, e.g. *point*, and a set of attributes. The attributes are denoted by names, e.g. *x*, *y* and *z*, and are given a type. This can be a base type, such as REAL, INTEGER or STRING, or could be a reference to another entity such as *p0* which refers to a *point* entity. An attribute can also be multi-valued, as can be seen by the *points* attribute in the *curve* entity which consists of a list of '1 to many' references to *point*. There are four types of aggregate available: array, set, list and bag.

This simple example does not show any of the more powerful facilities which are available. EXPRESS has constructs for categorisation (ie. sub- and supertypes). It also includes powerful rules which may be applied to attributes, entities and relationships.

5. Applications Programming Interface

A significant proportion of the work in interface writing consists of transforming entities from the internally used form to the standard form and vice versa. Once code has been written to perform these transformations for a particular application's reading and writing of a neutral file, it should not be necessary to rewrite the code to read and write from a database. The code for this work should be kept separate from the code to access the neutral data.

One way of doing this is to define a standard applications programming interface. This would consist of a set of subroutine definitions covering the tasks of obtaining

146

a piece of data and writing a piece of data. These should be completely independent of the storage mechanism and to ensure this they should be based on the EXPRESS model. For example, a subroutine to obtain a piece of data could require three parameters: the EXPRESS entity name, the attribute name and the identifier of the particular entity required. The subroutine should return the value or values found. Different sets of subroutines could be provided to access the data from whatever storage mechanism is being used. The program using these subroutines need have no knowledge of how the data is stored. When object oriented databases become more readily available then only these subroutines need to be rewritten to allow all existing interfaces to use the new databases. This is illustrated in figure 3.

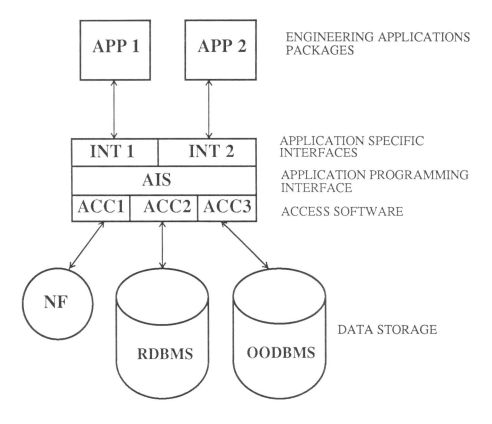

Figure 3. Independence of interface software from data storage means

The only information that is fed to the subroutines is based on the data model, therefore for this to work it is necessary for the mapping from the data model to the physical storage mechanism to be well defined. A proposed mapping to an implementation in a relational database is defined in section 6.

The STEP physical file committee is just beginning to consider the definition of a standard interface [1] and this will eventually become part of the standard. Some of the functions which the interface is expected to provide are:

- query capabilities
- insert capabilities
- modify capabilities
- delete capabilities
- navigation through entity instances
- schema information
- error handling
- open and close data management services

6. EXPRESS to SQL Mapping

The ISO STEP physical file committee is starting work on other implementations which will eventually form part of the standard. One such is an implementation into a relational database. This work will be based on the ISO standard relational database query language, SQL [3]. Some initial work was done by Joe Eggers [4] on a mapping from EXPRESS to SQL. This was taken and expanded by RAL into a fully implementable mapping [5].

The mapping generates SQL commands to create a relational database schema automatically from an EXPRESS data model. The mapping is intended to be implemented into an EXPRESS compiler and used to automatically generate an empty database. It is not intended that there should be any human intervention.

This mapping is based on the first ISO standard of SQL. It does not take into account any variations in actual vendor SQL products. In practice, different vendors do not conform completely to the standard and slight modifications will need to be incorporated for specific packages. The mapping also does not take into account the efficiency of the resulting database structure; when experience has been gained using this mapping then ways to improve access speed will be considered.

It is believed that many of the problems encountered in the mapping are resolved by SQL Addendum 1 and by the proposed SQL2. However, as these are not yet widely available in commercial products they have not been considered for this initial work. Further versions will need to take these into account.

EXPRESS describes objects of interest (entities) in terms of a set of associated attributes, where each attribute has a data type. The RDBMS stores information as relations, or simply tables. Each entity definition in the EXPRESS corresponds to one or more tables in the RDBMS, each attribute usually corresponds to a column

148

in the entity relation, and an instance of that entity corresponds to a tuple in the relation. The tables will be generated using the SQL command *CREATE TABLE*.

Example 2 shows the SQL commands which would be created from the EXPRESS given in example 1 using the mapping. This example will be used to illustrate the mapping which is described in more detail in the following paragraphs. Appendix 1 shows the database tables created from example 2 together with some sample data.

```
CREATE TABLE POINT
( POINT_ID          SMALLINT    NOT NULL    UNIQUE,
  X                 REAL        NOT NULL,
  Y                 REAL        NOT NULL )

CREATE TABLE POINT_Z
( POINT_ID          SMALLINT    NOT NULL    UNIQUE,
  Z                 REAL        NOT NULL )

CREATE TABLE LINE
( LINE_ID           SMALLINT    NOT NULL    UNIQUE,
  P0                SMALLINT    NOT NULL,
  P1                SMALLINT    NOT NULL )

CREATE TABLE  CURVE
( CURVE_ID          SMALLINT    NOT NULL    UNIQUE )

CREATE TABLE CURVE_POINTS_LI1
( CURVE_ID          SMALLINT    NOT NULL    UNIQUE,
  LIST_INDEX        INTEGER     NOT NULL,
  POINTS            SMALLINT    NOT NULL )
```

Example 2. Automatically Generated SQL Commands

6.1 Table and Column Names

Each EXPRESS entity will generate one main table and, for the purposes of this document, this table will take the name of the entity. Likewise attribute names usually map directly onto the respective column names. There are many instances where additional tables are generated, for example, to support list and array constructs; in these cases table names are generated which are formed from a combination of owning entity and attribute names plus, in some cases, a suffix. In fact, the convention used in this document does not guarantee uniqueness of table names (a combination of entity name plus suffix could match another entity name). It is recognised that, in practice, some transformation will be necessary between the names used in EXPRESS, which are long and purposely descriptive, and the names

149

required by SQL, which are limited to 18 characters. The exact form of this transformation is open to discussion, the two main contenders being:

- Names are generated automatically by the SQL writing code according to an appropriate algorithm. Generated names will not bear any resemblance to the originals. A proposal for this is detailed in a RAL internal report [6].
- Names suitable for the RDBMS are decided by human intervention. ('Aliased' from the EXPRESS). There is currently no facility in EXPRESS for this. An EXPRESS compiler could perhaps read a file containing a list of aliases before generating any SQL statements.

Both of these options could ensure uniqueness of table names. In either case, a table should be created in the RDBMS to describe this transformation. This table should be populated by the EXPRESS compiler as and when a new name is generated. Thus application codes using the data in the database will have access to the original names as decided by the EXPRESS schema writer. See section 7 for more detail.

6.2 Entity Identifiers, Keys

Although there is a *UNIQUE* construct in EXPRESS, entities may have any combination of attributes defined as *UNIQUE* or none at all. In a RDBMS, each tuple in a table must be unique from every other tuple in that table. However, because EXPRESS does not force each entity to have at least one *UNIQUE* attribute, a unique identifier must be added to each entity instance to ensure uniqueness. The creation of the tables includes an extra column for this identifier, and a program loading information into the database must invent an identifier for each entity instance that is unique over that table. For convenience, we will use a short integer. The column will be given the name of the table plus the suffix '_ID'. For example, a column *LINE_ID* is created for the entity *line* as shown in example 2.

6.3 Attributes with Base Types

There is a good, although not exact, correspondence between base types allowed in EXPRESS and SQL. Their mapping is shown in table 1.

Note that SQL has no logical type so the values TRUE, FALSE, UNKNOWN are mapped as enumerations of these strings. The one problem area is with strings. In ISO standard SQL it is possible to omit the length parameter from the character type but it then takes a default value of 1. There is not a type to deal with variable length strings and hence nothing on which to map the EXPRESS base type

STRING. In practice, most commercial systems have some sort of variable length string which may be used.

EXPRESS	SQL
Integer	INTEGER
Integer(n)	NUMERIC(N)
Real	REAL
Real(n)	REAL
Logical	FLOAT(N
Number	ENUMERATION
String	REAL
String(n)	CHARACTER(N)

Table 1. Mapping of base types

An attribute of base type appears directly in the entity relation. See the attribute *X* in the *POINT* table in example 2 which has a base type of *REAL*.

6.4 Attributes with Entity Types

When an entity references another entity, the owning entity has a column to hold the identifier of the entity referred to. For example, the column *P0* in the *LINE* table in example 2 which contains a key to an entry in the *POINT* table. Unfortunately referential integrity is not yet supported in SQL, so it is not possible to enforce that the identifier actually exists in the referenced table.

The column is given the name of the owning attribute, not the name of the entity referred to. This is to allow the same entity to be referenced more than once in different roles within an entity. To record the fact that *P0* is in fact a key to the *POINT* table a 'system' table is used (see section 7). This enables an application to find the correct table more easily.

6.5 Attributes with Aggregate Types

SQL does not have any base types to deal with aggregates, indeed every column in a table must be single valued. However, it is possible to implement aggregate types by creating extra tables.

Attributes with Array Types

The array is an indexed aggregation of data objects having the same data type. An array declaration in EXPRESS specifies a lower and upper index. The lower index must evaluate to an integer, while the upper index may take an undefined value greater than the lower index.

The array attribute itself does not appear in the owning table but instead, for each array declared in the EXPRESS schema, a table is created in the database for each dimension. The table names are generated by a combination of entity name, attribute name and a suffix denoting the level in the array. This algorithm is known to application programs so that values in the array can be searched for.

For a single dimension array, the extra generated table contains three columns. The first column contains the key of the owning table and the second contains the index of the array. The last column contains the actual item contained in the array and is given the name of the original attribute. This item could be a base type value or could be an integer reference to an instance of another entity. A tuple will exist in this table for each index in the array. If the array is of *OPTIONAL* items, for example, ARRAY [1:10] OF OPTIONAL REAL, then a tuple will only exist if the value is present.

The value in the index column must lie between the bounds declared for the array but this cannot be enforced by SQL. However, the array bounds could be stored in the generated 'system' table described in section 7 and this would allow an application program to easily check the values.

Attributes with List Types

Lists can be treated very much as arrays. The important difference is that lists do not have a fixed number of members, but this constraint (on arrays) cannot be supported by a RDBMS anyway. Neither can the required length of a list be supported. Lists should be treated as arrays, except that the lower bound is always 0 and the increment is always 1 (no gaps may appear as a result of deletions). The second column in the generated table will be named *LIST_INDEX*.

Example 2 shows the table *CURVE_POINTS_LI1* which is created to hold the list of references to the points which make up the curve.

Attributes with Set Types

The set is the simplest aggregate type to support in a relational database. A set is unordered, as are the tuples in a relation, and the entries are unique within the set - this is guaranteed by a relational implementation. The mapping is similar to that for arrays and lists but there is no need for an index so this is omitted. As with arrays and lists, the limits of a set are only retained in the system table.

6.6 OPTIONAL Attributes

All non-optional attributes should be declared as *NOT NULL* columns in the generated SQL.

Optional attributes may be dealt with by simply omitting this *NOT NULL* qualifier. However, there are some problems with the implementations of *NULLS* [7] and also with space considerations for entities with sparsely populated optional attributes. Therefore, an extra table is generated to hold the optional attribute. The table is given the name of the owning entity plus the attribute name.

This table contains the key of the owning entity and the value of the attribute. The column holding the key is again declared as *UNIQUE* which ensures that, at most, there can only be one tuple in the optional attribute table for each tuple in the owning table. Using this mapping, the optional attribute does not appear in the owning table, therefore the fact that it is an attribute of that table is stored in a 'system' table.

Example 2 shows the table *POINT_Z* which is created to hold the optional attribute Z from the *point* entity.

6.7 UNIQUE Attributes

Attributes mentioned in a *UNIQUE* clause should be specified as such in the corresponding *CREATE TABLE* operation. SQL requires that they also be declared *NOT NULL*. Joint uniqueness is applied to multiple columns by using the SQL *UNIQUE* construct at the end of the *CREATE TABLE* definition. Uniqueness on a single attribute may be done in the same way as joint uniqueness or may be included in the column definition. Uniqueness may be applied to an optional attribute by designating the actual value column as *UNIQUE* in the extra table created to hold that attribute. If one or more of the columns in an EXPRESS *UNIQUE* declaration is also optional then joint uniqueness may not be applied using this mapping.

6.8 Local Rules

SQL has no way of enforcing (or even 'understanding') local rules (EXPRESS *WHERE* clauses). It would be the task of an application program acting on the database to apply local (and global) rules. This problem is not considered further here.

7. System Tables

In most cases, the mapping from EXPRESS *ENTITIES* to SQL *CREATE TABLE* commands is quite straightforward but in some situations more information is required to enable subroutines to automatically access the database. One way of doing this is to provide one or more 'system' tables which contain information about the original EXPRESS model. These system tables will be created and filled by the compiler.

It is proposed to create two such system tables. The first will contain the mapping between the EXPRESS entity names and the compiler generated short table names (as mentioned in section 6.1). All the table names will be contained in this table, including extra tables which are created to support arrays, optionals etc. The short table names used in Example 3 are based on the name generation algorithm proposed by K Duffey [6]. There are two additional columns in this table which contain the attribute name, when an extra table has to be created, and a tag to denote the type of extra table. For example, for a three dimensional array there will be three tuples each with the same entity and attribute names but with different tags, to denote the levels of the array, and different generated table names.

The second table will contain one tuple for each column in the generated tables. In the case of aggregate attributes, a row is included for each of the columns generated to support the aggregate. The information included is as follows:
- table name - short name generated by compiler.
- attribute name - full EXPRESS attribute name.
- data type - type of attribute.
- sequence number - position of attribute within entity in EXPRESS schema, this is used by the name generation algorithm to generate the short column names. If a different system is used then this sequence number may be omitted but the mapped short column name must be given instead.
- reference - if attribute is of entity type then this column indicates the entity to which it is a reference. See section 6.4. Note that the primary component of the short table name is given here, not the full EXPRESS name.
- optional - switch to designate whether or not the attribute is optional, 1 for optional and 0 for not. See section 6.6.

Example 3 shows the SQL statements to create the two empty system tables. Appendix 2 shows the tables created by the SQL in example 3 together with some sample data corresponding to example 2.

```
CREATE TABLE SY_NAMES
(TABLE_NAME          CHAR(8)        NOT NULL    UNIQUE,
ENTITY_NAME          CHARACTER      NOT NULL,
ATT_NAME             CHARACTER,
TAG_FIELD            CHARACTER(4) )

CREATE TABLE SY_ATTRIB
(TABLE_NAME          CHAR(8)        NOT NULL    UNIQUE,
ATT_NAME             CHARACTER,
DATA_TYPE            STRING(8),
SEQ_NO               SMALLINT,
REFERENCE            STRING,
OPTIONAL             SMALLINT)
```

Example 3. System Tables

154

8. Current Status and Future Work

The project at RAL is still in its initial stages. It will be using an existing semi-conductor device modelling package to test out the feasibility of the ideas presented. This package at present uses the RALBIC neutral file [8] to transfer data to and from other packages. The STEP data model for finite element data is not yet in a stable enough form for implementation, so an EXPRESS model has been generated from the RALBIC neutral file [9]. As stated earlier, the methods described here will work for any EXPRESS data model.

The mapping from EXPRESS to SQL is now in a suitable form for initial implementations, and is being coded into the EXPRESS compiler written at RAL. A database schema has been generated from the RALBIC based EXPRESS data model using the mapping.

The initial coding of the subroutine interface is complete but not fully tested. This has been kept simple at first to prove the concepts. The first aim is to extract a piece of data from the database. The subroutines that have been written receive information based on the EXPRESS model only, ie. entity name, attribute name and identifier. They then use the EXPRESS to SQL mapping to determine in which table and column the information is stored. As it has been found impossible to write a general subroutine for this purpose using embedded SQL, because variables are not allowed for table and column names, dynamic SQL has been used within C. It was during this work that the necessity of the 'system' tables was realised.

The next stage of the work is to adapt the semi-conductor device modelling package to use the subroutine interface to obtain its data from the neutral database instead of the RALBIC neutral file. The results from this work will feed back to the development of the Application Programming Interface and to the refinement of the mapping from EXPRESS to SQL. At a later stage of the work the efficiency of the interface will be considered.

Close contact is being kept with the ISO STEP implementation committee and the results of the work are expected to influence the STEP database implementation amd application programming interface.

9. References

1. ISO TC184/SC4/WG1 N448, 'Functional Requirements for an Application Software Interface to STEP Data', R Cheever and L Slovensky, December 1989

2. ISO TC184/SC4/WG1 N442, 'Information Modelling Language EXPRESS', D Schenck, December 21 1989.

3. ISO 9075:1987, Database Language SQL

4. Joe Eggers, 'Implementing EXPRESS in SQL', McDonnell Douglas internal report, October 1988.

5. D Thomas and M Mead, 'Mapping from EXPRESS to SQL', RAL internal report, January 1990.

6. K P Duffey, 'Proposed Name Generation Algorithm, suitable for implementation in an EXPRESS-SQL compiler', RAL internal report, October 12, 1989.

7. C J Date, 'Relational Database - Selected Writings', Addison-Wesley, 1986

8. RALBIC - A Simple Neutral File for Finite Element Data, Emson, Greenough, Diserens & Duffey, RAL-87-102.

9. 'A Mapping from RALBIC to CAD*I Data Formats', K P Duffey, RAL-88-107.

Appendix 1.

This appendix shows the database tables created by the example in the main text together with some sample data.

POINT		
POINT_ID	X	Y
1	12.5	14.7
2	23.1	84.3
3	24.76	22.1
4	13.2	4.3

POINT_Z	
POINT_ID	Z
1	15.1
2	22.4
4	24.76

CURVE
CURVE_ID
1
2
3

CURVE_POINTS_LI1		
CURVE_ID	LIST_INDEX	POINTS
1	1	1
1	2	4
2	1	3
2	2	4

Appendix 2.

This appendix shows the system tables created by the example in the main text together with some sample data.

SY_NAMES			
TABLE_NAME	ENTITY_NAME	ATTRIB_NAME	TAG_FIELD
AAAA0_000	POINT		
AAAA0_003	POINT	Z	
AAAB0_000	CURVE		
AAAB1_001	CURVE	POINTS	LI1

SY_ATTRIB					
TABLE_NAME	ATTRIB_NAME	DATA_TYPE	SEQ_NO	REF	OPTL
AAAA0_000	X	REAL	1		0
AAAA0_000	Y	REAL	2		0
AAAA0_003	Z	REAL	3		1
AAAB1_001	POINTS	REFERENCE	1	AAAA	0
AAAB1_001	LIST_INDEX	SMALLINT	1		

Object-Oriented Database Design for the Ozone Software Development Environment

Greg Nichols and Steven A. Demurjian

Dept. of Computer Science and Engineering
Box U155, 260 Glenbrook Road
University of Connecticut
Storrs, Connecticut, 06269-3155 USA

Abstract

There are a number of significant issues that arise when the fields of software-development environments (SDEs) with database support and the object-oriented paradigm are combined, such as: support for a myriad of data types (i.e., source code, control-flow diagrams, parse trees, symbol tables, designs, specifications, etc.), the availability of a clear, concise public interface for tool designers and builders via data encapsulation and information hiding, and the ability to support extensibility by modifying both the public interface (i.e., data and methods available to users) and the private implementation of the environment data. These issues are currently under investigation as part of the design and prototyping of Ozone, an SDE for C programs with object-oriented database support. Ozone is being developed to support tools for project editing, text editing, compilation, and program questioning for querying the program information that is stored within the environment. This paper presents a significant portion of an object-oriented database design for the environment data required by Ozone for supporting its tools. Along with the explanation of the object-oriented design, the extent to which Ozone supports extensibility, tool integration, software-methodology and programming-language independence, and tool development, are also addressed.

1. Introduction

In recent years, the investigation of software-development environments (SDEs) with integrated database support has drawn the attention of researchers. Garden [19] which presents conceptual program design and development, Arcadia [24] which investigates a joint effort for environment integration and process programming support, Workshop [4] which examines environments from a knowledge-representation perspective, and Graspin [27] for syntax-directed support of software

159

development, are all examples of such SDEs. The incorporation of database system support within SDEs, specifically, Arcadia, Workshop, and Graspin, has also been proposed. In an alternative approach, the work on the Cactis object-oriented database system [12] proposes the development of database applications for supporting the software-development process. Regardless of the approach, the integration of a database system provides a variety of new features that enhance the software-development process, including transaction support for multiple concurrent users, integrity for data consistency, security to control data access, recovery in the event of system failure, and of course, querying to access the stored data of the SDE [3].

In step with this increased attention in SDEs with database support has been a resurgence of interest in the object-oriented paradigm. Historically, the object-oriented paradigm gained popularity with the development and introduction of Smalltalk [10]. More recently, object-oriented programming languages such as C++ [23] have come into wide usage. In the database domain, hybrid object-oriented database systems have also been proposed and developed. Gemstone [15], an extension of Smalltalk, is an integrated programming language/database system with typical database features such as data persistence, transaction processing, recovery, etc., and supports the Opal object-oriented model for developing applications. The ORION system, developed at MCC [13]and Cactis [12], both provide support for the object-oriented paradigm. Finally, ODE, under development at AT & T [1], attempts to extend current object-oriented programming language concepts (i.e., C++) with database primitives to support persistence, versioning, and set creation and access.

In attempting to develop integrated SDEs with database support, a number of issues are critical. From a database perspective, there must be support for the myriad of data types (i.e., source code, control-flow and data-flow diagrams, parse trees, symbol tables, designs, specifications, etc.) that are required [3]. Consequently, traditional database solutions (i.e., relational, hierarchical, and network) do not appear to have the modeling power that is required to represent these complex types. So, the object-oriented paradigm becomes a logical choice for supporting these diverse data needs. From a tool-integration perspective, the data encapsulation and information hiding that is available in the object-oriented paradigm provides a clean public interface for tool designers and builders. Finally, from the perspective of the environment, the object-oriented paradigm offers the ability to both extend the public interface (i.e., data and methods available to users) and to modify the private implementation to support dynamic environment extensions (i.e., adding new tools, new programming languages, etc.).

The issues outlined above are currently under investigation as part of the design and prototyping of Ozone [16], an SDE for C program development integrated with an object-oriented database system. Ozone is being developed to support a number of tools including a project editor for managing software projects, a text editor, a C compiler, and a program questioning tool that allows Ozone users to query the program information (i.e., source, parse tree, symbol table, etc.) that is stored within the environment. This paper presents a significant portion of the Ozone design, specifically, an object-oriented database design for the environment data required by

Ozone for supporting its tools.

In the process of presenting the database design, a number of goals that can be utilized to evaluate the design become evident. These goals may be posed as questions:

1. Can the object-oriented paradigm be successfully utilized to model SDE data?

2. Can the tradeoff between the integration of the environment and system extensibility be reconciled using the object-oriented paradigm?

3. Can extensibility be supported by the addition of types and methods to the existing environment?

4. Can a single set of operations be defined that are then combined and composed into a more powerful set of operations for supporting tool access to environment data?

5. Do the operations on the data and the ability to compose operations tend to reduce the complexity and redundancy of tool code?

6. Can a clear, conceptual model of the environment data be presented for tool designers and builders to use when interacting with the SDE?

7. Are programming-language and software-methodology independence attained using the object-oriented paradigm, at least for imperative programming languages?

This paper addresses these goals in the context of the object-oriented database design for the environment data of Ozone. The remainder of this paper is organized as follows. Section 2 presents an overview of the Ozone SDE by detailing its architectural structure and outlining its capabilities. Section 3 of this paper examines the object-oriented database design of the environment data and includes both descriptions of data structures and operations. In Section 4, examples of how the operations or methods can be utilized to support program questioning via operation composition are discussed. Finally, Section 5 concludes this paper and discusses both related issues in Ozone and other work currently underway.

2. The Ozone Software Development Environment

Ozone is a SDE consisting of three major parts, as shown in Figure 1: the collection of tools that operate within the environment, the Ozone Server that coordinates tool communication, and the object-oriented database system used to manage the environment data. The tools use a library of environment types as the means of access to the environment data.

The Ozone Server coordinates communication between the tools and the underlying storage system. The collection of object types used by Ozone to represent SDE data is the *environment schema*. The Server manages the collection of objects conforming to this environment schema. The Server also provides a central location for the implementation details that are specific to the storage system, translating between the environment schema and the model of the underlying database management system.

161

This minimizes the changes necessary to accommodate different storage subsystems. The Server also provides functionality that may not be offered by the storage system, e.g., the check-in/check-out of objects. The use of a Server eliminates the restriction of the storage subsystem's data language in defining the types of the environment, allowing programming language flexibility in defining the object types of the environment. The Server also provides a central user interface of the environment, for the user invocation of the tools.

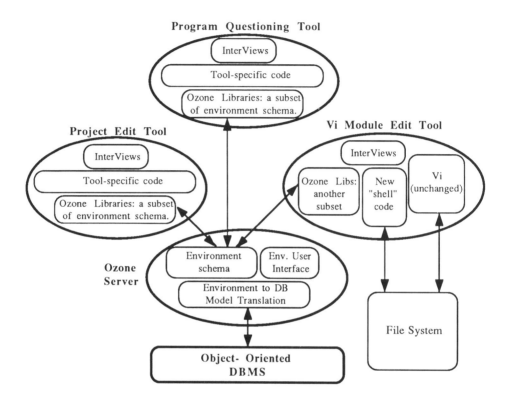

Fig 1. The Ozone System Architecture

Ozone is being prototyped on Sun workstations under the UNIX operating system. Ozone has been designed and is being implemented using the object-oriented paradigm and the C++ programming language. C programs that are developed using Ozone are represented conceptually as "modules" that are collected together to form "systems" and "projects". Ozone is an integrated environment in that it provides uniform methods of tool invocation and data access. The tools appear as windows in a multi-window environment; Ozone uses X windows through the C++ InterViews library. In addition, basic commands enable the user invoke the tools of the environment. Commands to import and export source files to and from the operating system are also included.

Four tools are included in the Ozone prototype: a Project editor, a new Program-

162

Questioning tool, an existing UNIX text editor, and a C compiler. These tools are being written in C++, and utilize a library of Ozone types (i.e., a subset of the environment schema) to interact with the environment. Server/Environment communication is hidden within the the library types, freeing the tool designer/writer from these details. The library types are used to present an SDE-specific interface to the tool writer.

The Project Editor allows software projects to be composed from programs made up of component collections of systems of modules. This tool allows the elements of these collections to be viewed, added or removed. In addition to tool-specific code, the Project Editor uses the InterViews library for its user interface and utilizes types and operations of the Ozone libraries for access to environment data.

The Program-Questioning (PQ) tool allows the user to ask general questions about the programs stored in Ozone [8]. For example, the user might want to know what procedure a certain variable is defined in, or what functions call a certain function. The PQ tool requires the associative access methods of the underlying database system in order to answer questions efficiently. This tool is a new tool being written for the environment. It relies on the operations defined on the environment types for much of its functionality. The tool itself presents an interface to the user and translates the user's questions into the appropriate database and type operations needed to answer the questions. The user interface of the tool is organized using menus. Each menu choice will facilitate a category of the questions. When a certain menu choice is made, additional information is requested to make the question specific. Answers to the questions are textual or pictorial, as appropriate. The composition of this tool is similar to the Project Editor.

To provide editing of the source code, the vi editor is being integrated into Ozone. This tool is made up of the unchanged vi editor, the new "shell" code written for the tool, types and operations included from the Ozone library, and a display for the tool using the InterViews library. vi can be invoked from within Ozone to edit the textual representation of the source code within Ozone. When Ozone receives a command to invoke vi on a module, an actual operating system file is created containing the text of the module to be edited. Ozone then starts vi to edit the operating system file. Upon termination of the editor, Ozone translates the operating system file into the objects used by Ozone to represent program information.

An existing C compiler is being integrated into Ozone for the compilation of C programs. The C compiler is invoked from within Ozone on a software project. When the compiler is run, Ozone creates operating system files containing the source or object versions of the program objects as dictated by the file dependencies of the project. The C compiler of the underlying operating system is then invoked. After the compiler runs, new object versions of the files are written back into Ozone.

To facilitate the storage of the abstract types necessary to support the software-development process, an object-oriented database system or an object manager will be utilized. Ozone uses the C++ programming language for modeling SDE data, since there is increasing evidence that a database system capable of directly supporting the storage of C++ classes will be available soon. Servio–Logic has recently announced a C++ interface for its Gemstone DBMS, and the University of Connecticut is slated to

163

be a beta test site. Other developments focus on systems that extend C++ to include persistent objects, such as ODE [1] and the Ontos persistent C++ system [17]. The ability of these alternatives to support SDEs, in general, and Ozone, in particular, is currently being evaluated.

In a SDE where collections of tools use data stored as objects in a central DBMS, there are two options for the execution of operations on the types (i.e., object methods). Either the object is checked-out to the tool and the method is run by the tool, or the method is run by the DBMS on the object within the database. Object check-out has the advantages of better system performance and simpler tool to server communications, while executing the methods in the DBMS would provide finer concurrency and more efficient data access. Ozone incorporates both techniques, with most of the data manipulation operations performed by the tools on checked-out objects, and most of the data location and access methods performed by the database system. Tools manipulate checked-out objects using object methods defined by the libraries. The library methods also make server calls, causing operations on types within the server. Associative access of object collections, analogous to database queries, can be handled effectively in this manner.

3. Object-Oriented Database Design for Environment Data

Ozone utilizes the object-oriented paradigm for the design of the object types representing the environment data and its behavior. The definition of each type includes both data and operations to achieve data encapsulation and information hiding. The set of types defined to represent the data of the environment collectively form the *environment schema*. The structure of the environment schema is the configuration of the network of objects that are instances of the types. The implementation details of the objects are hidden from the users of the objects.

As outlined in the introduction, Ozone's environment schema has several design goals. The operations of the environment schema form the tool interface. This interface must be uniform and concise; all of the operations of the interface must reflect a clear conceptual model of the data within the environment. The environment schema must also be defined to allow the sharing of environment data, promoting concurrency while preserving the integrity of the data. In addition, the environment schema must provide powerful operations on the environment data in order to meet Ozone's goals of extensibility and integration.

Language independence is one of the most important design goals. The environment schema design should not be restricted to a particular programming language, but should reflect a more abstract model of software and software projects. Ozone's prototyping effort focuses on providing support for the C programming language. To some extent, Ozone's environment schema (as defined in this section) reflects this orientation. While Ozone does model software at a abstract level, aiding language independence, the particular conceptual model Ozone uses may be more appropriate for C and C++ than for other imperative programing languages. The use of the object-oriented methodology should ease the task of extending the design of the environment schema to support other languages, especially through the use of inheritance to define types that are specialized for a particular programming language.

There have been a number of other efforts in modeling environment data in SDEs. Two of these efforts were concerned with the modeling of programs. The work of Linton [14] stores programs as a collection of relations in Ingres to create an environment where programs can be browsed and queries may be posed. The storage schema consists of relations and predefined views for storing information, including symbol tables. The work of Horowitz and Teitelbaum [11] examines the automatic generation of language-based editors, where a program is stored as an attributed abstract-syntax tree and a set of relations. In addition to browsing, they also provide the incremental updating of the various views of a program using relational operations whenever the program text is changed using the language-based editor. Both efforts indicate that the relational model has very limited semantics, complicating the modification process (e.g., required for incremental update of program content in the event of modifications) and degrading performance.

Other work in the area has modeled SDE data at the environment level. The Workshop System [4] examines environments from a knowledge-representation perspective. Workshop provides the SE-KRL rule-based language to specify software objects, and includes a SE-KRL kernel class hierarchy of objects. PCTE [25] is a tool interface standard for SDEs using an entity-relationship model for specifying environment data and interaction. This model, called OMS, is used to define schemas that are divided into "schema definition sets" structuring the environment data. The OROS type model [20] uses *objects*, *relationships* and *operations* as primitive types, and provides a type definition mechanism to compose them into more complex types.

The remainder of this section presents an overview of the object-oriented database design of the Ozone environment schema. As mentioned in Section 2, Ozone organizes data into projects, systems, and modules. After an initial discussion of the overall concepts, a discussion of the different object types in the environment, namely, modules, systems, and projects, is given. Since an object-oriented paradigm is being utilized, the discussion examines the structure, relationships, inheritance characteristics, and associated operations for the major types in the design. The section concludes with a discussion on sets and an examination of their utility in supporting the required actions of Ozone and its tools. One last note: throughout the section, references are made to the seven goals outlined in the introduction with the focus on how these goals are attained using the described design.

3.1. An Overview of Ozone's Environment Schema

Software within Ozone takes the form of *Projects* that are composed of *Systems* and *Modules*. *Projects* represent all software and other data that is part of a software product. *Systems* represent the parts of a project that produce a single executable program or process. *SubSystems* are groupings of components of a *System*, and *Modules* are the components of a *SubSystem* or *System*.

Figure 2 shows the structure of this portion of the environment schema. The structure of the environment schema can be represented as types, linked together with *references*. For the purposes of this paper, a *reference* is a unidirectional (from a source to a destination), one–to–one, or one–to–many relationship between objects (as specified by the types). References are owned by the source object and are not directly accessible outside the object. *Projects* are made up of a number of *Systems*, as indicated by the one-to-many *UsesSystem* reference. The *UsedBy* reference indicates that a *System* may be used by a number of different *Projects*. Similarly, *Systems* are composed of a number of *Modules* and *Subsystems*, *Modules* may be used by one or more *Systems* or *Subsystems*, and *Subsystems* may be used by one or more *Systems*. Figure 2 also indicates that the *ProjectSet* is made up of a number of *Projects*, *SystemSets* are made up of a number of *Systems*, *SubSystemSets* are made up of a number of *Subsystems*, and *ModuleSets* are made up of a number of *Modules*. The need for such sets is discussed in Section 3.4.

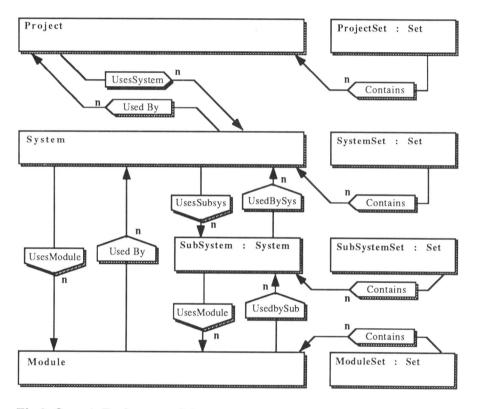

Fig 2. Ozone's Environment Schema

3.2. Modules

All software projects in Ozone are made up of *modules*. A module is the unit of compilation for the software in Ozone. The module is a conceptual unit of software in that they are not limited to any particular representation, such as a the source text or parse tree of the program. Modules in Ozone are defined by the type *Module*, consisting of a definition of its structure (describing the data it contains), a hierarchy of types related through inheritance, and the operations defining the interface of the type.

Figure 3 shows the definition of the *Module* type. Objects may contain objects, meaning that the internal object is accessible only through the operations on the object that contains it. *Module* objects contains objects for the various representations of the module needed by the system. The *Source* object is the source code text of the module. This form of the Module might be used by text editors. The *ParseTree* object is the parse tree of the source code. The *ParseTree* is made up of *Nonterminals* and *Tokens*, representing the nodes of the parse tree. *Nonterminals* are the nonterminal symbols of the parse tree, and *Tokens* are the tokens scanned from the source code text that form the leaves of the parse tree.

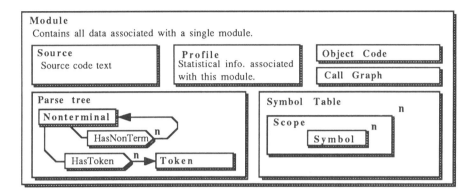

Fig 3. The Module Type

The *SymbolTable* object is made up of the symbols of the module. Symbols are grouped by scope; one for the global scope and one each local scope in the case of C modules. Figure 3 indicates that the *SymbolTable* object contains multiple *Scope* objects (as indicated by the **n**), and that the *Scope* objects contain multiple *Symbol* objects. The *ObjectCode* object represents the object code that is the result of the source code's compilation. *Modules* also contain a *Profile* object for statistical information. The *Profile* object includes information such as the size of the module in terms of the number of lines of source code, the name of the person who wrote the module, and the total time spent editing the module. Note that these objects are contained within *Module* objects and are not directly accessible outside. They are depicted here to provide a conceptual view of the data that the *Module* represents.

The *Module* type is the most general in an inheritance hierarchy. Types are related through inheritance, where a type inherits structure and operations from another type. Figure 4 shows the types in the hierarchy specialized for C modules. *CModule* is derived from *Module*; it contains specializations needed for modules written in C. *CImpModule* and *CIncludeModule* are derived from *CModule*. *CImpModule* is for implementations of C functions, or the traditional contents of the ".c" file. *CIncludeModule* is for declarations, definitions, and "#defines" normally in the ".h"

167

files of C programs. Further specializations of the include module are provided by *CDefineModule* for "#defines" and type definitions, *CDeclarationModule* for global declarations, and *CExternDecModule* for external declarations.

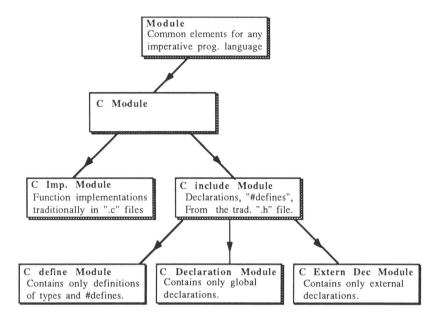

Fig 4. Module Inheritance

The *Module* type hierarchy illustrates the use of inheritance to aid language independence, grouping the types based on their similarities. New types may be added to this inheritance hierarchy, providing for the extension of Ozone to support new languages. For example, a new type *ADAModule* might be defined to support the ADA programming language, and added as a derived type of *Module*. Thus, both extensibility (Goal 3) and programming-language independence (Goal 7), are supported.

The type *Module* has operations that produce the various representations of the module's data that is used by the tools, operations needed for analysis of the module, and operations to allow the contents of the module to be changed. Figure 5 shows a representative set of these operations, using C++ notation to describe the operations' parameters and output (i.e., return type).

The *readSource* operation reads in a new version of the source code of the module. The *getSourceCode* operation produces the character stream that is the Module's source code. The *getSourceText*, *replaceSourceText* and *insertSourceText* operations are provided to allow access to portions of the source code based on line numbers. The *getObjectCode* operation produces the object code of a module.

Other operations are provided to support analysis of the module. The *getSymbols* operations return information about the symbols used within the module. These operations locate symbols based on scope, symbol name, or symbol kind. The *getSymbols* operation uses operator overloading to produce a set of operations performing similar functions with the same name. The *Symbol* type returned by these operations contains information about the symbol accessible through operations on *Symbols*. The *getNonterms* operation returns parts of the module's parse tree, based on scope and the terminal kind (corresponding to the nonterminal symbols in the grammar of the language). The *Nonterminal* object returned contains the information in the subtree were the nonterminal is the root, including the tokens that are the leaves of the tree. The *Module* type also has operations to gain information about its relationships to other objects, such as the *getUsers* operation that returns the *Systems* that use the module.

```
void readSource(istream& in);
void writeSource(ostream& out);
void writeObjCode(ostream& out);
String getSourceText(int fromLine, int toLine);
void replaceSourceText(int fromLine, int toLine, String newLines);
void insertSourceText(int atLine, String newLines);
SymbolSet* getSymbols(String name, String scopeName);
SymbolSet* getSymbols(SymbolKind kind, String scopeName);
NonterminalSet* getNonterms(NontermKind kind, String scopeName);
SystemSet* getUsers();
int        numLines();
Time*      totalCheckOutTime();
Person*    owner();
```

Fig 5. Operations on Modules

The last three operations, *NumLines*, *totalCheckoutTime*, and *owner*, are examples of operations that allow access to information about the module. The *NumLines* operation returns the number of lines of source code in the module. The *totalCheckoutTime* operation can be used to determine the amount of time a Module object has been in use by tools. The *owner* operation returns the person that is designated as the owner of this module. It is through these, and all earlier operations, that a clear, concise model of the environment data is presented to tool designers and builders (Goal 6).

An important aspect of the design of the *Module* type is that the consistency of the various representations of the software are maintained internally by the operations on the type, and are not the concern of the users of the type. For example, if a user were to call the readSource operation on a particular module, a subsequent call to getNonterminal would reflect the revised source code. The implementation of the *Module* type includes the transformations between the different representations. The implementation of the *CModule* type includes a scanner developed using LEX and a parser produced by the Bison parser generator. Ideally, the *CModule* type would encompass a complete C compiler, but for this prototyping effort, a UNIX compiler will be called to produce the object code from a temporary source code file. None of this will be visible to the tools that use the *CModule* type.

The operations of the six types of objects contained within the *Module* objects are not described here due to space limitations. The operations on modules heavily utilize the operations on the contained object types. For example, the *getSymbols* operation calls the *findSymbol* operation on the *Scope* object indicated by the *scopeName* parameter of *getSymbol* in order to return information about Symbols.

3.3. Projects and Systems

Figure 6 shows the portion of Ozone's environment schema composed of *Projects*, *Systems*, *Subsystems* and *Modules*. *Modules* are grouped into *SubSystems*, which are collections of modules provided to organize the software. *SubSystems* and individual *Modules* are organized into *Systems*.

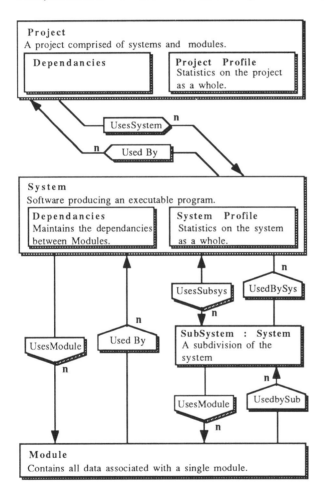

Fig 6. Projects, Systems, and Modules

A *System* represents all software needed for a single executable program. *Systems* may be grouped into *Projects*, which are collections of one or more executable *Systems* that make up a software project or product. These types are described by their definition, their inheritance hierarchy, and their operations.

A *Project* object contains a *Dependancies* object and a *ProjectProfile* object. The *Dependancies* object maintains information on the dependancies between the *Systems* that are part of the project. The *ProjectProfile* object contains statistical information about the project, such as its size and cost to date. The *UsesSystem* reference shows that a *Project* has a number of *Systems*, as indicated by the n at the pointed end of the reference rectangle. Note that the *Project* object owns this reference. The *System* object has a *UsedBy* reference, indicating which *Projects* use a particular *System*. *Systems* contain *Dependancies*, an object maintaining dependancies between the *Modules* and *SubSystems* of the *System*, and a *SystemProfile* object similar to the *Profile* object of the *Project*. Systems have references to their component *Modules* and *SubSystems*.

By modeling software projects as Projects, Systems, SubSystems, and Modules, Ozone has the ability to represent a wide range of software system architectures. These types can represent projects that range from a small program to a large multi-process, multi-computer system. The ability to manage large software projects is a requirement for SDEs to achieve methodology independence, and satisfy, in part, Goal 7.

Figure 7 shows an inheritance diagram for the type *System*, indicating that there is a type *CSystem* that inherits structure and operations from the *System* type, and has additional specializations needed for systems written in C. SubSystem is also a derived type of system, since it shares much of the data and operations of the System type. CSubSystem is a specialization for subsystems written in C.

The *System* type hierarchy shows the utility of type inheritance in achieving language independence. Also, the derivation of the *SubSystem* type illustrates the more general use of providing a more specialized type. Once again, inheritance provides both extensibility (Goal 3) and programming-language independence (Goal 7).

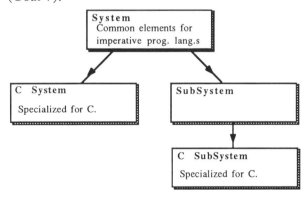

Fig 7. Systems Inheritance

The *Project* type includes operations for determining what Systems and Modules it uses, and for allowing the contents of these collections to be changed. *Project* also has operations for accessing information about the project. Figure 8 shows a portion of these operations.

```
SystemSet* getSystems();
System* getSystem(String name);
System* getSystem(Module usesModule);
int totalLinesOfCode();
void addSystem(System* newSystem);
void removeSystem(System* aSystem);
```

Fig 8. Operations on Projects

The *getSystem* operations allow the *Systems* of a *Project* to be located. For example, Systems may be located on the basis of name or its use of a particular module. The *addSystem* and *removeSystem* operations allows existing *Systems* to be added or removed from a project. Some operations are provided to access statistical information about the project, such as *getLinesOfCode* that returns the total number of lines of source code in the project.

The *System* type has operations similar to the *Project* type. Figure 9 shows some additional operations of interest. The *getSubSystem* operations allows the *SubSystems* used by the *System* to be accessed, and *getUsers* returns the projects that use the system. The *getModule* operation allows modules that the system uses to be located on the basis of the module's name. The *addModule* and *removeModule* operations allow changes to the set of modules used by the system. In addition, it has a *makeExecutable* operation that causes the compilation and linking of the system into an executable program. The operations on the SubSystem type are similar. Collectively, operations on systems and projects form a tight, succinct interface (Goal 6).

```
SubSystem* getSubSystem(String name);
ProjectSet* getUsers();
Module* getModule(String name);
void addModule(Module* newModule);
void removeModule(Module* aModule);
void makeExecutable();
```

Fig 9. Operations on Systems

3.4. Collections of environment objects

Ozone's environment schema also defines collections of the objects, as shown in Figure 2. These types allow objects to be grouped together, and provide operations for associative access. These sets contain very little data themselves, but serve to collect instances of their element types and provide a means of access to these collections. The

172

types ProjectSet, SystemSet, and ModuleSet are derived from a common type Set. Within the environments database, a single instance of each of these types is used to collect all instances of their respective element types. Other instances of these Set types are used in the course of Ozone's operation, such as when operations on types return collections. The *getUsers* operation on the *System* type is an example of this, returning a *ProjectSet* that is the collection of projects that use the system.

Provisions for associative access are needed in the environment schema. In work relevant to these needs, Shaw and Zdonik describe a query algebra for object-oriented databases [21]. The query algebra is defined for the Encore data model. Encore has three parameterized types for collections of objects: Set, Multiset, and Tuple. The query algebra consists of operations defined on these collection types. For example, "select" chooses objects from a collection that satisfy a predicate. An "ojoin" operation is defined that produces a collection of "tuple" objects given two collections of objects.

Ozone uses operations on set types to provide the tools using the environment schema with associative access capabilities on collection of objects. Figure 10 shows a portion of the operations on *ModuleSet*. This type has operations to locate modules that meet a given criteria through calls to operations on the Module type. For example, *getModule* takes a module's name as a parameter, and uses it to compare to the results of a call to the *getName* method of the *Module* objects. The *ModuleUsing* and *ModuleDefining* operations allow modules to be located on the basis of symbols they use or define. The *ModulesUsedBy* operations return modules that are used by a particular project or system. Similar operations are provided for the *ProjectSet* and *SystemSet* types to allow *Projects* and *Systems* to be located based on a variety of parameters. In addition, basic set operations, such as *Union* and *Intersection*, and *Membership* are provided, inherited from the *Set* type.

```
Module* getModule(String name);
ModuleSet* ModulesUsing(Symbol aSymbol);
Module* ModuleDefining(Symbol aSymbol);
ModuleSet* ModulesOwnedBy(Person& owner);
ModuleSet* ModulesUsedBy(Project& userProject);
ModuleSet* ModulesUsedBy(System& userSystem);
```

Fig 10. Operations on ModuleSet

4. The Use of Operations on Environment Types

The operations of the types that are defined in the environment schema are the means by which tools access and manipulate the data of the environment. The methods used to locate objects can be composed to provide a large variety of possible queries against the environment data. This section of the paper presents examples of the use of these operations to illustrate their ability to provide this access, thereby demonstrating the attainability of Goals 4 and 5.

Suppose that the Program-Questioning tool must answer a user's question about the global variables used in a particular *System*. First, the system must be located. The type *SystemSet* defines an operation *getSystem* that takes the system's name as a parameter and returns a pointer to the *System* object. The *getModules* operation on the *System* object may then be called to obtain a the set of modules used by the system, either directly or indirectly through *SubSystems*. For each of the modules the system uses, the *getSymbols* method is called with "global" as the name of the scope, returning the set of global symbols defined in the system. The Program-Questioning tool may then use operations on the Symbol type to produce a display of the information desired by the user. Note that these operations may be composed, as shown using C++ syntax:

```
symbols =   ((allSystems->getSystem(name))->getModules())->
                                     getSymbols( nil, "global");
```

Where *allSystems* is the instance of the SystemSet type that contains all the systems in the environment.

As another example, suppose a user wants to know the names of all systems that use a particular module. The PQ tool would begin by calling the getModule operation of ModuleSet to locate the module by its name. The tool would then pass the module as a parameter to the getUsersOf operation of SystemSet. This operation returns the set of systems that use a particular module. Finally, the getName operation would be called on the systems to make a list of the names of the systems that use a module. In its composed form, this is:

```
names
  =(allSystems->getUsersOf(allModules->getModule(name)))->getName();
```

Clearly, in both of these examples primitive operations can be composed into more powerful ones (Goal 4). However, the extent to which these compositions reduce tool complexity (Goal 5) is only partially answerable at present, and must rely on a postmortem of the prototyping effort to determine the degree to which this goal is attained.

These examples also show that the tools can compose the operations of the environment schema into powerful query expressions. These expressions can be evaluated by the Server or the underlying database management system, freeing tools from the need to check-out large numbers of objects from the database. The ability to compose operations also supports the extensibility of the system, since new query expressions can be formulated from the operations to meet the requirements of additional tools. The composition of operations is a powerful concept that has been demonstrated in the functional data model [22], and in programming languages such as LISP and ML.

5. Conclusions

This paper presents an object-oriented database design for the environment data of Ozone. The object-oriented paradigm was chosen since it offers support for a wide-range of data types, for tool integration via a well-defined public interface to environment data, and for environment extensibility by the modification of types and operations. The database design that was presented organizes software into projects, systems, subsystems, and modules. This organization coupled with the object-oriented design provides, in general, affirmative answers to the questions/goals posed in the introduction. Specifically, Goal 3 (extensibility), Goal 4 (composition), Goal 5 (reduce complexity via composition), Goal 6 (clear, concise model), and Goal 7 (programming-language and software-methodology independence) have all been positively addressed in Sections 3 and 4. The degree to which the object-oriented paradigm reduces tool development complexity and redundancy (Goal 5) is only partially addressed. The tradeoff between the integration of the environment and system extensibility (Goal 2) has not been considered. However, both of these goals tend to be the motivating factors for utilizing an object-oriented paradigm, and are only answerable given the experience of building Ozone and the subsequent evaluation of the prototyping effort. Nevertheless, the ability of the object-oriented paradigm to model SDE environment data (Goal 1) has been clearly demonstrated.

Currently, the design for Ozone is complete and prototyping has already begun. The first version of Ozone should be operational by May of 1990. As a test environment, Ozone will be utilized to allow the exploration of ideas on program questioning, tool integration, tool development, database support, and extensibility. To evaluate both the capabilities and limitations of Ozone, experiments will be made on an already-developed, medium-scale software system that contains 50,000 lines of C code. Specifically, the code of the multi-lingual/multi-backend database system [5, 7], an experimental, multiple-computer and multiple-process-per-computer system, will be used. This code will be loaded into Ozone and experiments will be conducted to determine how well Ozone can handle large volumes of data and still support program questioning in a timely fashion.

Another important aspect of Ozone's design that has not been presented in this paper, involves the issues and considerations that are necessary to support both sharing and concurrent access of environment data. Data may be shared between users, between tasks, and between tools. Often the sharing of data will involve the concurrent use of data. Concurrent access of environment data will be frequent. A single user on a workstation will often edit two different modules of a project simultaneously. Multiple users will often need to check library interface definitions or source code. Different users will often be using the same piece of information, or related pieces of information. Any successful SDE must promote a high degree of data-sharing. The design of the environment schema must also consider concurrent use of SDE data. All of these issues are currently being studied in order to determine their impact on Ozone's design and implementation.

The work reported in this paper is part of our ongoing effort by the SEEDS research project at the University of Connecticut [6]. SEEDS, short for Software-Engineering Environments and Database Systems, is an inter-disciplinary collection of faculty members and graduate students whose goal is to develop a software-development environment with database-system support that is both software-methodology and programming-language independent. There are a number of other related projects currently underway in the SEEDS group.

One major focus of the research group is the enhancement of object-oriented data models with active or propagation semantics. These new capabilities can then be used to more accurately model behavior between classes in a schema. Most object-oriented models support intra-class behavior definition by the encapsulation of methods within class or data type declarations. However, inter-class relationships and behavior are supported in only a limited sense by object-oriented models, i.e., ISA or inheritance hierarchies. This capability is critical for SDEs. With inter-class relationships, the modeling paradigm can be extended with the ability to represent the complex collection of behavior that would exist between the large number of data types in a SDE. This work of the SEEDS group is well underway [9, 18].

Other work within the SEEDS group addresses the database system needs of SDEs. A traditional single-processor database system architecture may not be sufficient to handle the large volumes of semantically-rich data required for SDEs. Some estimates of SDE-data size reach the 1 gigabyte range for storing all of the information in its various forms for a single project. The work of this group investigates database machine architectures for SDEs, with the goal of distributing system functionality while still providing for a centralized core of data on all projects that can be globally accessed [26].

References

1   R. Agrawal and N. Gehani, "ODE (Object Database and Environment): The Language and the Data Model", *Proc. of the 1989 ACM SIGMOD Intl. Conf. on Management of Data*, June 1989.

2   D. Barstow, H. Shrobe, and E. Sandewall (eds.), *Interactive Programming Environments*, McGraw-Hill Book Company, 1984.

3   P. Bernstein, "Database System Support for Software Engineering, An Extended Abstract", *Proc. of Ninth Intl. Conf. on Software Engineering*, March 1987.

4   G. Clemm, "The Workshop System", *Proc. of the ACM SIGSOFT/SIGPLAN Software Engineering Sym. on Practical Software Development Environments*, November 1988.

5   S. Demurjian, D. Hsiao, and J. Menon, "A Multi-Backend Database System for Performance Gains, Capacity Growth, and Hardware Upgrade", *Proc. of the Second Intl. Conf. on Data Engineering*, February 1986.

6   S. Demurjian, G. Beshers, R. Ammar, and T.C. Ting, "The SEEDS Project at the University of Connecticut", *Proc. of the Second Intl. Workshop on Computer-Aided Software Engineering*, July 1988.

7   S. Demurjian and D. Hsiao, "Towards a Better Understanding of Data Models Through the Multilingual Database System", *IEEE Trans. on Software Engineering*, Vol. 14, No. 7, July 1988.

8   S. Demurjian and H. Ellis, "The Storage and Management of Software in an Object-Oriented Database System to Support Program Questioning", Technical Report CSE-TR-89-25, Department of Computer Science and Engineering, University of Connecticut, 1989.

9   H. Ellis, S. Demurjian, F. Maryanski, G. Beshers, J. Peckham, "Extending the Behavioral Capabilities of the Object-Oriented Paradigm with an Active Model of Propagation", *Proc. of 1990 ACM Computer Science Conf.*, February 1990.

10   A. Goldberg, "The Influence of an Object-Oriented Language on the Programming Environment", *Proc. of 1983 ACM Computer Science Conf.*, February 1983; also in [2].

11   S. Horowitz and T. Teitelbaum, "Relations and Attributes", *Proc. of ACM SIGPLAN Sym. on Language Issues in Programming Environments*, July 1985.

12   S. Hudson and R. King, "The Cactis Project: Database Support for Software Environments", *IEEE Trans. on Software Engineering*, Vol. 14, No. 6, June 1988.

13   W. Kim, et al., "Features of an Object-Oriented Database System", in *Object-Oriented Concepts, Databases and Applications*, W. Kim and F. Lochovsky (eds.), ACM Press, Addison-Wesley, 1989.

14   M. Linton, "Relational Views of Programs", *Proc. of the ACM SIGSOFT/SIGPLAN Software Engineering Sym. on Practical Software Development Environments*, May 1984.

15   D. Maier, et al. "Development of an Object-Oriented DBMS", in *Proc. of the 1986 OOPSLA Conf.*, September 1986.

16   G. Nichols and S. Demurjian, "Ozone: A Software-Development Environment with Object-Oriented Database Support", Technical Report CSE-TR-89-30, Department of Computer Science and Engineering, University of Connecticut, 1989.

17   "ONTOS Object Database Documentation", Release 1.0, Ontologic, Inc., Burlington, MA, 1989.

18   J. Peckam, F. Maryanski, G. Beshers, H. Ellis, and S. Demurjian, "Constraint Based Analysis", *Proc. of Tenth Annual Intl. Conf. on Information Systems*, December 1989.

19   S. Reiss, "Working in the Garden Environment for Conceptual Programming", *IEEE Software* Vol. 4, No. 6, November 1987.

20   W. Rosenblatt, J. Wileden, and A. Wolf, "OROS: Toward a Type Model for Software Development Environments", *Proc. of 1989 OOPSLA Conf.*, October 1989.

21   G. Shaw, S. Zdonik, "A Query Algebra for Object-Oriented Databases", Brown University, Tech. Report No. CS-89-19, March 1989.

22   D. Shipman, "The Functional Data Model and the Data Language Daplex", *ACM Trans. on Database Systems*, Vol. 6, No. 1, March 1981.

23   B. Stroustrup, *The C++ Programming Language*, Addison-Wesley, 1986.

24   R. Taylor, et al., "Foundations for the Arcadia Environment Architecture", *Proc. of ACM SIGSOFT/SIGPLAN Software Engineering Sym. on Practical Software Development Environments*, November 1988.

25   I. Thomas, "PCTE Interfaces: Supporting Tools in Software-Engineering Environments", *IEEE Software*, Vol. 6, No. 6, November 1989.

26   D. Wong and S. Demurjian, "An Analysis of Database Machine Architectures for Software Development Environments", Technical Report CSE-TR-89-28, Department of Computer Science and Engineering, University of Connecticut, 1989.

27   C. Zaroliagis, et al., "The GRASPIN DB - A Syntax Directed, Language Independent Software Engineering Database," *Proc. of 1986 Intl. Workshop on Object-Oriented Database Systems*, September 1986.

A Geoscientific Database System Supporting Cartography and Application Programming

Friedrich Lohmann, Karl Neumann

Informatik/Datenbanken
Technische Universität Braunschweig
Postfach 3329, D-3300 Braunschweig

Abstract

This paper presents a survey of a database management system which has been designed to offer appropriate database support for geoscientific applications. We propose a novel, high-level database management language which permits storing, managing and retrieving information about geoscientific objects in a convenient way and which also supports automatic cartography. A broad variety of geoscientific applications can be supported, as the user is enabled to define his own specific geoobject classes and even to add new geometric data types. In application programs, the database language is available as an embedded data sublanguage, and sets of objects read from the database can be manipulated by operations offered in abstract data type modules. A sample application serves as an illustration of our approach to modelling and manipulating geoscientific data.

1. Introduction

In recent years, it has been recognized that traditional, commercially available database management systems such as IMS, SQL/DS, or ORACLE are not well suited for so-called non-standard applications [DD86, Ba88, Di88]. Therefore, many research groups have started to develop new data models (cf. survey in [PM88]), database languages (among others [RS87, ALPS88,

179

AG89, Gü89]), and storage structures [Gu84, NHS84, Sa84, HSW88, GW89, HSW89]. These new concepts are intended to be appropriate for areas like office, manufacturing, engineering design, and geoscientific applications.

Within the priority project "Digital Geoscientific Maps" [Vi88a], which was supported by the German Research Foundation (DFG), it has been our task to propose a novel database management language which permits storing, managing, and retrieving geoscientific data and which also supports automatic cartography. Hence, this sub-project, can be seen as a small part of the area of non-standard database research activities sketched above.

We started our project in 1984/1985 by first designing a special non-standard database language. Then we implemented a partial prototype in order to be able to demonstrate the features of the language by means of realistic geoscientific applications. With these experiences in mind, we carefully designed a second improved prototype. The following chapter gives a survey of the database language, while chapter 3 outlines the application programming facilities. The architecture of the second prototype is described in chapter 4. Finally, in chapter 5, we give some conclusions concerning the whole project.

2. Database Language

The geoscientific database language is based on a specific *geoobject model* which is an extension of the well-known Entity-Relationship model (ER model, [Ch76]). Hence, geoscientific worlds are modelled in terms of object classes and relationship classes. While objects have to be atomic in the classical ER model, the geoobject model also allows *complex objects* which are composed of a hierarchy of subobjects (or sets or lists of subobjects). Within the database, all objects are represented by their attribute values.

The geoobject model supports a conceptual distinction between information about geoscientific objects *(geoobjects)* and their graphic representation in maps *(map objects)*. While the user may define arbitrary geoobject classes according to the requirements of his specific application, the attribute scheme of maps and map objects is predefined and fixed. The database language offers special constructs for transforming geoobjects into corresponding map objects.

A significant feature of geoscientific objects is that they usually have a spatial extent. In order to support this important characteristic, the geoobject model offers special *geometric data types* in addition to the conventional alphanumeric data types. Thus geometric data can be manipulated just as conveniently as standard data. The types *Points* (sets of single points in the plane), *Lines* (sets of lines in the plane) and *Polygons* (sets of polygonal areas in the plane) are already predefined in the database system, together with a variety of operations, e. g. for computing intersections, for computing the size of a line or an area, etc. Furthermore, the user is enabled to define additional geometric data types and to introduce them into the database system, like spline curves, rasters, or space points. Subsequently, these new types can be used in database statements in the same way as the predefined data types.

In its data definition part, the database language enables the user to model his view of a geoscientific world by defining (and dropping) atomic or complex geoobject classes and relationships; in its data manipulation part, the language includes statements for creating, retrieving, updating and deleting geoobjects, relationships, maps and map objects as well as statements for alphanumeric and graphic output. The database language shows some resemblances to the relational database language QUEL [SWKH76]; like QUEL, the geo-database language uses range variables to refer to objects stored in the database.

To illustrate the use of the database language, we now present a few typical statements taken from a sample application. We consider a database in which base data for the computation of soil erosion and deposition in a certain test area are to be stored (cf. [BH88]). The geoobject scheme for this database may be defined as follows:

```
DEFINE_GEOOBJ Field
    (Name              String,
     Geometry          Polygons,
     CropsPerYear       LIST_OF GEOOBJ CropPerYear
        (Year              Integer,
         Crop              String));

DEFINE_GEOOBJ DrillHole
    (Geometry          Points,
     SoilTexture       String,
     Layers            SET_OF GEOOBJ Layer
        (Depth             Real,
         OrganicMatter     Integer));

DEFINE_GEOOBJ SoilArea
    (Name              String,
     Geometry          Polygons);

DEFINE_REL PointInArea (DrillHole, SoilArea);
```

In the first object class we store information about the fields situated in the test area and their agricultural use (cf. Fig. 2.1). Each field has a

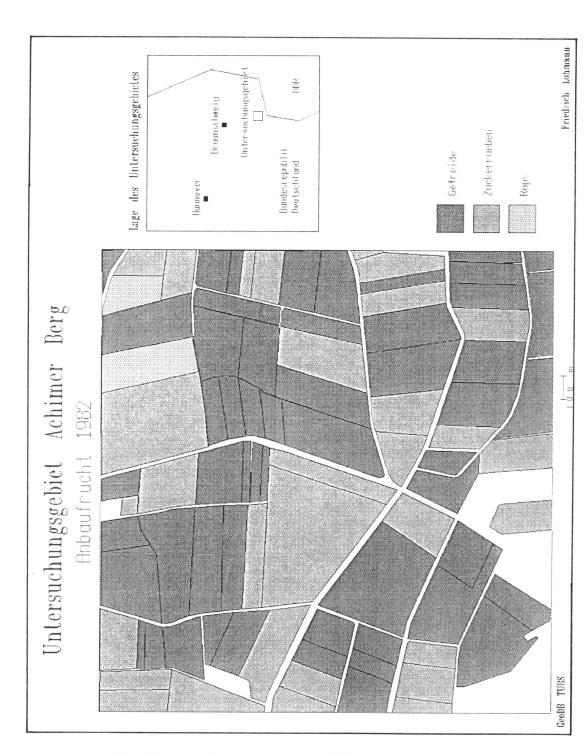

Fig. 2.1: Map of agricultural use in 1982.

unique name and a geometric shape (which is a polygonal area); furthermore, for every field, we want to store the list of the crops which are grown in the field during the course of several years: cereal (Getreide), sugar-beets (Zuckerrüben), or rape (Raps).

The second kind of objects are drill-holes. For every drill-hole, we want to store its geometric location and the soil texture found at this point: loamy sand (lehmiger Sand), loam (Lehm), clayey loam (toniger Lehm), or clay (Ton). Additionally, we store the mass fraction of organic matter found at this point in different layers . Each drill-hole and its respective soil texture is considered representative for exactly one area (according to the *Reichsbodenschätzung*), called `SoilArea`. The association between drill-holes and soil areas is given by the relationship `PointInArea`.

After the definition of the geoobject scheme, data can be inserted into the database and can subsequently be evaluated by retrieval operations. The following query computes a temporary geoobject class named `IntersectionArea`:

```
RANGE_OF f IS Field;
RANGE_OF c IS f.CropsPerYear;
RANGE_OF d IS DrillHole;
RANGE_OF s IS SoilArea;
RETRIEVE_GEOOBJ_INTO IntersectionArea
     (Name        = f.Name CAT s.Name,
      Geometry    = Intersection (f.Geometry, s.Geometry),
      SoilTexture = d.SoilTexture,
      CropsPerYear = SET_OF GEOOBJ CropPerYear
          (Year        = c.Year,
           Crop        = c.Crop))
WHERE Cut (f.Geometry, s.Geometry) AND
      PointInArea (d, s) AND
      c.Year >= 1982;
```

The actual `RETRIEVE` statement is preceded by the declaration of range variables which are needed to refer to the objects stored in the respective geoobject classes. Each object of the temporary class computed by the query represents an area with a uniform soil texture and a uniform agricultural use (cf. Fig. 2.2).

The geometries of these areas are computed by intersecting the fields f and soil areas s using the geometric operator `Intersection`; the names are formed by concatenating the names of the respective field and soil area. The `Cut` operation in the qualification part of the query specifies that only non-void intersections are to be stored. The soil texture of an area is given by the soil texture of the drill-hole d which is situated within the soil area

183

Fig. 2.2: Map of soil texture and agricultural use in 1982.

s. The `CropsPerYear` attribute is given by a set of tuples consisting of the years from 1982 onwards and the crops grown in the field f in the respective years.

The semantics of the database language is given by an underlying *object calculus* [LN87], which has been defined by extending the well-known tuple calculus [Ma83]. As queries may result in complex objects which may be arbitrarily nested, our calculus does not show the usual hierarchical structure of terms, atomic formulas, and formulas. Rather, the recursive structure of complex objects is reflected in the fact that terms may be set-valued, which implies that they are constructed by using formulas in their turn. A similar non-hierarchical approach to a calculus for complex objects is given in [HG88]. Despite their unusual structure, the resulting expressions are intuitively understandable; as an example, we consider the following expression which states the semantics of the query discussed above:

```
{ result | ∃ f ∈ Field ∃ s ∈ SoilArea ∃ d ∈ DrillHole
     (Cut (Geometry(f), Geometrie(s)) ∧
      PointInArea (d,s) ∧
      Name (result) = CAT (Name(f), Name(s)) ∧
      Geometry (result) =
              Intersection (Geometry(f), Geometry(s)) ∧
      SoilTexture (result) = SoilTexture (d) ∧
      CropsPerYear (result) =
              { sub_result | ∃ c ∈ CropsPerYear (f)
                   (Year (c) ≥ 1982 ∧
                    Year (sub_result) = Jahr (c) ∧
                    Crop (sub_result) = Crop (c)) } )}
```

After the computation of the class `IntersectionArea`, the results can be output in alphanumeric form, or they can be transformed into map objects for graphic display. Map construction is supported by the database language; the following **CREATE_MAPOBJ** statement gives a flavour of how it works. This statement creates map objects of all the areas where sugar-beets were grown on loam in the year 1982 and inserts them into a map named `SoilCrops82`:

185

```
RANGE_OF i IS IntersectionArea;
RANGE_OF c IS i.CropsPerYear;
RANGE_OF m IS MAP;

CREATE_MAPOBJ_FROM i
    INSERT_INTO m.FACE
    (POLYGONS: Type   = SOLID,
               Colour = 7  (* red*) )
WHERE m.Name = "SoilCrops82"  AND
      i.SoilTexture = "loam"  AND
      c.Year        = 1982    AND
      c.Crop        = "sugar-beets";
```

Note that the geometries of the map objects are computed implicitly by transforming the geometries of the underlying geoobjects from world coordinates into coordinates of the map sheet. The creation of the map SoilCrops82, which is initially empty and into which map objects are successively inserted, has not been shown here. The database statements provided for map construction can be found in [ELNR88], which also contains more details about the underlying graphic data types.

3. Application Programming

At the application programming interface of the geoscientific database system, the database language is available as an *embedded data sublanguage* of a general purpose programming language. Hence, application programs consist of statements of the programming language which are interspersed with database statements. Compared with other approaches to application programming—call-interfaces or integrated database programming languages, cf. [LP83, ESW88]—the embedding approach has two major advantages: On the one hand, one database language can be used both in application programs and at the dialogue interface, and on the other hand, there is no need to change an existing programming language and its compiler, as database statements can be translated into calls of respective modules of the database management system by a special precomiler (named *database language compiler* in the following). In application programs, database statements may be parametrized, which means that program variables may be specified instead of constant data values.

As the geo-database system allows the manipulation of arbitrarily nested complex objects, it is desirable that also application programs be able to process data read from the database in an object-oriented manner. To achieve this, we have chosen an approach which is based on the ideas of *data abstraction* (or *data encapsulation*, cf. [LG86, TRE88]): For all objects, sets

186

of objects and lists of objects which a user wishes to process within an application program, appropriate types and operations are made available to the programmer in abstract data type modules (ADT modules). Modula 2 was chosen as the application programming language, as it supports data abstraction by its concept of definition and implementation modules.

As an example, we suppose that the temporary object class `IntersectionArea` is to be read and processed by an application program. To this end, ADT modules have to be generated for the object type `IntersectionArea` and the set type `SetOfIntersectionArea` as well as for the sub-object type `CropPerYear` and its corresponding set type `SetOfCropPerYear`. The generation of the ADT modules occurs largely automatically by the aid of tools, the *object type generator* and the *object type compiler*. The object type generator takes the `RETRIEVE` statement from chapter 2—together with the necessary `RANGE` declarations—as its input. The object type generator reads the object schemes of the classes `Field`, `DrillHole` and `SoilArea` (which are referenced by `RANGE` variables) from the database catalogue and generates the following specification of the the object and set types required for processing the class `IntersectionArea`:

```
OBJECTTYPES
    SetOfIntersectionArea = SET_OF (IntersectionArea);
    IntersectionArea = OBJECT
                        Name          String,
                        Geometry      Polygons,
                        SoilTexture   String,
                        CropsPerYear  SetOfCropPerYear
                    END;
    SetOfCropPerYear = SET_OF (CropPerYear);
    CropPerYear = OBJECT
                        Year          Integer,
                        Crop          String
                    END
END_OBJECTTYPES
```

From this pseudocode specification, the object type compiler generates definition and implementation modules for the specified four types. The ADT modules for the object types `IntersectionArea` and `CropPerYear` include—among others—operations for creating objects and for reading or changing attribute values; the ADT modules for the set types `SetOfIntersectionArea` and `SetOfCropPerYear` include operations for creating an empty set, for inserting and removing objects, for checking if a given object is contained in a given set, for computing the number of elements currently contained in a given set etc.

187

In a similar way, another system component, the *data type compiler*, generates ADT modules for geometric data types specified by the user.

The integration of all required types in the form of ADT modules makes it very easy for the application programmer to process data read from the database. As an example, we consider the following program fragment, which is based on the examples quoted in chapter 2; we compute the percentage of the size of loam areas compared to the size of the entire test area:

```
(* declaration of program variables *)

VAR setintersec: SetOfIntersectionArea;
    singlesize, entiresize, loamsize, loampercent: REAL;

(* computate the temporary object class IntersectionArea
   (database statements) *)

...  as in chapter 2   ...

(* copy the temporary object class into the
   program variable "setintersec" (database statements) *)

RANGE_OF s IS IntersectionArea;
WRITE_GEOOBJ s INTO :setintersec;

(* compute the size of the entire test area and the sum of
   the sizes of all loam areas situated in the test area *)

entiresize  := 0.0;
loamsize    := 0.0;

FOR_ALL intersec: IntersectionArea  IN  setintersec  DO
    (* process each object *)
    singlesize   :=
            Area (IntersectionArea.ValueGeometry (intersec));
    entiresize   := entiresize + singlesize;
    IF IntersectionArea.ValueSoilTexture (intersec) = "loam"
    THEN loamsize := loamsize + singlesize
END;

(* compute the percentage of the size of loam areas
   compared to the size of the entire test area *)

loampercent := loamsize * 100 / entiresize;
...
```

188

By means of the `WRITE` statement, the geoobject class `IntersectionArea`—which was computed by the `RETRIEVE` statement shown in chapter 2—is copied into the program variable `setintersec`, which is of appropriate type. The loop construct `FOR_ALL` permits processing all the objects contained in the set in a system defined order; all objects are successively assigned to the loop variable `intersec`. The `FOR_ALL` construct extends the primary features of Modula 2; before the program is processed by the database language compiler, another preprocessor, the *language construct compiler*, replaces the `FOR_ALL` loop by standard Modula code, which includes calls to special procedures contained in the ADT modules for the respective set type. The operations `IntersectionArea.ValueGeometry` and `IntersectionArea.ValueSoilTexture` are contained in the ADT module for the object type `IntersectionArea`; these operations yield the geometry resp. soil texture value of the object currently identified by the variable `intersec`.

For a more extensive discussion of our approach to application programming the reader is referred to [Lo88], which also includes a detailed treatment of the ADT operations for geometric data types.

4. Architecture of the Second Prototype

A subset of the database language presented in chapter 2 was implemented in a first provisional prototype [ELNR88]. The maps shown in Figs. 2.1 and 2.2 have been constructed solely by using this first prototype; unfortunately, they can only be shown in black and white here for reasons of reproduction.

Our experiences with the first prototype, which was actually very slow, as well as discussions with geoscientists influenced the design of a second prototype, which is currently being implemented. Its overall architecture is sketched in Fig. 4.1.

As mentioned in the previous chapter, special tools, the *object type generator* and the *object type compiler*, are provided to generate abstract data type modules for all geoobject classes which the user wishes to process in an application program. Similarly, the *data type compiler* generates ADT modules for geometric data types. Application programs with embedded database statements are preprocessed by the *database language compiler*, which searches the program for database statements, checks their syntax and semantics and also performs all inter-language type checking. For each database statement, the database language compiler generates a module with the "implementation" of the statement. Within the application program, the database language compiler replaces every database statement by

189

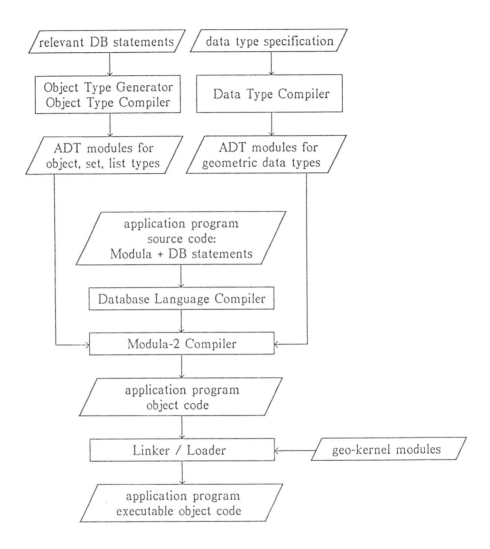

Fig. 4.1: Overall architecture of the second prototype.

a call to the respective module, in a way that the resulting program can subsequently be compiled by a standard Modula 2 compiler.

The second prototype is being implemented on a SUN3 workstation under UNIX; programming is done in Modula 2. The implementation is based on a special geo-database kernel [SW86, HSWW88, WWH88], which is a member of a "family" of database management systems called DAS-DBS [PSSW87]. As the geo-kernel supports nested relations (NF2-Relations [ScS86]) with geometric attributes and spatial indexing, we expect a considerable improvement of response times, compared to the first prototype.

5. Conclusion

In this paper, we have outlined a database language which is particularly suited for geoscientific applications. Geometric data types and complex objects are supported, and the semantics of the database language can be stated by an underlying object calculus. For application programming, the database language has been embedded into the programming language Modula 2; sets of atomic or complex geoobjects read from the database can be manipulated by operations offered in abstract data type modules.

A first partial prototype was implemented as a means to gain experience with the practical use of the database language; several realistic geoscientific applications proved our concepts to be appropriate. Currently, we are implementing a second, improved prototype.

We are very grateful to all the students who have worked and are still working within the project. During the last four years, about 25 of them prepared their term papers or diploma theses mainly by implementing the first and second prototype. Without their contributions, the geoscientific database system would have remained a "paper project".

The cooperation with the geoscientific research groups brought about some interesting challenges for us. Thus, for instance, the realization of the geometric data types Points, Lines and Polygons with associated operations, such as intersection of polygons, seemed to be one of our hardest tasks in the beginning. Then, all of a sudden, the users asked for arbitrary geometric types, including graphic representations of 3dimensional surfaces. On the other hand, the geoscientists also had to learn some "difficult" things, like modelling their worlds in terms of our database definition language and understanding the mechanisms of retrieving relevant data. So the interdisciplinary project was of interest to all participating groups.

Acknowledgement

We are very grateful to our "boss" H.-D. Ehrich. He did very hard work in the initialization phase to get the project started. It was easy to do good work under his liberal supervision.

References

[AG89]   AGRAWAL, R.; GEHANI, N.: ODE: The Language and the Data Model. – Proc. ACM SIGMOD Conf. on the Management of Data, Portland 1989; CLIFFORD, J./ LINDSAY, B./ MAIER, D. (eds.); SIGMOD Record 18:2 (1989), 36–45.

[ALPS88]   ANDERSEN, F.; LINNEMANN, V.; PISTOR, P.; SÜDKAMP, N.: Advanced Information Management Prototype – User Manual for the Online Interface of the Heidelberg Data Base Language (HDBL) Prototype Implementation. – Technical Note TN 86.01, IBM Heidelberg Scientific Center, Heidelberg 1988.

[AW89]   APERS, P. M. G.; WIEDERHOLD, G. (eds.): Proc. 15th Int. Conf. on Very Large Data Bases, Amsterdam. – Morgan Kaufmann Publishers, Palo Alto 1989.

[Ba88]   BANCILHON, F.: Object-Oriented Database Systems. – Proc. Principles of Database Systems, Association for Computing Machinery, New York 1988, 152–162.

[BH88]   BORK, H.-R.; HENSEL, H.: Computer-aided Construction of Soil Erosion and Deposition Maps. – In [Vi88b], 357–371.

[Ch76]   CHEN, P. P.: The Entity-Relationship Model – Toward a Unified View of Data. – ACM Transactions on Database Systems 1 (1976), 9–36.

[DD86]   DITTRICH, K.; DAYAL, U. (eds.): 1986 Int. Workshop on Object-Oriented Database Systems, Pacific Grove (CA), Proceedings. – IEEE Computer Society Press, Washington D. C. 1986.

[Di88]   DITTRICH, K. (ed.): Advances in Object-Oriented Database Systems. (Proc. 2nd Int. Workshop on Object-Oriented Database Systems, Bad Münster am Stein). – Springer, Berlin 1988.

[ELNR88]   EHRICH, H.-D.; LOHMANN, F.; NEUMANN, K.; RAMM, I.: A Database Language for Scientific Map Data. – In [Vi88b], 139–152.

[ESW88]   ERBE, R.; SÜDKAMP, N.; WALCH, G.: An Application Program Interface for a Complex Object Database. – Proc. 3rd Int. Conf. on Data and Knowledge Bases, Jerusalem 1988.

[Gu84]   GUTTMAN, A.: R-Trees – A Dynamic Index Structure for Spatial Searching. – Proc. ACM SIGMOD Annual Meeting, Boston 1984; SIGMOD Record 14:2 (1984), 47–57.

[Gü89]   GÜTING, R. H.: Gral: An Extensible Relational Database System for Geometric Applications. – In [AW89], 33–44.

[GW89]   GÜNTHER, O., WONG, E.: The Arc Tree: An Approximation Scheme to Represent Arbitrary Curved Shapes. – Proc. 3rd Int. Conf. Foundations of Data Organization and Algorithms (FODO), Paris 1989; LITWIN, W./ SCHEK, H.-J. (eds.); Springer, Heidelberg 1989, 354–370.

[HG88]   HOHENSTEIN, U.; GOGOLLA, M.: A Calculus for an Extended Entity-Relationship Model Incorporating Arbitrary Data Operations and Aggregate Functions. – Proc. 7th Int. Conf. on Entity-Relationship Approach; BATINI, C. (ed.); North Holland, Amsterdam 1988, 1–20.

[HSW88]   HUTFLESZ, A.; SIX, H.-W.; WIDMAYER, P.: Twin Grid Files – Space Optimizing Access Schemes. – Proc. ACM SIGMOD Int. Conf. on Management of Data, Chicago 1988; SIGMOD Record 17:3 (1988), 183–190.

[HSW89]   HENRICH, A.; SIX, H.-W.; WIDMAYER, P.: The LSD-Tree: Spatial Access to Multidimensional Point and Non-point Objects. – In [AW89], 45–54.

[HSWW88]   HORN, D.; SCHEK, H.-J.; WATERFELD, W.; WOLF, A.: Spatial Access Paths and Physical Clustering in a Low-Level Geo-Database System. – In [Vi88b], 123–138.

[LG86]   LISKOV, G.; GUTTAG, J.: Abstraction and Specification in Program Development. – MIT Press, Cambridge (Mass.) 1986.

[LN87]   LIPECK, U. W.; NEUMANN, K.: Modelling and Manipulating Objects in Geoscientific Databases. – In: Entity-Relationship Approach: Ten Years of Experience in Information Modelling (Proc. 5th Int. Conf. on the Entity-Relationship Approach, Dijon 1986); SPACCAPIETRA, S. (ed.); North-Holland, Amsterdam 1987, 67–86.

193

[Lo88]   LOHMANN, F.: Processing Non-Standard Database Objects in a Higher Level Programming Language – An Abstract Data Type Approach. – Proc. Int. Workshop on Software Engineering and its Applications, Toulouse 1988, 1141–1159.

[LP83]   LACROIX, M.; PIROTTE, A.: Comparison of Database Interfaces for Application Programming. – Information Systems 8:3 (1983), 217–229.

[Ma83]   MAIER, D.: The Theory of Relational Databases. – Pitman, London 1983.

[NHS84]   NIEVERGELT, J.; HINTERBERGER, H.; SEVCIK, K.C.: The Grid File – An Adaptable Symmetric Multikey File Structure. – ACM Transactions on Database Systems 9:1 (1984), 38–71.

[PM88]   PECKHAM, J.; MARYANSKI, F.: Semantic Data Models. – ACM Computing Surveys 20 (1988), 153–189.

[PSSW87]   PAUL, H.-B.; SCHEK, H.-J.; SCHOLL, M.H.; WEIKUM, G.; DEPPISCH, U.: Architecture and Implementation of the Darmstadt Database Kernel System. – Proc. ACM SIGMOD Annual Conference, San Francisco 1987; DAYAL, U./ TRAIGER, I. (eds.); SIGMOD Record 16:3 (1987), 196–207.

[RS87]   ROWE, L.A.; STONEBRAKER, M.: The POSTGRES Data Model. – Proc. 13th Conf. on Very Large Data Bases, Brighton 1987; STOCKER, P. M./ KENT, W./ HAMMERSLEY, P. (eds.). Morgan Kaufmann Publishers, Los Altos (CA) 1987, 83–96.

[Sa84]   SAMET, H.: The Quadtree and Related Hierarchical Data Strutures. ACM Computing Surveys 16:2 (1984), 187–260.

[ScS86]   SCHEK, H.-J.; SCHOLL, M.H.: The Relational Model with Relational-Valued Attributes. – Information Systems 11 (1986), 113–133.

[SW86]   SCHEK, H.-J.; WATERFELD, W.: A Database Kernel System for Geoscientific Applications. – Proc. 2nd Int. Symp. on Spatial Data Handling, Seattle 1986, 273–288.

[SWKH76]   STONEBRAKER, M.; WONG, E.; KREPS, P.; HELD, G.: The Design and Implementation of INGRES. – ACM Transactions on Database Systems 1 (1976), 198–222.

[TRE88]   THOMAS, P. M.; ROBINSON, H.; EMMS, J.: Abstract Data Types – Their Specification, Representation and Use. – Oxford University Press, Oxford 1988.

[Vi88a]   VINKEN, R.: Digital Geoscientific Maps – A Research Project of the Deutsche Forschungsgemeinschaft (German Research Foundation). – In [Vi88b], 7–20.

[Vi88b]   VINKEN, R. (ed.): Construction and Display of Geoscientific Maps derived from Databases (Proc. Int. Coll. Dinkelsbühl 1986). – Geologisches Jahrbuch A104, 1988, Hannover.

[WWH88]   WATERFELD, W.; WOLF, A.; HORN, D. U.: How to Make Spatial Access Methods Extensible? – Proc. 3rd Int. Symp. on Spatial Data Handling, Sydney 1988, 321–335.

The Arrival of
IRDS Standards

D J L Gradwell

Data Dictionary Systems Limited

Abstract

CASE tools place a new set of requirements on data dictionary (or Information Resource Dictionary System) design. An open architecture is needed to enable a variety of CASE tools to share information in an IRDS. The range of tools that any one site may wish to use will come from more than one vendor. Thus standards for IRDS are necessary.

The author is Rapporteur (Chairman) of both the International Standards Organisation's Information Resource Dictionary Systems Rapporteur Group, part of ISO/IEC SC21/WG3 responsible for all database standards and of the British Standards Institution's IRDS Panel Rapporteur Group. The author is Editor of the ISO IRDS Framework that is shortly to be published as IS10027.

1. CASE Tools and Information Resource Dictionary Systems

The market for CASE tools has expanded very dramatically in the last two years. Central to any complete CASE tool is a dictionary, sometimes known as a repository or Information Resource Dictionary System (IRDS). CASE tools place a much higher demand on dictionary facilities for storing information than has been supported by some of the older dictionary products. This is because a CASE tool needs its data to be better structured and accessible with high performance. Further, CASE tool users are demanding products that share the same dictionary over a local area network. Thus there is the possibility that CASE Tool dictionaries will overtake some of the older mainframe based dictionaries as repositories of analysis and design information.

The key problems that such tools bring are those of complexity of data structure and of distribution of analysis and design data. Both DP staff and vendors are keen to exploit workstations with large screens with high resolution graphics. It is becoming technically possible to build good dictionaries on such workstations. However, the need is not for stand-alone systems, but for the support of multiple projects each with many analysts and designers.

In order to meet the need for sharing of information between CASE Tools a lot of work has been going on in the IRDS standards arena. This paper describes the work by both the American National Standards Institute (ANSI) and the International Standards Organisation (ISO) to develop standards for Information resource Dictionary Systems.

In addition, IBM are developing their own 'repository' interface. Any realist will see the possibility of a de-facto 'IBM standard' emerging from this situation. Further, Digital are developing a counter interface to the IBM work. This then raises the possibility of there being four 'standards' for IRDS, one from ANSI, one from ISO, one from Digital and one from IBM. Both vendors appear to be seeking to replace the existing ANSI work by their own.

In the author's view only a strong series of ISO standards will bring cohesion to this fragmenting marketplace. This paper examines these developments in some detail.

2. Scattered Dictionaries

The result of the trend towards CASE tools mounted on powerful micro-computers, coupled with a diversity of hardware and dictionaries supplied by mainframe vendors, is that many organisations now have a confusion of data dictionaries with a few weak links between them. Figure 1 shows a few of the products and links that one finds. Several of these often appear in one organisation.

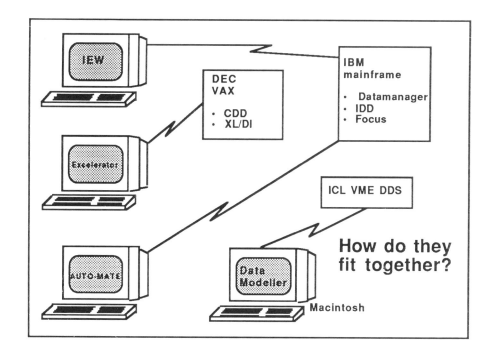

Fig 1: Multiple, scattered Dictionaries

Clearly many organisations wish to exploit a variety of products, but would much prefer one dictionary with good links to all the different tools. Only by developing standards for dictionary content and the access to that content can this be achieved.

3. Goals of Standardisation

In this paper we examine the progress so far and the progress expected in the future in the development of standards for Information Resource Dictionary Systems and their relevance to the development of the practical use of CASE tools. Some of the problems are examined and where available, possible solutions identified.

In the author's view, it is essential that the IRDS standards are aimed at the needs of the 1990's and beyond. Whereas the data dictionaries of the late 1970's were syntax driven and fairly stand-alone, the data dictionaries of the 1990's will be central repositories accessed by many kinds of man machine interfaces. Some of these interfaces will be analysis support systems, some will help the designer. Yet others will generate database design or program code and some will assist the operational running of systems. This span of tools covers the CASE market and beyond. The tools will clearly come from many vendors but will share certain information. The role of standardisation is to make this fitting together and sharing of information possible.

Some will argue that it is possible for one vendor to produce an integrated product set and that hence there is no need for a dictionary standard. The author notes that a few products do indeed span much of the project development life cycle for one or two environments. Such products are to be applauded. However, reality in many companies consists of diverse hardware, a range of operating systems, different database management systems of varying vintages, a scattering of data dictionaries and a plethora of application generators. Such confusion is now being added to by a range of CASE tools. Reality is that this diversity of systems must exchange analysis and design information if we are to overcome the inefficiencies of current application development.

4.   ANSI

Between 1978 and 1984, the American National Standards Institute (ANSI) X3/H4 committee developed a 1200 page specification of an IRDS Command Language Interface and a Panel Interface. Part of the reason that this document was so large and complex is that it specifies a data modelling facility that is different from any other. When work started on the document the relational versus network model debate was raging. It must have seemed to X3/H4 to be the right thing to do to choose a different model, unrelated to either the relational or the network models. Now however, with considerable hindsight, we can see that it would have been better to have chosen either one of these two carefully thought out and well specified data modelling facilities, or the other, than to start again and come up with something weaker. Both NDL and SQL have reached ISO standard status and are well understood. The SQL model is extremely strongly supported by ANSI X3/H2, the ANSI SQL committee. The ANSI X3/H4 IRDS Committee's model and its limitations are however is not so well understood. The ANSI X3/H4 model is similar to that supported by the TOTAL database management system in that it is not possible to model multi-level structures. However, it is even more limited. Only binary relationships with attributes are supported. This combines with the X3/H4 IRDS naming rules that do not allow concatenation of attributes to build up identifiers.

It is important to understand why this is a significant problem. Consider figure 2, which shows a typical stock control data model. This model exhibits both multi-level hierarchies and networks. Typically, *stock* would be identified by part number and warehouse id, taken together. In the relational model *stock* would be a table. In the network model, *stock* would be a record, related by sets. In the entity relationship model commonly used in the United Kingdom and in the USA by products such as the Information Engineering Workbench and the Information Engineering Facility and in the CCTA's SSADM[1], *stock* would be represented by an Entity related by relationships to *Part* and *Warehouse*. In the X3/H4 model, *stock* would be represented by a relationship with appropriate attributes.

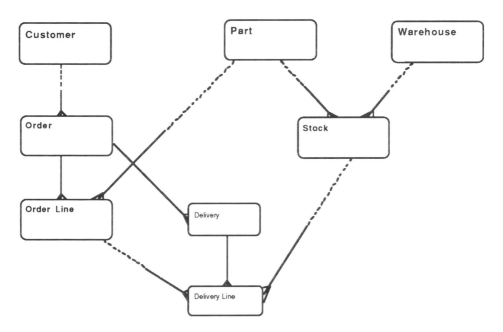

Fig 2: Typical stock control data model showing multi-level hierarchies and networks

When we then come to add in *delivery line* it is simple in all the above mentioned models, except the X3/H4 model, where it is not possible.

This example is an example at the Information Resource Dictionary (IRD) Level (the concept of levels is explained more fully in section 7 of this paper) rather than at the Information Resource Dictionary Definition level. The example was chosen at this level for ease of explanation and comprehension. Nevertheless, it is important to say:

---

[1] The Central Computer and Telecommunications Agency developed their Structured Systems Analysis and Design Method (SSADM) which has now gained wide acceptance in the UK and other markets.

a) because of the extensible nature of the emerging IRDS standards, **any** methodology can be supported at the IRD level. If a particular user wishes to use a particular complex or simplistic methodology he is rightly free to do that.

b) at the IRD definition level we face a database design task. An IRD is one of the most complex applications one can envisage. Precision in IRD data structure specification is extremely important if we are to be able to share design data amongst many software products. Stability of those data structures is also essential. The relational model lends itself well to addition of new data without perturbing existing structures. The ANSI model is weak in this respect. In the example of figure 2, if we designed *stock* as a relationship and a later designer wished to add delivery line, this would be easy with the relational model. With the ANSI model it would be impossible without changing a relationship to an entity, with the consequent impact on the programs using that information.

Similar examples of data structuring do of course appear in the design of the data structures for an Information Resource Dictionary. Figure 3 shows a structure to be found in two current commercial dictionaries.

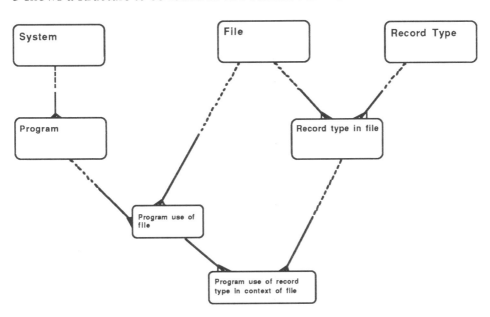

Fig 3: Example of the use of multi-level hierarchies and networks in the IRD to show context dependent information

This example clearly shows that an IRDS designer needs the full data structuring power to be found in SQL in order to be able to specify IRDS data structures.

ANSI offered their specification to ISO but agreement could not be reached because of the problems mentioned above.

Nevertheless, the ANSI work is now an ANSI standard (X.138). ANSI have also developed an IRDS Services Interface (the different kinds of interfaces will be described later in this paper in section 7) for CASE tool builders to use. Indeed, some of the ISO work on an IRDS Services Interface is based upon the ANSI X3/H4 work.

5.   IBM

IBM have been working for several years on a 'repository'. At first the task of producing a data structure to support the complete development cycle seemed beyond comprehension. Although the early work was narrowed in scope to make it implementable, the product now seems to have been broadened again to meet the needs of the methodology oriented European market and the rapidly developing requirements of CASE tools.

Although all will not be clear until IBM publish the final specifications, it appears that many CASE tools will be able interface to the repository. Now that IBM have launched the Repository, the level of detailed information available will increase rapidly over the next few months. It is believed that a number of CASE tool vendors are co-operating with IBM so as to have interfaces between their products and the repository available soon after the repository is available. By the time of BNCOD-8 more detailed specifications may be available in the public domain.

IBM offered a cut down version of their repository interface to the ANSI X3/H4 and ISO IRDS meetings in 1989. Neither body have yet made a formal response. The IBM repository interface is interesting in that it offers a hierarchical view of an underlying network data structure. This is similar in concept to IBM's IMS product. Such an interface might make it easier to retrieve information efficiently from an IRDS and with a high degree of data independence. However, a program updating the dictionary would still have to deal with the underlying structure. Once the work on the IBM Repository is more publically available, we will be able to better assess what IBM have offered to ANSI and ISO. At present it appears that it is only a portion of the full repository interface specification. It is also not clear how it would fit in with existing ISO and ANSI work.

The ISO IRDS Rapporteur Group noted that IBM are likely to build the repository on top of a relational database. In the ISO discussion of the IBM proposal the question was asked as to whether this kind of hierarchical view of data would be equally useful (or not) for application data as well. Perhaps the interface should be proposed as an interface to SQL as well.

6. Digital

Digital Equipment Corporation have been working with a USA company called Atherton to develop a tools interface. This has resulted in the Atherton Backplane, now renamed ATIS or A Tools Interface Standard.

ATIS is a programmatic interface to a dictionary. The concepts in ATIS are somewhat different from those in either the ANSI work or the IBM Repository. The model is very object oriented. Figure 4 shows the key ATIS concepts modelled using standard entity modelling conventions.

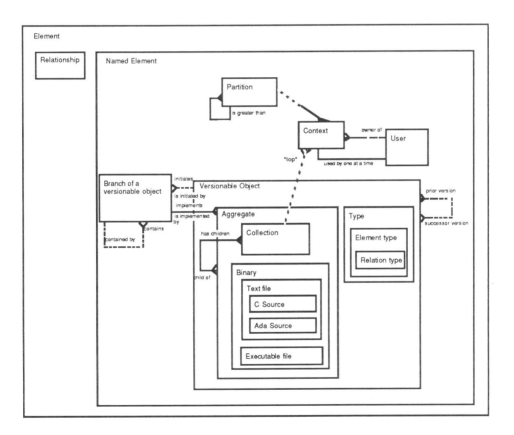

Fig 4: A model of the ATIS Concepts

203

In the author's view, some of the ATIS concepts match well with what is already in the emerging ISO IRDS Services Interface. The object oriented facilities of ATIS should be added to the IRDS Services Interface as an addendum or a revision to the current work.

However, the ATIS document is weaker than SQL in its data structuring approach and thus the best concepts of ATIS should be added to the ISO work rather than replacing it with something weaker.

ANSI have stated that the ATIS document is the basis for their future work. This brings in to question the status of the current X.138 standard since the two are not clearly reconcilable.

However, the ATIS concepts may lead to the development of a path forward to reconcile the ISO and ANSI differences.

7. ISO

The emerging International Standards Organisation (ISO) work on IRDS standards is concentrating on the following areas:

- The IRDS Framework;

- The IRDS Services Interface;

- Export/Import; and

- IRDS Support for the ISO SQL standard

The IRDS Framework has now been approved for advancement to an International Standard and has been sent to Geneva for publication. The ISO IRDS Framework defines an architecture for extensibility, based on a four level architecture shown in Figure 5.

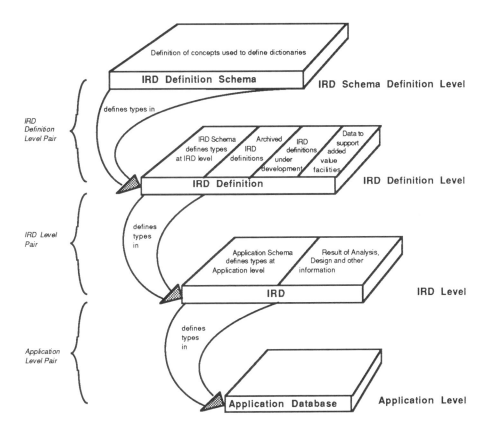

Fig 5: IRDS Levels

Figure 5 shows the following four levels:

- the Fundamental level;
- the IRD Definition level;
- the IRD level;
- the Application level.

In addition there are three level pairs, each of which consists of a higher data level and a lower data level:

- the IRD Definition level pair;
- the IRD level pair;
- the Application level pair.

It should be noted that the name of each pair is based on the lower of the two data levels comprising the level pair.

An understanding of data levels and level pairs is critical to an understanding of how an IRD related to its environment and of how an IRDS provides the services defined in the standard.

Concepts of Types and Instances

Before discussing the data levels and level pairs and describing them in more detail, it is useful to review the basic concept of "type" and "instance" (also referred to also as "occurrence").

The idea of types and instances is well established in many programming languages and in database management systems. A "type" of data, such as an EMPLOYEE is defined either in a program or, in the case of a DBMS, in a separate language used for defining data. This definition of a type of data essentially creates an open-ended container. Sometimes this container is identified as a record type, sometimes as a table, and sometimes in other ways. A container is of relevance even when it is empty. It is important to note that the term "container" is used here in the sense of a "logical container" rather than in the alternative sense of a "physical container". (A drum or a diskette is an example of a physical container).

Application programs, which may be separate from the data definition or may embrace it, will refer to EMPLOYEE in their executable code. When such programs are executing, they will subsequently cause data about specific EMPLOYEES (each of which is an instance of the type referenced) to be stores in a file or in a data base.

When data about a specific EMPLOYEE needs to be accessed, it is necessary to refer to the type of data in a program. In this case, the type of data would be EMPLOYEE. Subsequently, when a program is executing, it will pick out one or more specific instances of the type.

These instances might, for example, be the EMPLOYEE records for J Smith and P L Jones. If EMPLOYEE refers to a table, not a record, then there should be rows in this table for J Smith and P L Jones. In either case, EMPLOYEE is the "type" and data about J Smith and P L Jones are examples of "instances of this type".

The preceding explanation should not be difficult to follow by anyone with a previous exposure to basic data processing concepts. The terminology used to refer to these basic concepts in various sub-cultures of data processing varies. Nevertheless, the underlying concept is the same and pre-dates the advent of data processing technology by some considerable time.

Level Pairs

The concept of an application program in its source form referencing a defined type of data, such as EMPLOYEE, and when executing accessing an instance of that type provides the basis for understanding the concept of "level pair". One could claim that all data belongs on a single level. However, in general parlance, the description of any piece of data is always regarded as being on a level "above" that of the level of the data itself.

Carrying the example of the previous section further, if it is necessary to find out information about P L Jones, it helps to know that he is an EMPLOYEE rather than, say, a SUPPLIER or a CUSTOMER. The program is written to refer to EMPLOYEE. The selection of P L Jones, as opposed to any other instance of EMPLOYEE, is controlled by the logic of the program and by parameter values referred to by the program.

The important fact is that the source program refers to concepts on the "type" level, such as EMPLOYEE. When the program is executing, it affects (in some sense) data on the associated "instance" level. When discussing what a program does and how it works, it is necessary to refer to a level pair.

In traditional data processing, there is only one level pair. This is the one referred to in Figure 4 as the Application Level Pair. It is the addition of two more level pairs that gives the IRDS its broad and powerful extensibility.

IRDS Interfaces

The IRDS Framework identifies a number of interfaces as shown in Figure 6.

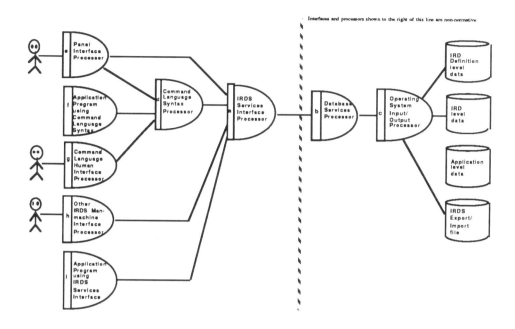

Fig 6: Major IRDS Processor Interfaces

This architecture shows both human user (lettered e, g and h in figure 5) and programmatic interfaces. From the CASE tool developer's perspective it is the programmatic interfaces that matter. These are the interfaces he will use to write his product so that it can access a common dictionary and thus share design data with other products. In particular, the CASE tool vendor will use the IRDS Services Interface (lettered a in the figure).

Status of the current work

The IRDS Framework has now been recommended for advancement to the status of an International Standard and is expected to be published by ISO in the next few months.

The IRDS Services Interface is still at Working Draft stage, but is expected to be recommended for registration as a Draft Proposal in 1990.

One of the key issues that has been debated is the choice of data modelling approach to be adopted. The choice is between using SQL entirely or taking a more object oriented approach. Currently the draft text uses SQL with some object oriented extensions. In this short paper it is not possible to discuss all the aspects involved in this debate. We are also discussing the differences between the PCTE object model and the ATIS object model. Anyone interested in contributing to these important discussions, which ultimately will shape the CASE tool industry is invited to contact the author to arrange to attend the regular British Standards Institution's meetings.

Work on an ISO Command Language and Panel interface is suspended until the IRDS Services Interface, upon which these depend, reaches DIS status.

7. Summary

The development of data dictionary standards is a very difficult task. This is perhaps the first true database application to be standardised and possibly the most complex application for which a standard will ever be attempted. This paper has outlined some of the problems and set out a way forward where possible. It is important that we achieve adequate IRDS standards if the need for integrated CASE tools and active dictionaries is to be met. In the author's view these form an essential part of the drive both for Open Systems and for better productivity in application development.

If we are to avoid the possibility of a range of conflicting standards that limit our ability to make software products interwork, I believe that we as purchasers must put our weight behind the ISO standard. If not, the only standard to survive will be the IBM standard running on IBM mainframe hardware.

A Modelling Paradigm for Retrieval of Office Documents

Augusto Celentano[1], Maria Grazia Fugini[1,2], Silvano Pozzi[3]

(1) Dipartimento di Automazione Industriale, Università di Brescia
(2) Dipartimento di Elettronica, Politecnico di Milano
(3) CEFRIEL, Milano

Abstract

Modern information retrieval systems share with expert systems a knowledge based approach to document modelling. Document classification and indexation based on lexicon and thesauri are inadequate to support complex queries about documents in office environments: operational dependencies, documents relationships and references to regulations and laws require direct access to the document semantics and knowledge about concepts which are not explicitly stated in the text. This paper discusses the guidelines for the development of a suitable semantic model for office documents classification and retrieval.

1. Introduction

The computer assisted management of documents in office automation applications is built on two platforms. At one side there are the concrete properties of documents, that is the shape, the layout and the graphical attributes: they are transformed by text processing programs which do not access the meaning of the embodied information. At the other side there are the semantic properties, that is the concepts expressed: little processing can be automatically done with current technology but for very narrow application domain.

Nevertheless, most of the processing of documents is related to the classification of documents for subsequent retrieval: this requires a deeper insight into the information meaning, because the lexical and structural properties are not appropriate to describe at the required level of accuracy the purpose, the relationships with the procedures and the environment, the dependencies from the domain rules, that is the semantics of documents.

210

It is important to introduce a distinction between the goal of a retrieval system, because sometimes the document and the information contained in it are items oriented to different purposes. Therefore we will use the term *information retrieval* to denote the retrieval, from a heterogeneous and unstructured database, of pieces of information whose presence, number, and relevance are not a priori known; they can be whole documents or fragments, as the goal of the search is the information itself, independently of where it is found. Conversely, we will use the term *document retrieval* to denote the retrieval of specific documents and document types from a document database whose structure is related to a particular application environment; the goal of the search are the documents themselves.

Typical information retrieval queries are oriented to bibliographic searches, such as "retrieve the articles about Information Retrieval in Office Automation submitted to international conferences in the last two years", while typical document retrieval queries are concerned with office procedures, such as "retrieve the budget approval forms for projects carried by the Research Department during the last year".

In this paper we discuss the main features a document model must have in order to constitute the basis of a document retrieval system able to answer queries related both to the application domain and the procedural context where documents are used. We propose a knowledge based approach to document modelling and we give rationale for such a choice. In particular we can notice that the model of this kind has to comprise three basic types of knowledge, namely: (1) knowledge about the structure of documents, (2) knowledge about the relationships among concepts and documents, among documents, and among documents and procedures which produces or uses them, (3) knowledge about the relationships among documents and laws and regulations (either internal or external to the application domain) which constitute the theoretical and pratical basis for document existence.

2. Related works

The use of knowledge based techniques in information retrieval is not new; in fact, knowledge based techniques are used in query processing, natural language understanding, text understanding and classification, to augment the identification of text contents, but little attention has been devoted to the modelling of documents as semantic components of office procedures [5].

In RUBRIC [13], production rules are used to map semantic concepts used for retrieval into text patterns. The goal of the system is to provide more automated and relevant access to unformatted textual databases.

211

The idea of retrieval as an inference process is exploited in the OFFICER system [7], according to the approach proposed in [17]. Indeed the system treats retrieval as a process of plausible inference and uncertainty is part both of query specification and of the process of the query-document matching. The user is presented with a ranked list of documents satisfying his query, each document being labelled with a degree of relevance with respect to the presented information needs. Ranking strategies for documents are also described in [10]: document descriptions are improved by repeatedly performing the description process basing on observation of the inquirers' requests. The idea of document re-description according to system adaptative capabilities of learning, for example using alternate search terms or modified relevance weights, has been variously investigated (for example in [2] and [9]).

In some other systems, a database is used to support document storage and retrieval, exploiting database mechanisms such as transaction management, back-up, concurrency control. In these systems, information in a document is seen as partially structured to simplify management and retrieval. An example is given in [6], where basic search and retrieval capabilities of traditional information retrieval systems are coupled with database search mechanism: a document manipulation language is defined to query the document base, on which keyword indexes are constructed. In [11], indexing technique for document retrieval on top of the INGRES database system are described.

Knowledge based classification of documents and automatic identification of the conceptual document structure is discussed in [8]. In [18] analogy between expert systems and retrieval systems is discussed: an information structure called concept space is introduced and a semantic model is defined to use the knowledge contained in such a concept space. The paper [16] presents a knowledge based browser that helps users to access a statistical database through a semantic model of the domain.

3. Document modelling requirements for retrieval

Document retrieval aims at identifying documents whose contents match the meaning required by the user (figure 1). From a logical point of view the document retrieval process consists of the following steps:

- semantic document modelling, which produces the conceptual document;
- elaboration of user's information needs, to produce a set of semantic properties needed;
- match between the two sematic representation to possibly obtain the required documents.

212

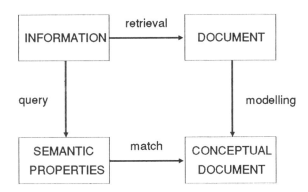

Fig. 1. A conceptual schema of information retrieval

In office environments the relationships between contents and semantics are often complex, since they heavily depend on the way in which the documents are used, and on the reasons that justify them in specific procedures. In particular, document retrieval system should consider two different cases: in the former case the semantics carried by a document is completely described by its contents, that is the document alone is sufficient to identify its purpose and the role it plays in a specific office procedure; in the second case the semantics carried by a document is mostly defined by its role in the office, by the relationships with other documents, and by the justifications provided by general rules such as regulations or law, information which is not contained in the document text.

The retrieval of information and documents in complex office environments relies in the two cases upon two different attitudes; indeed both require identification of documents carrying a specific meaning, but the selection of documents according to their roles in the office, rather than according to the content alone, requires a description at the conceptual level of the environment in which the document are used. Therefore a more thorough document model is needed which enables to consider objects like procedure, agents, temporal events and to express relationships among such objects and the documents itself.

Suggestions about the definition of such a model can come from the wide literature on office modelling [15]. On the other hand we argue that a whole office model is not needed since, for example, an office model describes in detail the execution flow of procedures and the rules for their activation, which do not concern directly the processing of documents.

A formal representation of the concepts associated with the life and the evolution of the documents allows one to design document retrieval systems which overcome the limits of traditional information systems, that is, the inability to process in the same way queries or navigations related to different targets: instances of documents ("retrieve all scientific paper about Information Retrieval and Office Systems"), types of documents ("what documents shall I submit to ask for a business trip"), document usage context ("retrieve the procedure which has output the financial plan"). While they appear, from a design point of view, related to three distinct types of information systems, from the user point of view they are very similar.

An example supporting the idea of knowledge based conceptual modeling in retrieval applications is the identification of the documents that are necessary to complete a particular procedure, say for example a contract with the Public Administration. This search has two apparently similar but very different facets: if the search concerns a procedure to be executed, the target is a set of document types (since they must be filled in with instances during the procedure execution), if the search concerns a specific procedure already completed, the target is a set of document instances.

In the former case it is obvious that traditional information retrieval techniques are not suitable; indeed, the search is closer to a database search (since the answer is a structured and short information, and concerns a domain, the types of the documents, which is classifiable in advance) or to an expert answering system query (if the office procedure involved is complex, and subjected to many logic constraints).

Also the latter case reveals a number of inadequacies in information retrieval based on text or tags: the knowledge about the relevance of a document as a component of a procedure is seldom described by the document itself. Registration numbers or classification codes that usually link documents cannot always guarantee that all relevant documents will be retrieved; external signatures or tags are usually restricted to code marks applied for classification purposes, unrelated to the deep knowledge about the document purpose; while it could be foreseen an extension of signatures to include this category of information, it seems to lead to a large growth of complexity.

4. Representation of knowledge and document modelling

The knowledge used by a system which aims at satisfying the document retrieval requirements above outlined, i.e. the capability to identify a document both through its specific meaning and according to its roles in office procedures, can be classified in *static knowledge* and *dynamic knowledge*. We call *static* the semantic information regarding the document types, the document contents, and the hierarchical relationships among document types and subtypes. We call *dynamic* the knowledge pertaining to the conceptual description of the domain to be considered. Such kind of knowledge includes also a description of the procedures in which documents are created and used; such description is limited to the features relevant to document retrieval.

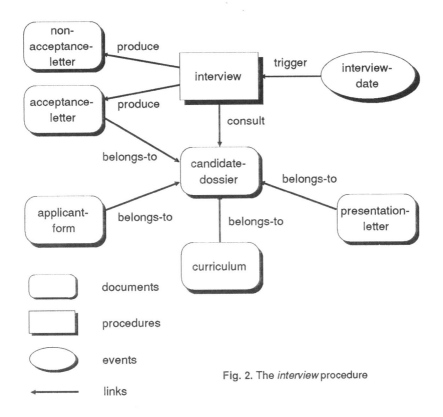

documents	
procedures	
events	
links	

Fig. 2. The *interview* procedure

In the following we illustrate a reference example which shows how such a knowledge can be represented. Then we describe the document retrieval model features; the model is illustrated on the reference example.

4.1 Reference example

The example refers to the student application procedure at the Master course of CEFRIEL, which is a research center supported by Industries, University and Public Administration in Milan. In figure 2 a graphical representation of the elements involved in the procedure is depicted. To join the master course an applicant must fill in a predefined applicant form, which can be requested to the secretary of CEFRIEL. Every filled applicant form arrived at the secretary causes a dossier to be opened: it contains the curriculum of the candidate, the presentation letter (if any) of a professor and other documents. The applicant is examined by a commission of professors to evaluate his capability: if the result of the examination is positive, the applicant is accepted at the course (an admittance letter is therefore send to him), otherwise a non-acceptance letter communicates to the candidate his failure. We focus our discussion

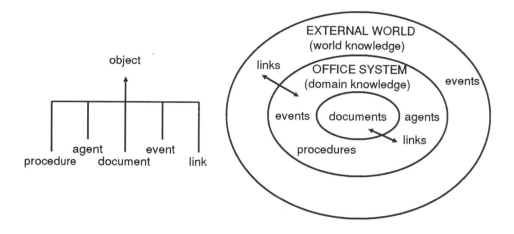

Fig. 3. (a) The basic elements of the model. (b) Scopes in the document retrieval model

on the interview phase during which the candidate is examined by the commission.

4.2 Document retrieval model

The document retrieval model can be described by an object oriented or frame based approach: frame slots can be used to describe structural aspects of schema based documents (such as sender, receiver, date and subject in a letter), concepts defined by prose text (such as curriculum and previous experiences in the presentation letter of our example), and strictly related document families (such as a dossier). The model describes also aspects relating to the behavior of a document considered alone, such as the update frequency or the lifetime; the procedural context where the documents are used is also modelled.

The basic elements of the document retrieval model are the following:

- procedure
- agent
- event
- document
- link.

These types are shown in figure 3a in a IS-A hierarchy of inheritance; the root element is the *object*.

The model obviously focuses the *document* element which is described in detail in its contents and structure. The other elements of the retrieval model are represented in as much detail as is needed for expliciting the relationships among documents. These relationships are modeled by the *link* object.

216

Figure 3b shows the environmental location of the elements in the retrieval model. The core is constituted by the *Documents* region. The Office System is modeled through procedures, events (facts whose occurrence trigger procedures, e.g., the decision of holding an interview on a certain date), and agents (roles of office workers that are relevant because they create, manipulate, transmit, etc. documents). *Links* are the bridge objects between the System and the Document worlds. Links exist also among system objects (e.g., between procedures) and are illustrated in the following of the paper.

The representation of the Office System is the representation of *domain knowledge* needed to allow users to retrieve documents basing on procedural elements (e.g. to issue a query like: "Retrieve all documents manipulated by the CEFRIEL Secretary when scheduling an interview"). The External World is modelled only using the *event* object to represent facts whose occurrence triggers office procedures on documents (*world knowledge*).

4.3 Static knowledge about documents

Any type of document in the office is modelled using a predefined set of basic objects (for instance document, letter, form and dossier) and exploiting typical class relationships (e.g. is-a, is-member, is-part relations) to establish classification hierarchies among documents in terms of specialization or membership. Any real document used in the office would then result in an instance of a particular class. In figure 4 the IS-A relationships which holds among the documents of the model are depicted. We have reported the document specializations that hold in the reference example.

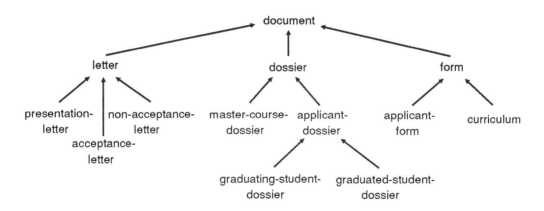

Fig. 4. The IS-A hierarchy of the reference example

217

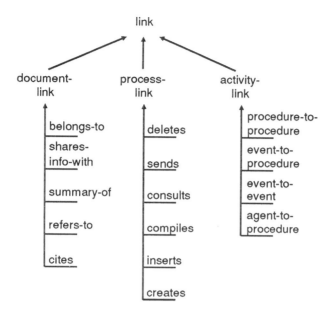

Fig. 5. The IS-A
hierarchy of the
link objects

Figure 5 shows the *link* object. *Document links* connect document pairs
to represent relationships between document contents and structures.
We have identified a set of predefined document links, as shown in figure
5; they can be further specialized in the IS-A hierarchy in order to be
tailored to specific application environments. In particular, the
is-neighbor-of links are used for navigation in the semantic network of
knowledge for retrieval purposes.

    Process links connect procedures and documents, therefore
connecting the Office System world and the Document world.
Considering the direction of the links to be from procedures to documents,
figure 5 shows a sample set of predefined system links. The inverse links
from documents to procedures also exist (e.g. is-input-of) but they are not
shown in the figure; inverse links allow a broader spectrum of queries
and navigations to be performed, such as "Retrieve documents that
contain a signature and are input of the applicant evaluation procedure".

    Activity links relate objects of the domain knowledge each other, i.e.
procedures with procedures, events with procedures (basically the
triggers predefined link), events to events and agents who are involved
in the execution of procedures.

    The *procedure-to-procedure* and the *event-to-event* link types of figure
5 represent mainly temporal relationships (e.g., before, after,
upon-completion) and causal relationships (e.g., derives-from,
is-caused-by).

4.4 Links and navigation

The *link* object is fundamental for navigating in the semantic network of the knowledge. This navigation is performed by a navigation tool. This tool, whose basic functionalities are presented in [5], is composed of a *browser* and of a *filter*; both components are based on the mechanism of link traversal and the link carries all the semantics necessary to explore the network nodes and to get orientation in the network (where am I, where have I been, where do I go from here) [16].

The *link* object has the following properties:

type	one of the types shown in figure 5
inverse	name of the inverse link type
status	traversed, to be traversed, being traversed, selected
presentation	graphical representation properties

The *status* property is used to discriminate among the actions that can be undertaken by a navigation tool, depending on the status of the links that are connected (depart or arrive) to the *current node* of the network (the node that has been reached in the navigation and is being explored). In particular, the *selected* value of the status means that the information associated to a link has been considered interesting by the user and therefore moved to a workarea for further elaboration and search.

The *presentation* property describes how the link appears on the screen, according to its type. For example, IS-A links are shown by displaying the parent and the children objects: the presentation property describes the number of descendants in the IS-A hierarchy that are to be shown, how to see the parents and children properties, which information is maintained on the screen when scrolling up and down the hierarchy.

Default presentations are given for predefined link types; however, the mechanism should be flexible enough to allow the system administrators to define the presentation modes for new link types.

4.5 Dynamic knowledge about document relationships

The relationships among documents and the procedural properties associated to their meaning can be formalized through a network based model (for example, a semantic net or a hypertext with typed links). Since documents are objects created and accessed by activities (operations, tasks, procedures), the network includes procedures, events and agents. This network relates objects of the model through the link types described previously. Every kind of link connects specific classes of entity, that is, every entity has a set of applicable links. Such assumption assigns a "strong" semantics to links, needed to navigate in such a complex structure. As shown before, links are objects with a class hierarchy and contain semantic information. Every link which can be established between documents (e.g. belongs-to, which links a document to a dossier; is-answer-to, which links two documents and so on) are document links. Every link which can be drawn between a document and a procedure (e.g. is-created-by, is-consulted-by) belongs to the process link class, while every link which connects two procedures (for example to establish temporal relationships) belongs to the activity link class.

Figure 2 is a sample of such a network model; the *interview* node represents a procedure, while the *interview date* node represents an event. Documents involved in the procedure are shown.

4.6 General knowledge about domain rules

The rules of the application domain which concern the role of the documents, and help in describing their meaning, constitute a layer of knowledge connected to the static and dynamic layers. A production rule approach seems suitable to describe relationships and constraints among concept: cause-effect dependencies, implication, generalization, exclusion. Such dependencies can be established in a simple and consistent way also among concepts stated in documents which are not directly connected in the network.

An example of a rule stating the possibility that an applicant can be issued a scholarship during the Master course is the following one (informally phrased):

> *if x is a Master student and his/her age is under 25*
> *then x must certificate he/she is unemployed*

Such rule concerns the documents which must be provided by the applicant, and it can be seen as a link to a more general law stated by the European Community, which governs the issue of scholarships.

Besides the office procedure context, such approach seems to be relevant in legal systems, but also technical environments of quality assurance, certification, definition and evaluation of standards benefit from a view of documents in terms of meaningful components of operational procedures. A simple but common example of retrieval based on operational meaning is to find all documents which must be processed to complete a specific office procedure (such as a store inventory); all the documents whose usage is dictated by operative rules and regulations must be retrieved, even if they do not mention the store inventory problem at all. Another example is derived from the treatment of laws and regulations, and allows one to retrieve documents which must be revised because a specific law has changed (this problem has been addressed in [4] in the domain of automated document generation); the

220

influence of a law on the set of documents handled in an office is far from being straightforward, especially in contexts inspired by main principles of law rather than by specific detailed regulations.

5. Final remarks

The usage of a document modelling paradigm based on knowledge representation is suitable for covering the requirements of retrieval systems in terms of accuracy and usability, and for covering a broad spectrum of situations typical of office environments. Beyond the information retrieval applications, additional benefits are gained in terms of understandability, uniformity of representation, and generalization to multimedia systems; a brief discussion of each of these items will point out the most relevant features.

The use of semantic modelling techniques for the conceptual description of documents has the advantage that the representation of the document is understandable also to non experts; instead of relying upon the use of a specific jargon, it is a way to assign a precise and unambiguous meaning to words and phrases, conventionally selected but formally used. Of course the model must be completed with a dictionary defining the asserted meaning in human understandable form. As a by-product, there is no need for synonym processing, each concept being expressed by exactly one piece of knowledge (for instance, a logic predicate).

The reasoning based on implication and logic inference allows one to approach the problem of identifying documents, procedures, and operational requirements in a uniform way: the retrieval of "documents needed for completing a specific dossier", of "documents to be issued before a specific date", of "documents concerning a specific topic", are several facets of a unique semantic characterization which focuses, in different cases, on procedural, operational or informative meaning.

As illustrated in the paper, the benefits of a knowledge based approach come up mainly from the operational and domain specific aspects: in those areas knowledge based techniques enforce uniform management of different kinds of information, good modularization and incremental update of the information system.

The proposed approach is also convenient for multimedia environments; these require a normalization phase in order to retrieve the documents in a way that does not depend on the appearance of the specific information: the conceptual modelling provides normalization through the identification of a unique language to represent different kinds of knowledge, hence different kinds of information.

References

1 E. Bertino, F. Rabitti, and S. Gibbs, Query processing in a multimedia document system, *ACM Trans. on Office Information Systems*, 6, 1, 1988.

2 T. Brauen, Document vector modification, in G. Salton, SMART Retrieval System Experiments in Automatic Document Processing, *Prentice-Hall*, 1975.

3 Brodie M., Mylopolous J., Schimdt H.J., On Conceptual Modelling: Perspectives from Artificial Intelligence, Databases, and Programming Languages, *Springer-Verlag*, 1984.

4 A. Celentano, P. Paolini, Knowledge Based Document Generation, in W. Lamersdorf, Office Knowledge: Representation, Management and Utilization, *Elsevier Science Publ. Co., North-Holland*, 1988.

5 A. Celentano, M.G. Fugini, S. Pozzi, Semantic Retrieval of Documents: a Framework for a Knowledge-based System, *AICA Conference*, Trieste, October 1989.

6 C. Clifton, H. Garcia-Molina, and R. Hagmann, The design of a document database, *Princeton Univ., Dept. of Comp. Sc. Int. Rep. CS-TR-177-88*, Sept. 1988.

7 W.B. Croft, R. Krovetz Interactive retrieval of office documents, *Proc. ACM-IEEE Conf. on Office Information Systems*, Palo Alto, March 1988.

8 H. Eirund, K. Kreplin, Knowledge Based Document Classification Supporting Integrated Document Handling, *Proc. ACM Conference on Office Information Systems*, Palo Alto, 1988.

9 G.W. Furnas, Experience with an adaptative indexing scheme, *Proc. ACM-SIGCHI Conf. on Human Factors in Comp. Sytems.*, S. Francisco, 1985.

10 M. Gordon, Probabilistic and genetic algorithms in document retrieval, *Comm. ACM*, 31, 10, 1988.

11 C.A. Lynch, M. Stonebraker, Extended user-defined indexing with application to textual databases, *Proc. 14th VLDB Conf.*, Los Angeles, 1988.

12 G. Marchionini, and B. Schneiderman, Finding facts vs. browsing knowledge in hypertext systems, *IEEE Computer*, 1, 1988.

13 B. P. Mc Cune, R. M. Tong, J. Dean, D. G. Shapiro, RUBRIC: A System for Rule-Based Information Retrieval, *IEEE Transactions on Software Engineering*, SE-11, 9, 1985.

14 J. Peckham, and F. Maryanski, Semantic data models, *ACM Comp. Surveys*, 20, 3, 1988.

15 B. Pernici, A.A. Verrijin-Stuart (editor), Office Information Systems: the design process, *North-Holland*, 1989.

16 D. Schwabe, E. E. Mizutani, A knowledge based browser to access complex databases, submitted to the *International Conference on Extending Database Technology*, Venice, March 1990.

17 C.J. Van Rijsbergen, A non-classical logic for information retrieval, *Computer Journal*, 29, 1986.

18 C. R. Watters, Logic framework for information retrieval, *Journ. of the American Soc. for Information Science*, 40, 5, 1989.

Trail Management in Hypertext: Database Support for Navigation through Textual Complex Objects

T.J. Sillitoe[1], B.N. Rossiter[1] & M.A. Heather[2]

[1] Computing Laboratory, Newcastle University,.
Newcastle upon Tyne, England NE1 7RU

[2] Sutherland Building, Newcastle Polytechnic,
Newcastle upon Tyne NE1 8ST

Abstract

The hypermedium is an information space filled with heterogeneous data and relationships. Present attention is focused on manipulating its human computer interface for a limited sub-class of mainly textual and pictorial data held in documentary form as chunks. This paper describes the benefits of present database technology for aiding the implementation of hypertext systems. In particular, a system implementing the storage, retrieval and recall of trails through hypertext comprising textual complex objects is described and discussed. Useful enhancements are discussed including the potential of object-oriented database systems for handling the complex modelling required.

1. Background

To introduce this work, the nature of hypertext systems will be briefly reviewed, the idea of recording trails or paths that users make through hypertext as fully-fledged data structures will be developed and the strengths and weaknesses of database systems in manipulating textual data will be discussed.

Present hypertext systems concentrate on the human computer interface including psychological aspects [19] and on physical addressing to represent links between one document and another [2]. Three main types of link are recognized in hypertext systems:

1. inter-document links representing citations,

2. lexical links in which the meaning of words is resolved,

3. conceptual links in which implicit semantic connections are made between one document and another.

This work is mostly concerned with symbolic links between one document and another. Lexical links pose greater difficulties in implementation because of frequent ambiguity in finding the definition of a word amongst its many usages in a text. Implicit links are obviously difficult for the machine.

The first attempts to implement inter-document links in hypertext systems were manually based with links being assigned on an individual basis. Subsequently, programs in languages such as C have been used to generate hypertext systems which employ as far as possible symbolic addressing to cope with pre-existing forms of citation and allow automated authoring of large quantities of text [30]. For static bodies of text, this approach may be satisfactory but with large amounts of text that are subject to continuous amendment, there are many problems associated with management of persistent data.

Thus hypertext systems of the first generation are generally self contained and cannot be easily integrated with other programs and data. Nor is it easy for them to be used concurrently by a number of different authors. They cannot, in general, be used for handling large amounts of persistent data. They can store multimedia data in physical form but the semantic structure is not captured: the design and construction of maintainable links is a major problem. There is limited opportunity for mapping and indirection between user views and storage structures: there has to be one fixed view - that of the author, with little scope for the preferences of individual readers. There is no independent level of control that can test or validate the data and which can track the navigation through documents. There is an emphasis on browsing through nodes via links rather than on content addressing where the facilities are often quite limited.

Database systems can assist in many of these problem areas: high-level end-user languages such as SQL can be embedded in standard programming languages such as C, COBOL or FORTRAN to integrate data base facilities with other functional aspects; transaction processing allows concurrent reading and writing of data by many users; management of large volumes of persistent data is a central tenet of the technology; semantic data models provide a conceptual framework in which to design an application; multi-level architectures with mappings from logical to physical levels provide different views of the same stored data; in some systems, content-addressing can be integrated with navigation to give facilities as sophisticated as those found in information retrieval systems with the use, for example, of Boolean operators, wild characters, weightings and iterative searching.

To enable larger amounts of data to be handled, some hypertext systems have already been augmented by a conventional relational database system as for example with the commercial system OWL [8] and in experimental work in France [18]. At Texas Instruments, a system PANORAMA based on the object-oriented database ZEITGEIST has been built to augment navigation facilities with searching functions [5].

1.1. Documents of Text in the Hypermedia

A document is a unit of text holding information in the form of structured data attributes. The size selected for a document is subjective and has been traditionally determined by the printing press and publishers to give often a very arbitrary division in information [13]. A more flexible view is that documents should be treated as complex objects and aggregation abstractions provided to vary dynamically the granularity of data addressed. Work by Raymond & Tompa [21] has indicated the need for an accurate representation of the fine structure of documents to allow fragments of documents to be referenced and treated as objects of data in their own right. Tompa's model [27] satisfactorily treats some aspects of the hypermedia through using a 6-tuple structure recording nodes, pages, readers, mapping from nodes to pages, labels and hyperedges. Such a structure has some advantages:

1. multiple readers can be positioned at arbitrarily many nodes at one time;

2. flexibility in data structuring can be achieved by the mapping between nodes that users see and pages in which the data are held;

3. symbolic labels can be used for cross-referencing purposes;

4. recording of all links can be made explicitly as hyperedges, each hyperedge comprising a source node, target node and a label.

However, there is a major problem with the model for real textual data: all references are between nodes mapped statically to a number of data pages with no scope for dynamic variation of unit size in the source and target objects. The model thus fails to capture the inherent complex object structure of multimedia data including the fragmentation features discussed by Raymond and Tompa in their earlier work.

1.2. Document Architecture

In order to examine document architectures, the example of English legal statutes will be used in this paper. Other work at Newcastle has also investigated models for legal dictionaries [12]. In England, Parliament enacts statutes and Figure 1 shows related documents which have a bearing on the meaning of a particular section in an Act of Parliament. A section represents the smallest self-contained free standing unit of text. It is a mere point in the textual hypermedium and can rarely be consulted alone or understood without reference to other documents. As any of the information in the Figure 1 may have a bearing on a section in question, it can readily be seen that advanced hypertext features are needed if all the relevant subject matter is to be available and easily reached in the electronic medium.

Further, it can also be seen that conceptual paths [3,31] will exist in the law following the same route through a text to be followed by many searchers over a period of time. These paths, which can be thought of as trails [28], should be preserved for a searcher to retrace his steps at a later date. Of great importance is the ability to vary the trail to gain additional insight into a particular area. It is envisaged that these trails will be held in database tables as persistent data fully integrated with the hypertext data.

The main objective of trails is to assist the human in communication with the machine by removing the need to memorise backward and forward references, unsuccessful routes through the database, search terms used, the search strategy, etc. Such mental effort, being non-automatic, interferes with ongoing conscious activities and requires extensive metamemory skills [4]. One of the major difficulties in current hypertext systems is the user becoming "lost in hyperspace" [7] as a result of losing his way along a trail as a result of the demands made on his metamemory. It is thus necessary to provide a conceptual framework for the machine to assist the human in his database searching [22].

Let us now consider database models for representing the internal structure of the statute.

Figure 1. A Section of Statute set in the European Legal Hypermedium

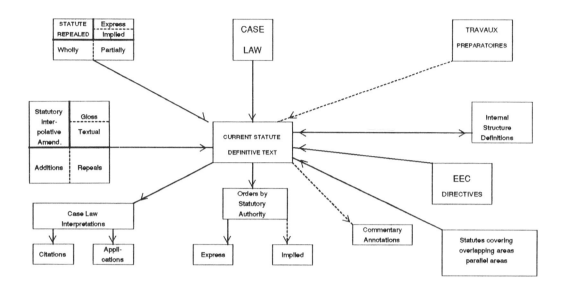

2. Database Models and Textual Structures

The basic DBMS models are implemented and work well for administrative data. Can they be extended to documents as complex objects? There are some difficulties with the relational model mainly due to the problems of normalization and aggregation of textual data [14,15] which in general terms result from an inadequate representation of complex objects [26]. At least for representing ideas, it is necessary to move on from the classical models to the semantic models because the required emphasis is on capability, expressiveness and abstraction.

A range of semantic models incorporating more features and constraints [25] than in the basic models has been proposed in an attempt to model more closely the real world. These include the Entity-Relationship Model [6] and Taxis [17], both of which have been employed in this work. Of

Figure 2. Class Structure for Objects Occurring in Legal Text

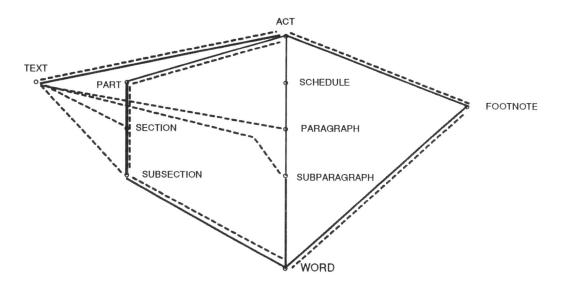

particular interest in hypertext systems is the modelling of dynamic aspects: events have to be controlled over long periods, as in the design, control and maintenance of the trails used to navigate the hypermedium. The division between function and data in classical database systems [29] extends to some semantic models such as the E-R model mentioned above [20] so that the model represents structural rather than behavioural characteristics. Thus, current systems analysis techniques employ E-R models weakly-integrated [16] with Data Flow Diagrams [10] to provide a unified approach. Whilst the actual implementation described here employs these techniques, other alternative fundamental options will be described later.

2.1. Class Structures

A Chen E-R model of English statutes has been presented elsewhere [14]. The basic structure can be viewed as the complex object shown in Figure 2 in which *word* is a subobject shared by several classes, each word being considered in its own right as well as in its use in a local and global context. Two types of hierarchy are embedded within the class structure:

- An aggregation hierarchy represented by the solid lines to indicate potential groupings of data. The complex object structure illustrates the problem of unit size in which a user may seek to aggregate data at any level of the structure or search for data in the context of any simple or aggregated unit.

- An inheritance hierarchy represented by dotted lines to indicate the automatic inheritance of properties (attributes) by lower level objects from higher ones. Thus *text* is a generic object from which the subobjects *section, subsection, paragraph* and *subparagraph* inherit properties such as text formatting attributes. Other forms of inheritance are for identifiers: thus *part* inherits the identifier for *act*.

2.2. Symbolic Addressing for Hypertext

For navigation in the hypermedium, it is important to be able to identify uniquely individual units of text so that cross-references can be resolved. This is the function of the primary key in database technology. The simplest form of key is a numerical index (slot key) which is convenient for the system but which bears no direct relationship to the contents of the data. Other possible forms of the key are the ordinary hard-copy identification of the unit (natural key) and a semantic description of the content (symbolic key). All three forms of the key have been tried in work at Newcastle [11] which has shown the advantages of the symbolic key for intelligent processing by the machine. Conversion routines between natural and symbolic keys provide a reasonable interface to users.

An important question is what form the symbolic key should take. In Figure 3 - an extract from the full E-R diagram described earlier, *cross.reference* (alias *XRef*) is an involuted relationship involving the generic entity-type *text*. This provides an appropriate abstract definition: the cross-referencing process where one of the occurrences of the entity-types *section, subsection, paragraph* and *subparagraph* may cite any other occurrence of the entity-types *section, subsection, paragraph* and *subparagraph* can be simplified into an occurrence of the *text* entity-type may cite another occurrence of the *text* entity-type. However, a concrete representation is essential for implementation purposes.

For the generalization *text*, the identifier is *symbolicID* which can be abstractly represented by the Taxis-like class structure shown in Figure 4. Each attribute qualifies one aspect of the content of an object so that the key represented by the attribute *symbolicID* of the class *SymbolicKey* is a polynomial consisting of the hierarchical sequence of an object in the statute law structure. In this study, all the attributes are integer within the permitted ranges shown. The attributes of the class *cross.reference* will be the key of the citing text unit, *citing.symbolicID*, and the key of the cited text unit *cited.symbolicID*. The form of these attributes therefore also

Figure 3. Extract from E-R Diagram for Statute Law
showing *cross.reference (XRef)* and *text* entities

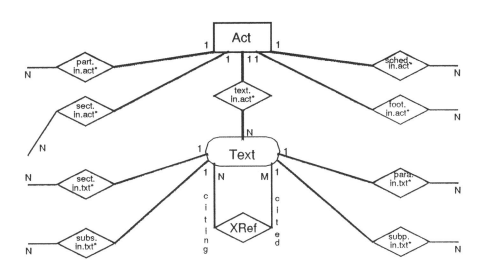

conforms to the structure of Figure 4. The obvious mechanism therefore
for concretization of the cross-referencing process is to employ a generic
symbolic key as in Figure 4 to provide a powerful mechanism for addressing
any unit in the complex object structure of Figure 2.

Figure 4. Taxis-like Specification of Symbolic Key for Statutes

```
define AnyDataClass SymbolicKey with
    subsection#: {| 0:99 |}
    section#: {| 0:999 |}
    part#: {| 0:255 |}
    subparagraph#: {| 0:99 |}
    paragraph#: {| 0:999 |}
    schedule#: {| 0:255 |}
    footnote#: {| 0:99 |}
    year: {| 1267:2000 |}
    chapter: {| 0:255 |}
  unique
    symbolicID: {year, chapter, part#, section#, subsection#,
            subparagraph#, paragraph#, schedule#, footnote#}
```

Database systems employing symbolic keys for identification of objects have an inherent advantage over less conceptual approaches in handling text whose content is continuously changing. In first–generation hypertext systems with physical node addressing, cross-references must in advance be fully identified as in a network database. In a value-oriented database approach to hypertext, links are made dynamically at run-time using symbolic key matching techniques. Both means provide for display and navigation through documents. The physically-oriented approach uses less resources but the early binding of identifier to data is more of a static method which allows less flexibility if, for example, data is being loaded in an uncertain order or key values are being changed or deleted. A more flexible approach is to exploit the dynamic power of lazy evaluation using the technology of value-oriented databases.

2.3. Models for Expressing Dynamic Aspects of Trail Management

Figure 5 shows a De Marco Data Flow Diagram for the trail management which indicates the control of events required in searching and navigating. The diagram shows an overview of the processes involved and how they reference three types of information: the hypermedium itself, a record of the searches made with results and the navigational activity of each user. Whilst execution of a particular process is not complicated, it is a matter of integrated management of the very large number of processes that are possible and their complex inter-relationships. Also shown is a description of the main data flows on the input side to illustrate the nature of the commands passed to the system for action.

2.4. Models for Expressing Static Aspects of Trail Management

Clearly, the trail status will be held and maintained as data. Therefore, as companion to the DFD of Figure 5, there is an E-R diagram which is shown in Figure 6. The machine records as data in separate database tables all information on the user's past and current searching of the hypermedium which can be interrogated either overtly or covertly by the system itself. The entity-type *Current.Record.Position* has been introduced to explicitly indicate the current selected object. The *Search.History* and *Navigation.History* data-stores of Figure 5 have been logically combined into a single *Trail.History* entity-type: each trail is initiated by a single content-based search which is followed by many navigations.

Figure 5. DFD for Trail Management in Navigation of Hypertext

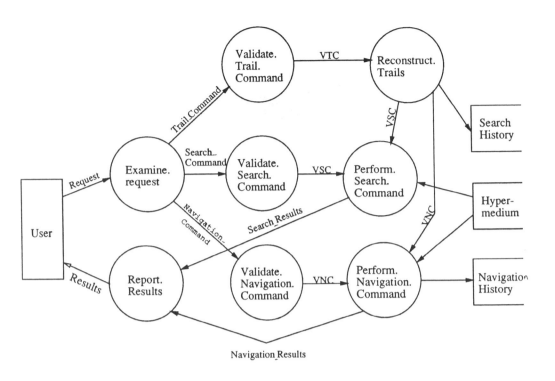

```
Request        = [Trail_command | Search_command |
                  Navigation_command | System_command]
Trail_command  = [trail_label str | first | last | fwd(n) |
                  bwd(n) | end]
Search_command = [find | and | or | not] attr str
Navigation_command  = [[+|-] n | ref | {subobject_id}]
System_command  = SPIRES_command
Subobject_id   = [subsection p | section q |
                  part r | subparagraph s | paragraph t |
                  schedule u | footnote v | year w | chapter x]
         n..x = integer_value
         attr = text_attribute
          str = string_value
Abbreviations:
         VTC = Validated_Trail_Command
         VSC = Validated_Search_Command
         VNC = Validated_Navigation_Command
Convention: [..] selection; {..} iteration; (..) optional
```

233

Figure 6. E-R Diagram for Static Aspects of Trail Management

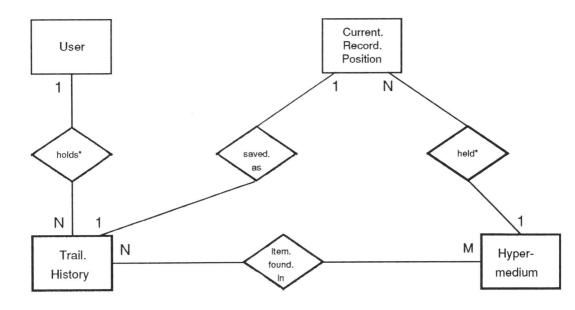

3. Implementation of Trail Management System

The system was implemented on the SPIRES[1] DBMS run on an Amdahl 5860 of the NUMAC service. The textbase STATLT holding the English statutes has been developed and refined in a series of projects since 1980 and at the start of the project described here already provided full text searching facilities, symbolic addressing in the manner of Figure 4 and a multivalued attribute *marg-note-xref* in each text unit to record cross-references made to other parts of the text.

The current work is concerned with the implementation of the dynamic aspects shown in Figure 5 and the static aspects of Figure 6 [24]. The additional tables created to record the status of navigation will first be described.

---

[1] SPIRES is a trademark of Stanford University

3.1. Tables to record the Navigational Status

The entity *Trail.History* shown in Figure 6 holds all information on the trails made by users through the textbase. The attributes describing this information are *command, success, current.unit, relevance* and *symbolic.key*. In addition, each trail needs to be labelled with a string for identification by the user. Each trail consists of many commands so that normalisation gives the following two table-types (key attributes in bold):

- path(**user.id, trail.num,** trail.label)

- pathitem(**user.id, trail.num, command.num,** command, symbolic.key, current.unit, success, relevance)

Figure 7 shows the definition of these two table-types in the SPIRES File Definer language. Structures *path.id* and *item.id* are used to hold the keys of the table-types *path* and *pathitem* respectively. In *pathitem, symbolic.key* holds the symbolic key of the current record after the command held in *command* has been both executed and successful. Success or failure is indicated by the value for the logical attribute *success*. The current unit size, indicating the extent to which the complex object structure has been aggregated to provide results to the user, is indicated by the value for *current.unit*. The attribute *relevance* can be used to record the desirability of taking a particular route. The tables and their attributes are extensively used by the processes described in the DFD of Figure 5.

3.2. Application of Transform Analysis to the DFD of Figure 5

The DFD of Figure 5 was converted to the structure diagram of Figure 8 by transform analysis. The process *Examine.Request* was considered to be the transaction centre as it triggers many courses of actions in the system. Figure 8 includes explanatory notes on the ten variables shown on the diagram including their correspondence with database attributes defined in Figure 7. The operation of the modules in the diagram is summarised below. The functions were implemented using the SPIRES Protocols language.

Control.module provides overall control of the reception and examination of requests; it receives user input strings from *Receive.request* and passes them to *Examine.request* which determines the type of function sought by the user. SPIRES system commands are passed to the database kernel without modification. Other commands are parsed and then sent to the appropriate process for the request, either *Search.command, Navigation.command* or *Trail.command*. Each of these processes subjects the request to validation

Figure 7. *Trail.History* Table Definitions in SPIRES
File Definer Source Language

```
subfile path
fixed
element path.id/length 6,exact/single/structure/key
   inproc $struc.in(2,'.')
   outproc $struc.out(2,'.')
   fixed
   element user.id/length 4,exact/single/immediate index
   element trail.num/length 2,exact/single/immediate index
   end
required
element trail.label/single/immediate index
end
*****
subfile pathitem
fixed
element item.id/length 8,exact/single/structure/key
   inproc $struc.in(3,'.')
   outproc $struc.out(3,'.')
   fixed
   element user.id/length 4,exact/single/immediate index
   element trail.num/length 2,exact/single/immediate index
   element command.num/length 2,exact/single/immediate index
   end
elememt symbolic.key/length 36,exact/single
required
element command/single
optional
element current.unit/single
element success/single/yesno
element relevance/single/yesno
end
```

---

and then passes the action sought for execution by one of the three main
procedures in the system described below. It should be emphasised that the
interpretation of users' actions is to some extent context-driven. Thus if the
Status of system variable holds the value REPLAY, the users' actions will be
interpreted as far as possible as involving the recall of a trail. If the value is
ACTIVE, the user is thought to be navigating and if INACTIVE performing
an initial search to locate a record on content prior to navigation.

1. *Perform.search.command* takes a valid search command, manipulates
   the search string according to certain rules and passes the result on to

Figure 8. Structure Chart for Dynamic Aspects of Trail Management

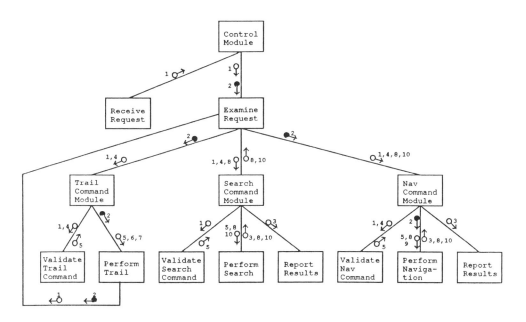

1. Request string	6. Position in trail
2. Status of system	7. Trail identifier
3. Result code	8. Unit type
4. Number of command	9. Current record key
5. Valid command split into fields	10. Search commands in one string

1. *Request string* is the instruction issued by the user;

2. *Status of system* can be:

    - INACTIVE when the user is performing an initial search by content,
    - ACTIVE when the user is navigating,
    - REPLAY when the user is reconstructing a trail;

3. *Result code* is a variable which is set to certain numbers to indicate when certain error conditions have occurred;

4. *Number of command* is set by *Examine.request*;

5. *Valid command split into fields* is the parsed validated command (= *command* in *Pathitem*);

6. *Position in trail* has the number of the current command in the trail being reconstructed (= *command.num* in *Pathitem*);

7. *Trail identifier* is the id for the current trail (= *user.id+trail.num* in *Path*);

8. *Unit type* is the current text aggregation size (= *current.unit* in *Pathitem*);

9. *Current record key* is the key of the current record in the textbase (= *symbolic.key* in *Pathitem*);

10. *Search commands in one string* is formed from concatenating all the user's iterative search commands.

237

Report.results. A search command *find* produces an initial result stack of items; other search commands are iterations with Boolean logic on the current stack. Navigation can only sensibly proceed when the user has identified a single record as of supreme importance from content searching.

2. *Perform.navigation.command* receives a valid navigation command and finds the required record in the textbase:

> [+|-]*n* changes the current record in the textbase to n units away in a positive or negative logical direction respectively. This command is typically used for browsing forwards or backwards through *sections* within a *part* or *paragraphs* within a *schedule* at a constant textual unit size.

> *ref* finds the record referenced by the current record. If several records are referenced from a single record, the user will be given a choice as to which one is required. If the reference is to a high-level unit such as a *part*, objects will be aggregated to retrieve a complete *part* for the user. This command can therefore dynamically change the current textual unit size.

> *subsection p, section q, ...* finds a record with symbolic key with new values p, q, ... for the designated components. The current textual unit size is adjusted accordingly.

With all three forms of the navigation command, execution results in updating the status tables defined in Figure 7 and, if successful, making the object found the current item.

3. *Perform.trail* receives a valid trail command and depending on the parameter passed performs the following action:

> *trail_label string* leads to a look-up in *Path* for a trail labelled with the appropriate string value. If the trail exists, the first action will be executed by passing the stored search command to *Perform.search* and the system status will be changed to REPLAY.

> *first* finds the key of the record found at the beginning of the selected trail and establishes it as the current record.

> *last* finds the key of the record found by the end of the selected trail and establishes it as the current record.

fwd(n) takes the navigation n steps forward from the current position.

bwd(n) returns the navigation back n steps.

end causes the status of the system to be changed from REPLAY to INACTIVE.

Finally *Report.results* sends the required information from the hypertext to the user or returns an error message.

4. Discussion

We have used current database techniques to satisfy our requirements without insuperable difficulties. Of particular interest is the availability of both powerful browsing and searching facilities, the recording of all information concerning user trails as persistent data in fully-fledged database tables, and the dynamic variation of text unit size to meet changing user demands.

However, our task was relatively hard in two areas:

1. the dynamic adjustment of unit size; and

2. the integration of dynamic and static models.

The definition of abstract data types as in Postgres [26] to represent the various aggregation possibilities would be of considerable assistance from the conceptual viewpoint. However, there are problems with closure in some extensions of the relational model which employ procedures as attributes: the return of a multi-valued set produces an unnormalized relation. Alternatively, an object-oriented database system such as GemStone [1] could have been employed. This would have improved the data modelling by allowing an accurate representation of the class structure of Figure 2 including in particular the inheritance abstractions. However, the aggregation abstraction is achieved externally as in the present work and there is a greater emphasis on procedurality than on declarativeness in current object-oriented systems.

The dynamic and static aspects have been implemented using diffferent models which are weakly-integrated. This lack of integration is an inherent feature of virtually all database systems in current use [29]. It is possible with the emerging object-oriented databases to provide a complete integration with a single model specifying definitions and functions in the same manner as classes or objects. Some semantic database models such as Taxis

239

also provide this capability and their expressiveness has been examined for text [23]. However, these integrated models are at the experimental stage for realistic amounts of data.

In addition, there is also a number of areas where further work is required:

1. The interface provided to users. Layered object-oriented techniques employing multi-windowing have been investigated with promising results for the development of interfaces to hypermedia and multimedia applications [9].

2. Development of a more general hierarchical trail system. It has been an assumption in the present work that trails to be held will be linear in structure. However, it is apparent from experimental tests that trails can be hierarchical with one trail comprising exploration to a terminal node, backtracking to an earlier point which had multiple citations, forward movement to a terminal node, and so on, in which all material seen is relevant to the user's quest. The trail structure shown in Figure 7 should be adjusted to allow the recording of such hierarchical trails.

3. Investigation of the semantics of trail integrity. The integrity of trails depends during their existence on no component object being deleted during maintenance of the hypermedia database. There is therefore a need for restrictions on the actions that are permitted on objects that participate in trails. Further work is needed at the conceptual level in this area to determine the constraints required.

5. Conclusions

Hypermedia systems are very complex: events have to be controlled over long periods, as in the design, control, maintenance and integrity of hierarchical trails used for navigation; text and graphical information comprises complex data objects with the need for aggregation and inheritance abstractions; and interfaces must employ multi-windowing techniques and be natural according to psychological models. A natural extension of the present work on hypertext at Newcastle is to investigate the use of object-oriented techniques with their claimed suitability for complex applications. Against the gains from more natural class structures and an integration of dynamic and static aspects will be measured the losses caused by a greater emphasis on procedurality in current object-oriented database systems.

References

1. Bretl, R, Maier, D, Otis, A, Penney, J, Schuchardt, B, Stein, J, Williams, E H, & Williams, M, (1989), The GemStone Data Management System, in: *Object-Oriented Concepts, Databases, & Applications,* (edd.) Kim, W, & Lochovsky, F H, Addison-Wesley 283-308.

2. Brown, P J, (1988), Hypertext: the way forward, in: *Document Manipulation and Typography,* (ed.) van Vliet, J C, Cambridge University Press 183-191.

3. Bush, V, (1945), As we may think, *Atlantic Monthly* **176** 101-108.

4. Ceci, S J, & Howe, M J A, (1982), Metamemory and Effects of Intending, Attending, and Intending to Attend, in: *Aspects of Consciousness, Awareness and Self-Awareness,* (ed.) Underwood, G, Academic Press **3** 147-164.

5. Chen, J C, Ekberg, T W, & Thompson, C W, (1989), Querying an Object-oriented Hypermedia System, *Proceedings Hypertext II,* York.

6. Chen, P P-S, (1976), The Entity-Relationship Model - towards a unified view of data, *ACM TODS* **1**(1) 9-36.

7. Conklin, J, (1987), Hypertext: An Introduction and Survey, *IEEE Computer* **20**(9) 17-41.

8. Cooke, P, & Williams, I, (1989), Design Issues in Large Hypertext Systems for Technical Documentation, in: *Hypertext, Theory into Practice,* (ed.) McAleese, R, Intellect, Oxford 93-104.

9. Cordes, R, Hofmann, M, & Langendorfer, H, (1989), Layered Object-Oriented Techniques supporting Hypermedia and Multimedia Applications, in: *Workshop on Object-Oriented Document Manipulation* (Rennes, May 1989), (edd.) André, J, & Bézivin, J, BIGRE no. 63-64 286-296.

10. De Marco, T, (1978), *Structured Analysis and System Specification,* Yourdon Press.

11. Heather, M A, & Rossiter, B N, (1987), *Database techniques for text modelling: the document architecture of British statutes,* University of Newcastle upon Tyne, Computing Laboratory Technical Report no 227.

12. Heather, M A, & Rossiter, B N, (1988), Specialist dictionaries in electronic form, *Literary & Linguistic Computing* 3(2) 109-121.

13. Heather, M A, & Rossiter, B N, (1989), A Generalized Database Management Approach to Textual Analysis, in: *Proc. 2nd Int. Colloq. Bible and Computer: Methods, Tools, Results,* Champion-Slatkine, Paris-Geneva 519-535.

14. Heather, M A, & Rossiter, B N, (1989), Theoretical Structures for Object-based Text, in: *Workshop on Object-Oriented Document Manipulation* (Rennes, May 1989), (edd.) André, J, & Bézivin, J, BIGRE no. 63-64 178-192.

15. Heather, M A, & Rossiter, B N, (in press), Syntactical Relations in Parallel Text, in: *Proceedings 15th International ALLC Conference,* (ed.) Choueka, Y, Jerusalem 1988.

16. Longworth, G, (1989), *Getting the System you want, A User's Guide to SSADM,* NCC Publications, Manchester.

17. Mylopoulos, J, Bernstein, P A, & Wong, H K T, (1980), A Language Facility for Designing Database-Intensive Facilities, *ACM TODS* **5** 185-207.

18. Nardot, J, & Pujolle, G, (1989), Une Interface de Type Hypertexte pour la Gestion d'Objets Complexes, in: *Workshop on Object-Oriented Document Manipulation* (Rennes, May 1989), (edd.) André, J, & Bézivin, J, BIGRE no. 63-64 383-386.

19. Pasquier-Boltuck, J, Grossman, E, & Collaud, G, (1988), Prototyping an Interactive Electronic Book System using an Object Oriented Approach, in: *Lecture Notes in Computer Science,* Springer-Verlag **322** 177-190.

20. Peckham, J, & Maryanski, F, (1988), Semantic Data Models, *ACM Computing Surveys* **20**(3) 153-189.

21. Raymond, D R, & Tompa, F W, (1988), Hypertext and the Oxford English Dictionary, *CACM* **31**(7) 871-879.

22. Rossiter, B N, (1987), Machine Awareness in Database Technology, in: *Proceedings Symposium VI*, Meta-intelligence and the Cybernetics of Consciousness, *XI International Congress of Cybernetics,* Namur 1-9.

23. Rossiter, B N, & Heather, M A, (1990), *Towards the Object-oriented Textbase,* University of Newcastle upon Tyne, Computing Laboratory Technical Report no 297.

24. Sillitoe, T J, (1989), *Navigation through Documents using Database Techniques to Emulate Hypertext,* M.Sc. Dissertation, Computing Laboratory, University of Newcastle upon Tyne.

25. Smith, J, & Smith, D, (1977), Data Abstraction, Aggregation and Generalization, *ACM TODS* **2**(2) 105-133.

26. Stonebraker, M, Anton, J, & Hanson, E, (1987), Extending a Database System with Procedures, *ACM TODS* **12**(3) 350-376.

27. Tompa, F W, (1989), A Data Model for Flexible Hypertext Database Systems, *ACM Trans Information Systems* **7**(1) 85-106.

28. Treu, S A, (1971), A Conceptual Framework for the Searcher-System Interface, in: *Interactive Bibliographic Search: The User/Computer Interface,* (ed.) Walker, D E, AFIPS Press, Palo Alto 53-66.

29. Tsichritzis, D C, & Nierstrasz, O M, (1988), Fitting Round Objects into Square Databases, ECOOP '88 Proceedings, in: *Lecture Notes in Computer Science,* Springer-Verlag **322** 283-299.

30. Wilson, E, (1988), Justus: towards a Workstation for Information Retrieval in Law, *Preproceedings 4th International Congress on Law and Computers,* Session X, Italian Ministry of Justice, Rome.

31. Zellweger, P T, (1989), Scripted Documents: A Hypermedia Path Mechanism, in: *Hypertext'89 Proceedings,* Special Issue - SIGCHI Bulletin 1-14.

Design and Construction of Graphical Database User Interfaces Using Surface Interaction

Alan W. Brown

Roger K. Took

William G. Daly

Department of Computer Science
University of York

Abstract

It is recognised that databases would benefit from *interactive graphical user interfaces*, yet that little development has taken place in this area. Part of the reason is the difficulty and expense of constructing such interfaces, given existing user interface services for application writers. A new paradigm for user interface services, **surface interaction**, is particularly suited to supporting interfaces to databases, in that it provides for persistent, user-manipulable graphical objects which can represent views on a wider underlying database. This is illustrated by reference to a number of prototype database applications which have been developed at York using **Presenter**, an implementation of the surface interaction principle. Issues raised by this approach are examined.

1. Introduction

The 1980's have seen a dramatic change in the power, price, and availability of computer systems. In particular there has been a move towards decentralised systems, with high power bit-mapped graphic workstations available on the desks of many end users. It is recognised that graphical user interfaces can dramatically increase the useability of computer applications. However, such user interfaces are critically subject to issues of *Human Computer Interaction (HCI)*: ease of use, ergonomics, aesthetics, and other pyschological aspects. It is therefore important that the services available to exploit the power of a graphical workstation should allow for rapid prototyping and modification of interfaces with the minimum investment of effort on the part of the application programmer.

243

Database systems are applications which have a particular need for efficient and effective user interfaces. In many organisations, the database system provides the main corporate resource, with the result that any techniques for improving the development, maintenance, or use of this resource will be vigorously pursued. However, far from accepting the benefits of graphical database user interfaces with open arms, there has been remarkably little work which addresses the particular ways in which this technology can be applied to database systems. In a recent meeting of a number of eminent database researchers at Laguna Beach, they noted that,[16]

> "There are virtually **no** researchers investigating better end-user interfaces to databases, or better database application development tools... Moreover, there was universal consensus that this was an extremely important area."

The Laguna Beach participants noted a number of reasons for this apparent lack of work in the database user interface area. One of the most important reasons identified was that "there is a mammoth amount of low-level support code that must be constructed before the actual interface can be built".

This paper directly addresses the issues raised in the Laguna Beach Report, describing work that has been taking place at the University of York to facilitate the design and construction of user interfaces to applications, and databases in particular. A new paradigm for user interfaces, *surface interaction* has been proposed[20] , and is being applied through a graphical user interface management system known as **Presenter**.

In this paper we examine some of the requirements that graphical database user interfaces must address, and show the way in which we are making use of Presenter as a tool for rapidly developing prototype database interfaces for experimentation.

2. Graphical Interfaces to Database Systems

A database system is a key component of many organisations. Indeed, some organisations view the business of the company as analogous to the development, operation, and maintenance of the corporate database system. In these circumstances, a great deal of effort is involved in ensuring the correctness of that data, both in terms of the internal integrity of the data, and external security of access to that data. Similarly, the database administrators are continually monitoring the database in an attempt to identify inefficiencies (in any of the normal database activities) and to effect changes to address those inefficiencies.

An important component in all of these areas is the database user interface. Typically, it is at the interface level that much of the confusion arises, leading to inefficient use of the database system, and issuing of incorrect commands which may not affect the database in the way anticipated by the user. For example,

- To delete a customer from a sales order processing database, does the end user first have to learn the syntax of a database query language such as SQL?

- When the user issues a "delete" operation for a customer, is it clear to the user what happens to any outstanding orders for that customer ?

A database system is also accessed by a variety of users, within many different roles, requiring distinct classes of operations. Typical roles include database developer, responsible for the initial design of the database system, database administrator in charge of the overall operation of the database system, and many classes of database end-user who require different kinds of access to the data. Each of these user roles has different interface criteria.

We briefly examine some of these issues for the three distinct classes of database user identified above.

2.1. Database Developer

The main functions of the database developer are to design the initial database schema, implement appropriate views of the database for different end users, and to develop database transactions which will be executed against those views. Until quite recently, very little computerised support has been provided to help the developer in carrying out these tasks. Typically, the developer would draw diagrams representing individual views on paper, try to construct a global schema by amalgamating those views, and then write the corresponding data definition language (DDL) statements for a particular implementation of a database system. These DDL statements would be executed, and the resultant database schema tested to remove errors which may have occurred during this manual process.

In the last few years attempts have been made to help automate the process of schema development. Through Computer-Aided Software Engineering (CASE), a number of CASE tools have been developed.[15] These tools usually help to automate schema development by providing graphical schema drawing facilities in most cases based on some form of the Entity-Relationship modelling formalism.[5] The better tools automatically validate the construction of the diagrams, allow previous diagrams to be browsed, and generate the DDL statements which implement the schema for a particular database system. CASE tool interfaces have been developed for most commercial database systems.

2.2. Database Administrator

The key role in database operation is the database administrator (DBA). It is the DBA's job to ensure the database system performs correctly and efficiently. Hence, aspects of this role include monitoring of database preformance, authorisation of new users, defining and implementing security constraints, and controlling the evolution of the database schema.

There have been few attempts to provide graphical facilities for enhancing the function of the DBA. This can be seen as an important area for database systems to address in the near future.

2.3. Database End-User

The wide variety of different database end user is a result of the many different application areas in which database systems are employed. A typical business data process application may use a database system for recording personnel or accounts records. Typical users will include data entry clerks, data enquiry personnel, and department managers. Each user has different requirements of the system, and hence different user interface needs. For example, a simple form fill interface may be appropriate for data entry, a simple query language for data enquiry, and a small number of pre-defined transactions ("canned-queries") for the department manager.

The introduction of fourth generation languages (4GL's) during the last few years has made the development of form fill interfaces much easier. A 4GL typically provides a simple set of commands for interacting with pre-defined screens set up via a screen painting facility. Hence, command line interfaces (through languages such as SQL) and form fill interfaces are most common. True graphical query languages are much less common. The only widespread example being Query-By-Example (QBE) which uses a relation template with a simple query language to perform queries.[8]

For more complex applications, more sophisticated user interfaces are required. One example involves the use of a database system as the central component of an Integrated Project Support Environment (IPSE). As a gross simplification, an IPSE can be thought of as an integrated set of tools for large scale software development. The user interface to an IPSE becomes a vital factor in the use of such a system. It is at the user interface level that the complexity of the underlying system must be controlled, otherwise the IPSE could become unusable. We shall examine this application in more detail in a later section.

3. User Interface Services

The writer of a database application cannot be expected to have the time or expertise to implement an optimal user interface, particularly if a direct-manipulation graphical interface is required. As in many other application areas, such a writer looks to a user interface service level to provide an environment within which user interfaces can easily be constructed, without worrying about device-level detail. Existing services fall into three broad categories:

1. *Window managers* provide screen management of large-grain workspaces. User input is split: operations such as moving or iconising the windows is captured by the window manager, while in-window events are passed raw to the application.

2. *Toolkits* provide a selection of ready-made and possibly customisable components, like menus or scroll bars. Some of these may handle small cycles of interaction, for example to provide feedback for menu selection.

3. *User Interface Management systems (UIMS)*[17] manage all user input, usually against an ideal template for user dialogue expressed as a state-

transition network or formal grammar. User errors are handled by the UIMS, while validated input is passed to the application layer for processing.

An application writer might be expected to have the following ideal requirements of a user interface environment:

- *Power*: the user interface level should handle the mechanics of maintaining the display, so that the application designer has simply a declarative access to the objects of interaction.

- *Freedom*: while there is an argument for constraining the application to a fixed style of interaction (or 'look and feel'[10]) in order to enforce consistency, experience shows that different application domains, different application designers, and different users, have very different user interface requirements. Criteria for usability and aesthetics are not yet so well developed that it is possible to standardise on a fixed interface style. We should therefore expect the user interface level to give freedom of design, whether that design is carried out by the application writer, a specialised interface designer, or even dynamically by the user.

- *Separation*: the user interface level should preserve a separation between the tasks of application and interface design[19] . These can then be carried out by different roles, if not by different people. Ideally a separation should also be preserved between the execution of interface and application, so that, for example, the interface may run on a mouse-driven workstation, while the application runs on a computation or storage intensive device. Such a separation means that interface objects persist independently of application execution, and can thus be stored, copied, or interactively edited without application involvement.

Existing user interface services fall short on a number of these criteria. A bare window manager provides no power to construct application interfaces within windows - all that may be provided are low-level raster operations. Typically, however, the window manager is bundled with support software which allows the drawing of simple shapes and text. These facilities are usually provided as a static library. To manage a dynamic interface, therefore, the application must handle much of the incremental redisplay, for example when objects change size or position. Even in object oriented toolkits[13] the application must often handle all raw input events.

On the other hand, the power of a UIMS to handle user input on behalf of the application is at the expense of design freedom - the application is constrained to the interface as generated by the UIMS. The services provided by window managers and toolkits are also limited in design freedom. The window manger interface is typically fixed, and while toolkit objects are often extendible, their general usefulness depends critically on the range of the basic set provided, and the extent to which they are parameterised.

Separation is also problematic. Libraries and toolkits have only static separation. While object-oriented toolkits are in theory dynamically separable, there is a tendency in such toolkits for the dividing line between application and interface to become blurred, since user interface objects may be extended with application semantics. Also, the separation of dialogue and application which is at the core of the classic UIMS is most suited to applications which are computationally intensive. The UIMS is used to compose a request from the user which is then sent to the application and the answer returned. Applications which are storage intensive, like databases, have, in contrast, a persistent state. Users of direct manipulation graphical interfaces expect this state to be visible, in some schematic form, and demand rapid incremental feedback from the application ('semantic feedback'[12]) as the state changes at intermediate stages of the dialogue. UIMSs cannot provide this without compromising separation.

3.1. Surface Interaction

Surface interaction is an alternative paradigm for the separation of interface and application. Its main premise is that a *separable* interface is one in which some state changes can acceptably occur independently of changes to the application state. Take the example of a slider or scroll bar: if the user moves the thumb button, then they may well expect the application to register some change as a result. However, the user might wish to change the position or size of the slider as a whole, for example to make the screen layout more comfortable or convenient. In this case the user does not expect to invoke application functionality, and thus there need be no change to the application state. Such surface manipulations can occur independently of the application by means of a control abstraction in which input events are filtered first by the surface. The application can decide in advance which surface events it wishes to be informed of, and give application meaning to.

There are thus two subsidiary premises for surface interaction:

- There exists a rich *surface* domain, that is, a domain which can be used for the presentation of application objects, but which is independent of application semantics (*deep* interaction). The domain consists of textual and graphical objects, their structure, rendering, and operations.

- The surface is highly *separable*, since its operations can often be performed without involving the application. We can therefore abstract surface control into a separate process with which both the application and the user can interact. By abstracting graphical and textual manipulation into an interface server we factor out what is commonly a major proportion of design and coding effort in direct manipulation applications.

For these two reasons, it is both possible and *worth* separating the surface. There are a number of corollaries:

- The surface becomes a protected *medium* which can be controlled equally by the user or by the application. It is protected because only the operations of the surface process are permitted on it.

- The *identity* of an application's surface objects is independent of contingencies like size and position. This means that the user can modify the size and layout of an application interface without affecting its functionality.

- Since the surface objects are independent of applications, and yet possibly

248

common to a number of these, they need to be *persistent*. Persistence allows surface configurations to be copied, saved and reloaded. With this capability we can build interactive editors to construct interfaces independently of applications. Persistence also supports higher level structures on the surface, for example document layout structures, connected diagrams like engineering or database schema diagrams, and hypertext networks.

There is thus a close analogy between the services offered by a user interface manager based on the principle of surface interaction, and those of a database engine. Both offer a developed algebra (objects and operations) and an efficient and protected implementation. Moreover, because of the persistent nature of the surface objects, and the importance of persistent state in a database, an interface manager based on surface interaction is particularly effective in presenting database functionality. The alternative using existing user interface services is for the database to continually redisplay its state each time this changes.

3.2. Presenter

Just as in database, there are many different algebras that can be developed as models for surface interaction. We now briefly describe a particular surface interaction model which has been implemented at York as **Presenter**. Presenter was developed as the interface medium to the ASPECT IPSE[1] . It was fully specified using the formal language Z^{18} , is implemented in C and runs on Sun workstations.

In short, Presenter handles tree-structured graphical and textual objects, and provides operations to construct, add content to, query and display this tree. Presenter has a single construct, *region*. Regions may be composed into an ordered n-ary tree structure. There is a single tree structure per workstation, and a distinguished root region.

This structure is *loaded* with visible content and properties. Content is loaded *at the leaves only*. Leaf regions can thus be arbitrarily composed into groups. For example:

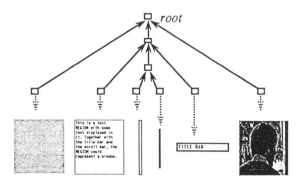

Leaf regions may contain text, line graphics, or bitmaps. Presenter has no built-in objects like windows, menus, icons, scroll bars etc. It therefore places no stylistic constraints on applications, while at the same time facilitating the construction of such objects.

The principal *property* of regions is a geometry. Regions are simply rectangular coordinate spaces which have a size and position with respect to their parent. Presenter places no restrictions on the relative size or position of child and parent. In addition, the ordering of the sequence of leaf regions is interpreted as surface layering. Thus the tree above, with appropriate sizes and positions, could be presented on the surface:

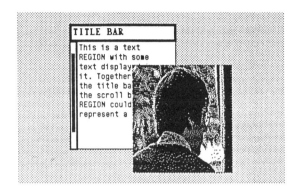

In addition to these basic properties, the *visualisation* of the surface object can be affected by a set of inheritable *attributes*. These determine, for example, the display modes of leaf regions (opaque, or transparent in OR, XOR or AND modes), and which regions clip their descendants. Regions with any property can be layered and manipulated arbitrarily.

Behaviour

Surface objects have *behaviour* to the extent that their control is abstracted from applications. There is thus a subset of the full set of operations which is also available interactively to the user. For example users can move and size regions, and enter, copy, delete, and move text and line graphics. Rescaling of graphics, and reformatting of text, are automatic. Tree operations (cutting and pasting), however, are only available to applications, not directly to users.

The default behaviour of regions can be modified by the application. Presenter provides simple geometric constraints which affect the movability and sizability of regions, and are set simply by (non-inheritable) attributes. Thus a region can be set to move or size only vertically or horizontally, or (possibly in combination) only within or outside another region. This is a basic capability, for example, for constructing scroll bars and the like. In addition, it is possible to set constraints which fix a region's size or position, irrespective of changes to the size or position of its ancestors on the tree.

Communication

The surface communicates with the application by informing it of events that have been generated by the user. Currently, these may be keyboard or mouse events such as the selection or attempted move of a region. The application is informed both of the event and the region in which it occurred. The application can then allow the default surface operation to take place, or cancel it or modify its target. It can also, based on its interpretation of the surface, perform any application-specific function, and modify the surface accordingly. For example, the user may select a button labelled 'QUIT', and on learning of this the application clears the surface and exits. The application thus provides the semantics for the surface.

Surface events are filtered on a per-region basis. That is, the application can request to be informed of selection events on one region, but only size events on another. In this way it can vary its involvement with surface interaction, only taking action when a semantic response is required.

Other Facilities

A linking mechanism is also incorporated which maintains both a logical and a graphical link between any two regions. This mechanism can model a wide range of connected diagrams. Through region behaviour, the diagrams can be manipulated directly by the user with or without the involvement of an application.

As the surface interaction paradigm predicts, it is possible to construct an interactive editor for Presenter objects which can then be stored and loaded at appropriate points in an application's interaction. An important initial application of Presenter has thus been *DoubleView*[11] , which allows the designer to construct and store interfaces or components of interfaces for later use in applications.

4. Applications of Presenter

Over the past two years Presenter has been used in a wide range of different application areas both within the Department of Computer Science at York, and at other academic and industrial research institutions. While interesting example applications include a graphical interface for an Ada debugger,[6] a Mascot 3 Paintbox,[21] and a CORE requirements and analysis workstation,[2] in this paper we shall concentrate on the database applications.

Even within the database field itself, Presenter has found a variety of uses. We shall briefly describe two of these, before discussing two further examples in a little more detail.

4.1. A Database Schema Design Tool

As a simple evaluation of Presenter facilities, a CASE tool style interface to an existing relational database system was developed. In this case we took our existing implementation of the Empress Relational Database Management System, and through combining Presenter with the Empress C language interface designed and constructed a graphical schema development tool based on the Entity-Relationship model.

This interface, designed and constructed by one person as an MSc project over a three month period, allows entity types to be interactively created, attributes to be assigned to entity types, and relationships defined between those entity types. Once completed, the ER diagram is automatically converted into a set of equivalent Empress relations. An example screen from this system is shown in figure 1.

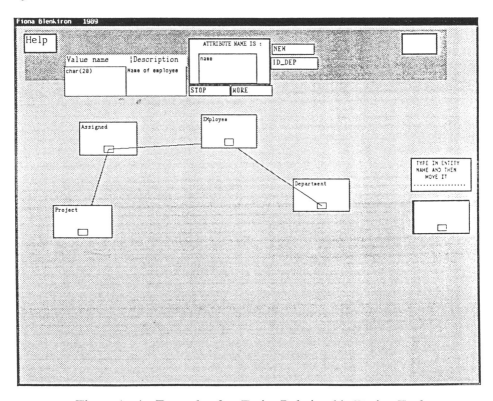

Figure 1. An Example of an Entity-Relationship Design Tool

4.2. A Database Query Tool

Currently under development is a simple graphical database query interface, again on top of the Empress Relational Database Management System. The initial aim is to try to implement a "Query-By-Example" interface, and then to try to extend this interface by taking advantage of the graphical facilities provided by Presenter.

The next step will be to try to integrate the schema development and database query tools that have been developed. This will form an initial graphical database workbench. It is intended that future projects will extend the workbench with more graphical database tools including a set of DBA performance monitoring and control tools.

4.3. A Database User Interface Management System

It is possible to specialise the UIMS philosophy to manage user interfaces to databases. In this way the graphical design of the database representation is incorporated in the generic UIMS, rather than being left up to the database implementor. There are a number of potential advantages.

1. A consistent interface may be given to databases developed on different DBMSs.

2. The integration of a number of different schemas, defined on the same DBMS or on different DBMSs, may be effected by providing an common graphical interface to the databases concerned.

3. Schema data may be represented in graphical form to end-users and integrated with database application interfaces to provide a concurrent view of database structure and database content. An understanding of data relationships is essential when using systems defined by semantic or object-oriented data models.

4. Different conceptual views of the same database can be provided, allowing both the schema interface and application data interfaces to be presented to end-users at different levels of complexity and detail.

5. A database UIMS may provide many of the services defined for the Information Resources Dictionary System such as the management of metadata and meta-metadata. This requirement is important for organisations which hold data in a number of different database systems.

A *graphical database management system (GMS)* is a database-specific UIMS which uses graphical interfaces and direct manipulation interaction techniques for database design, development and access. This has been implemented using the surface interaction paradigm on top of Presenter.[7] The GMS:

*   extends the functionality of current systems to include a *data modelling* function,

*   implements current functionality graphically,

*   integrates all functions into a graphical tool which manages the entire database life-cycle.

Specialising the UIMS in this way allows more powerful, direct manipulation interfaces to be supported since a higher level of semantic feedback between application and UIMS may be defined.

The GMS supports three main functions for three types of user. Each function is carried out using direct manipulation. *Schema creators* use graphical interfaces which are specified by an *interface designer*. *End-users* use graphical interfaces which are constructed by the schema creator.

The interface design process is an editing function carried out on system-defined surface objects called *structure definition interfaces*. Three structure definition interfaces are defined, consisting of object and operation *icons* which are used by the schema creator to carry out specific data definition tasks. The interface designer uses interface editors to alter the graphical characteristics of structure definition interfaces in order to tailor the interface for schema creators and end-users. Figure 2 shows objects of the data model graph structure definition interface being edited to support the definition of Entity-Relationship graphs during the schema definition task.

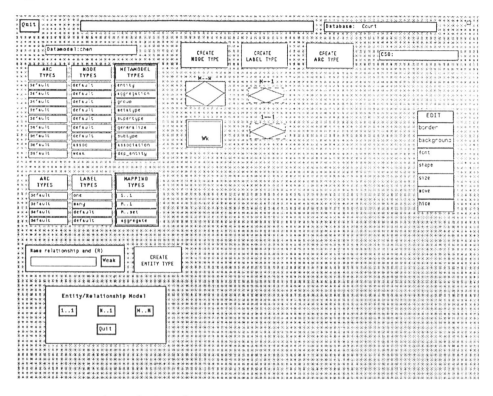

Figure 2. Interface Design of Graph Definition Objects

The schema creator's task is to define the schema of a database using a set of structure definition interfaces. This data definition task is partioned across three structure definition interfaces:

- a domain tree definition interface
- a data model graph definition interface
- a forms network definition interface.

These interfaces allow the schema creator to create three surface structures:

- a tree structure defining the data type hierarchy of the database

- a data model graph defining entity types and entity type relationships of the schema

- an interactive network of forms interfaces for database access.

These structures form the end-user interface. The data definition process may also be viewed as an *end-user interface definition* function. Figure 3 shows the interface which builds the Domain Tree structure.

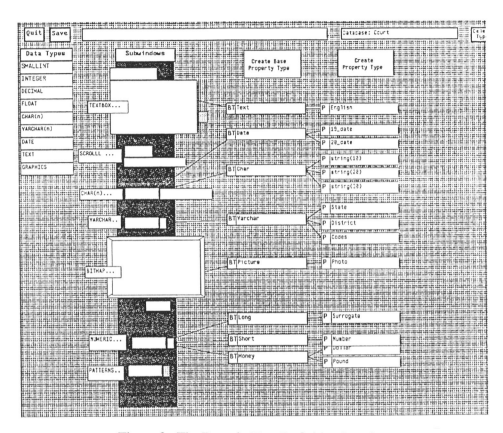

Figure 3. The Domain Tree Definition Interface

End-users access a database via a network of forms. They navigate the forms interface using a map of the schema in the form of a data model graph. A tree structure defining the type hierarchy (properties/attributes) of the database may also be viewed. Data manipulation operations are initiated from each form in the network. Forms themselves are graphical objects which may be manipulated. End-user interface management is provided by the GMS, while database management and storage is managed by an external DBMS which is coupled to the GMS. Figure 4 shows an example of the end-user interface managed by the GMS. Application data accessed by forms interfaces is integrated with schema data shown in a data model graph window (lower right). Form objects are selected for display by selecting a node object from the graph or typing its name in the form selection box.

255

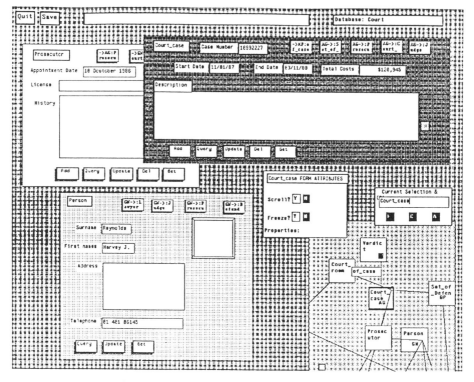

Figure 4. A Node/Window Session View

4.4. An IPSE Interface

The first project to be funded under the recent Alvey Programme was a project called **Aspect**.[9] The aim of this project was to carry out research into the development of an Integrated Project Support Environment (IPSE).

Central to Aspect is the Information Base, and it is the Information Base which achieves the integration between tools by providing a central, structured repository for all the information they manipulate.[3,4]

An important component of the Aspect system is the user interface. This must support complex interaction with the Information Base by a wide variety of users, assuming many different roles. The Aspect approach has been to tie together the data available to a user within a role to the *Task* that must be carried out within that role. Hence, Tasks can be viewed as "work packages" which may be assigned, executed, refined, and so on.

To define a Task, it is necessary to carry out a number of actions. In addition to defining the resources required for the Task, the view of the data that is appropriate to the task, and assigning pre- and post-conditions on the execution of the Task, a *user interface* must be defined for the Task. The Aspect IPSE uses the DoubleView editor to construct these interfaces, which are then loaded dynamically during interaction. The value of the surface interaction paradigm is that no code need be written to manage the user manipulation of the interfaces. All that is

256

necessary is to write code to define the *semantics* of the interface, that is, the IPSE functionality to be invoked upon particular user actions.

It is not possible in this paper to show an example in detail, but instead we take two snapshots within the project life-cycle and examine the user interface at those points, and the support provided by the Aspect Information Base.

Consider a large software system that has been under development for some time. Eventually, versions of the system will be released to customers who will be making use of the system with "live" data. We examine the role of the Aspect system at this stage in the software life-cycle.

Typically, no matter how comprehensive the testing procedures, when a system is used in the field a number of errors, omissions, and inconsistencies become apparent. Shown in figure 5 is the user interface for user "freda" in the role of customer services as she performs the Task of logging calls from customers concerning software errors.

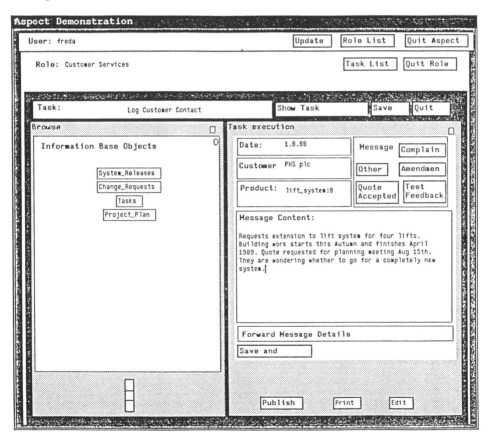

Figure 5. An Example Task Execution Interface

The left-hand side of a Task environment consists of a browse area. In this area objects in the Information Base which are available in this Task can be displayed on the screen and examined. The right-hand side of the screen is the Task execution panel. This area contains operators which are available to manipulate and update information in the Information Base. In this case a simple form-fill interface has been implemented as the most appropriate. The objects available in this Task (which can be either browsed or updated) are determined by the Task definition which has been defined during the setting up of the project, and the view of the Information Base which has been defined for that Task. The action to be taken when a region is selected could be to allow text to be entered into that region, to perform a query on the Information Base to validate the data entered, and then to report the result of the query to the user.

Later in the project life-cycle, when the senior programmer creates amendment specifications for work that is to be carried out in response to customer requests, the Task environment could be as shown in figure 6.

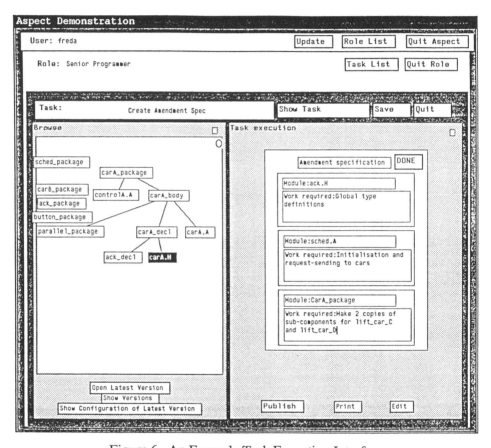

Figure 6. An Example Task Execution Interface

Here it was necessary to browse the structure of the software system being amended before identifying individual modules requiring change. Hence, a database query was performed and the results displayed as a connected graph. Any of the nodes in the graph can be selected (highlighting the region) and then selecting the region labelled "show versions" would retrieve the different version of that module that exist.

258

When the amendment descriptions have been completed they would be published to the correct roles. Each one would create a new Task within those roles and be associated with an appropriate view of the Information Base. This will normally be a semi-automatic operation in that much of the Task definition can be automatically derived from the parent Task, while user interaction may be required to resolve some ambiguities. A Task definition tool is available to help users define tasks.

5. Discussion

The above examples illustrate two important features of the surface interaction paradigm, and of its realisation, Presenter:

- *Persistence* - since surface objects exist independently of application execution, they may be edited and stored during an interface design stage.

- *Behaviour* - since the user can interact with surface objects independently of the application, the user is able to modify the interface to suit the needs of the moment. Surface object behaviour also allows the task of managing direct manipulation graphics to be factored out from application code.

We make a number of observations on the suitability of the surface interaction paradigm to the design and management of database interfaces, drawn from our experiences with Presenter.

- Database systems are typically accessed by a wide range of users. A simple query language interface may be adequate for some users, but difficult and unnatural for many others (eg. database-naive end users). The ability to easily generate and adapt graphical database interfaces will be an important part of future database application development environments.

- The current trend is towards extending the application areas of database systems typically for storing complex, highly-interrelated data (eg. design activities such as VLSI circuit design, and software development environments). New approaches to the creation, display, manipulation, and maintenance of these applications will be required. Such applications will undoubtedly be built on graphical displays using high powered bit-mapped workstations. Much more work is required to investigate the coupling of the user interface to the underlying database services for these applications.

- Database systems are often one component of a much larger 'Information System'. Office Information Systems (OIS) and Geographic Information Systems (GIS) are two areas which use database systems in this way. Graphical display facilities are important to these applications, and thus we must investigate the integration of a wide range of services in this context.

- Security and control of data with a database system is typically provided by limiting a user's *view* of the database. The data and operators which are displayed on the screen will obviously provide one approach to defining such a view. How do we combine the necessary control with sufficient flexibility to allow the end user to customise and adapt their own user interface? The answer appears to lie in a new form of data independence which we can call *display independence*. Hence, not only do we have physical and logical data independence which insulate end users from changes in physical and conceptual data organisation, we also have insulation from changes in the way in which that information is displayed to the end user. Through Presenter the main display characteristics of each screen region can be amended *without* changing the application program itself. The principle of display independence requires further investigation.

- Presenter has proved an excellent tool for rapid generation of prototype application systems. By perceiving data in a graphical form, new application areas and new approaches to existing applications become apparent. For example, browsing data by navigating a graph on the screen could apply to a hierarchical subject index for a library system, a software design in a structured methodology, a database schema, a version graph for a VLSI hardware design, a parts explosion, and so on. All of the above applications have been implemented using Presenter.

5.1. Open Issues

Finally, there are a number of unresolved questions which have arisen out of the work with Presenter for graphical database interfaces. We hope to address these issues in the near future. Of particular interest are the following questions:

- Presenter in effect maintains a *presentation database* which in addition to storing logical relationships between surface objects, also necessarily holds contingent information such as size, position, and other graphical 'frills'. Since speed of response at the interface is critical to user appreciation, Presenter is highly optimised to traverse and incrementally display its particular structure. We believe that recording this fine grained graphical data in a conventional DBMS would significantly impair performance of the user interface. Are there techniques which overcome these performance difficulties?

- Given the existence of a presentation database and a logical database, what are the problems of synchronising and maintaining the integrity of each database with respect to the other?

- Is there any formalisable relationship between the logical underlying database, and the presented interface, which presumably is some view, or visualisation, of the logical objects ? Is it therefore possible to 'mechanise' the viewing of a database ?[14]

- Clearly, some level of software must be written to interpret between the surface and the database. Minimally, two mechanisms are required: a projection mechanism which represents views of the logical database in terms of surface objects, and a mechanism which translates surface actions into database queries or updates. The degree to which this intermediate level can be made independent of the database, or even of the DBMS, is open to question. For example, the GMS system described above is an attempt to provide a UIMS which is specific to the domain of DBMSs, but independent of any particular database.

6. Summary

There is a generally held view that the user interface is of vital importance to the efficient and successful use of application programs. This is particularly true in large, complex applications with a wide variety of different classes of end user. Many database system applications typically fall into this latter category.

This paper has reported some of the work at York to investigate the principle of *surface interaction* as a user interface manipulation technique, and described the experiments taking place to make use of this approach within different database applications.

While the work at York is clearly in a preliminary stage, initial results are particularly encouraging. Use of Presenter user interface management system coupled with a proprietary relational database system has proved a very useful basis for experimentation. We plan to continue our investigation of this flexible approach to graphical database user interface management.

Acknowledgements

The development of the surface interaction principle, and the design and implementation of Presenter, are the work of Roger Took.

The database user interface management system of section 4.3 is the work of Bill Daly, who is now employed by *Hand, Whittington & Associates.*

References

1. *ASPECT: Specification of the Public Tool Interface*, System Designers PLC (1987).

2. *Assessment Report for the Aspect HCI*, British Aerospace PLC (January 1988).

3. A.W. Brown, A.N. Earl, P. Hitchcock, R. Weedon and R.P. Whittington, "The Use of Databases for Software Engineering", pp. 55-70 in *Proceedings of the 5th British National Conference on Databases (BNCOD5)*, ed. E.A. Oxborrow, Cambridge University Press (14th - 16th July 1986).

4. A.W. Brown, D.S. Robinson and R.A. Weedon, "Managing Software

Development'', pp. 197-235 in *Software Engineering '86*, ed. D. Barnes and P. Brown, Peter Peregrinus (1986).

5. P.P. Chen, ''The Entity-Relationship Model - Toward a Unified View of Data'', *ACM Transactions on Database Systems* **1**(1), pp. 9-36 (March 1976).

6. A.P. Cobbett and I.C. Wand, ''The Debugging of Large Multitask Ada Programs'', *Proceedings of Ada UK Conference* (September 1989).

7. W. Daly, *A Graphical Management System for Semantic, Multimedia Databases*, PhD Thesis, University of York (1989).

8. C.J. Date, *An Introduction to Database Systems - Volume I*, Addison-Wesley (1986).

9. J. A. Hall, P. Hitchcock and R. Took, ''An overview of the ASPECT Architecture'', pp. 86-99 in *Integrated Project Support Environments*, ed. J.McDermid, Peter Peregrinus Ltd. (1985).

10. T. Hoeber, ''Open Look Design Gaols'', *Sun Technology*, pp. 63-75, Sun Microsystems (September 1988).

11. S.J. Holmes, ''Overview and User Manual for Doubleview'', YCS.109, Department of Computer Science, University of York (January 1989).

12. S. E. Hudson, ''UIMS Support for Direct Manipulation Interfaces'', *ACM Computer Graphics* **21**(2), pp. 120-124 (April 1987).

13. Apple Computer Inc., *Inside Macintosh*, Addison-Wesley (1986).

14. J. Mackinlay, ''Automating the Design of Graphical Presentations of Relational Information'', *ACM Trans. Graphics* **5**(2), pp. 110-141 (April 1986).

15. C. McClure, *CASE is Software Automation*, Prentice-Hall (1989).

16. Laguna Beach Participants, ''Future Directions in DBMS Research'', *ACM SIGMOD Record* **18**(1), pp. 17-26 (March 1989).

17. *User Interface Management Systems*, Springer-Verlag, Berlin (1985).

18. J. M. Spivey, *The Z Notation - A Reference Manual*, Prentice Hall International (1989).

19. P. Szekely, ''Modular Implementation of Presentations'', *ACM SIGCHI Bulletin* **18**(2), pp. 235-240 (April 1987).

20. R. K. Took, *Surface Interaction: A Paradigm and Formal Model for the Presentation Level of Applications and Documents (PhD Thesis)*, Computer Science Department, University of York (1990).

21. K. Whiteley, M.J. Birch and A. Parker, ''A Mascot 3 Paintbox for Aspect'', *Proceedings of Software Engineering '88* (July 1988).